Twilight at Conner Prairie

Twilight at Conner Prairie

The Creation, Betrayal, and Rescue of a Museum

Berkley W. Duck III

ALTAMIRA
PRESS

A division of
ROWMAN & LITTLEFIELD PUBLISHERS, INC.
Lanham • New York • Toronto • Plymouth, UK

All author royalties from the sale of this publication are being donated to Conner Prairie.

Published by AltaMira Press
A division of Rowman & Littlefield Publishers, Inc.
A wholly owned subsidiary of The Rowman & Littlefield Publishing Group, Inc.
4501 Forbes Boulevard, Suite 200, Lanham, Maryland 20706
http://www.altamirapress.com

Estover Road, Plymouth PL6 7PY, United Kingdom

British Library Cataloguing in Publication Information Available

Library of Congress Cataloging-in-Publication Data

Duck, Berkley W., 1938–
  Twilight at Conner Prairie : the creation, betrayal, and rescue of a museum / Berkley W. Duck III.
    p. cm. — (American association for state and local history)
  Includes bibliographical references and index.
  ISBN 978-0-7591-2010-5 (cloth : alk. paper) — ISBN 978-0-7591-2012-9 (electronic)
  1. Conner Prairie (Museum)—History. 2. Historical museums—Indiana—Fishers—History. 3. Open-air museums—Indiana—Fishers—History. 4. Earlham College—History. I. Title.
  F523.D83 2011
  907.409772—dc22

                                                                    2011007249

Printed in the United States of America

This book is dedicated to all of the volunteers who served on the advisory council and the board of directors of Conner Prairie; to the members of the board of directors of Save the Prairie, Inc., and everyone who supported their efforts; and, with particular gratitude, to the staff who served at Conner Prairie following June 11, 2003. Without the dedication of the staff and the generosity and support of the Conner Prairie community, the museum would have been lost.

Many forms of conduct permissible in a workaday world for those acting at arm's length are forbidden to those bound by fiduciary ties. A trustee is held to something stricter than the morals of the marketplace. Not honesty alone, but the punctilio of an honor the most sensitive, is then the standard of behavior.

—Judge Benjamin N. Cardozo, *Meinhard v. Salmon*,
164 N.E. 545 (N.Y. 1925)

Contents

~

Preface

This is a story about trust. The Conner Prairie outdoor history museum in
Hamilton County, Indiana, was founded and nurtured by Indianapolis philanthropist Eli Lilly and later transferred by Lilly to a public charitable trust.
Earlham College, a Quaker-affiliated liberal arts college in Richmond, Indiana, was named as the trustee, and under the terms of the trust, the museum
was to be maintained and operated by Earlham for the benefit and education
of the public. Lilly later established a substantial endowment at Earlham that
was dedicated to the operation and development of the museum, but any income not needed for the museum could be applied to the college. The terms
of his gifts created a conflict of interest for the college.

As the story unfolds, the college struggles with the adoption and administration of policies for the museum that attempt to balance the museum's
claims on the endowment—the value of which increases over time from
about $30 million to over $150 million—with the college's growing financial
dependence on that same fund. Ultimately, the college's conflicts of interest
put in jeopardy the very future of Conner Prairie.

This also is a story about the volunteer leadership of Conner Prairie—
their views of their roles in a fluid and sensitive relationship in which they
had only the moral authority they brought to Conner Prairie as members
of the Indianapolis business and philanthropic community; their efforts
to effectively manage the museum under the circumstances in which they
found themselves; and their interactions with the administration and board
of trustees of Earlham College. The story culminates in the breakdown of

Earlham's increasingly tenuous hold on Conner Prairie, the struggle for the museum's independence, the tactics pursued by the Conner Prairie board of directors, Earlham's responses, and the roles played by the museum's staff, the media, the Indiana attorney general, and the courts in determining the future of the museum.

This story is part of the Lilly story and part of the events that shaped Earlham College, and histories of both the man and the institution have been written.[1] These books touch upon, but do not by any means exhaust, the facts surrounding the relationship between Lilly, the college, and the museum. This book examines those relationships in detail, and although this is not a comprehensive history of Conner Prairie, it seems appropriate that a contemporary record should be made of how the museum came to its present governance and funding arrangements.

In writing this book, I have drawn upon historic documents in the Conner Prairie archives; notes, memoranda, and correspondence generated over the course of approximately five and one-half years of discussions and negotiations between Earlham College and representatives of the board of directors of Conner Prairie regarding the governance of the museum; and the documents made available by the Indiana attorney general during two and one-half years of subsequent negotiation and litigation between his office and Earlham College. These contemporaneous materials also have been deposited in the Conner Prairie archives.

I was a participant in the events at Conner Prairie over the final 10 years of its relationship with Earlham College and deeply involved in the efforts to separate the museum from the college. This book is, therefore, a memoir. But it also is a history, and a history with legal content. There is no way to understand what happened at Conner Prairie without reference to legal concepts and legal strategies. The issues at Conner Prairie were created as a result of the terminology of legal documents, the governance crisis was shaped by the advice Earlham received from its lawyers, and leaders of the independence movement were (or had been) practicing attorneys. The issues ultimately were resolved as a result of the intervention of the Indiana attorney general and his access to the judicial system. I have attempted, however, to keep the legal jargon to a minimum and to explain terminology that may not be familiar to non-lawyers.

The Conner Prairie story also is a lesson in the limitations of the rule of law, and the resolution of the Conner Prairie crisis occurred at an intersection of law and public policy. As we will see, the options open to the attorney general in his management of the issues included the pursuit of legal remedies, but full-scale litigation could have had a dramatic adverse impact on

Earlham College and resulted in a Pyrrhic victory for Conner Prairie. How the attorney general managed the issues, in the face of sometimes strident advocacy from both sides, is a part of this story. We also will see the importance, in a dispute involving the public interest, of access to the media, of the roles that volunteer organizations can play in generating and sustaining media interest, and of the effect of media coverage in shaping both the tactics employed by the contestants and the outcome.

Finally, this is a cautionary tale for anyone considering a major gift to an eleemosynary organization for the purpose of funding some specific program or interest of the donor's. This book will examine in some detail what Eli Lilly said and did in funding the development and operations of Conner Prairie, and how those actions ultimately compromised his objectives and led to years of tension and uncertainty between the objects of his bounty.

⌒

The background that I brought to my role at Conner Prairie was that of a lawyer. I retired from the Indianapolis firm of Ice Miller in 2001, having practiced there for 38 years. It is coincidental, but fortuitous in relation to my role in the Conner Prairie dispute, that my practice included the management of questions of director fiduciary duty and conflicts of interest. I became a member of the board of directors of Conner Prairie, Inc., in December 1995. I was recruited to that position by Donald G. Sutherland, a law partner of mine at Ice Miller who was, at the time, the outgoing chairman of the Conner Prairie board. Sutherland was one of the architects of the changed relationship between Earlham and the museum that resulted in the organization of Conner Prairie, Inc., an Earlham College subsidiary charged with the operations of the museum from 1992 to 2003. In our conversations about the museum and its governance, Sutherland told me that the museum's relationship with Earlham College had a long history of uncertainty and skepticism, on the part of those involved at Conner Prairie, regarding Earlham's management policies and its compliance with the terms of the Lilly gifts. He also said that, viewed properly, the relationship was one of trust. I found his comments interesting at the time, but had no idea where that thread would lead.

Sutherland approached me in part because he was aware that my wife's parents, Warren and Frances Ruddell, had been significant contributors to Conner Prairie. Warren and his brother, James, had donated to the museum (from the family farm located a few miles south of the museum) what is now the Campbell House in the museum's 1836 village, Prairietown, and a number of historic artifacts, and Warren and Frances made a substantial monetary gift to Conner Prairie at the time of the construction of its Museum Center.

The library in the Museum Center was named for them. Warren also served for several years on the advisory council of the museum (the predecessor of the board of directors of Conner Prairie, Inc.) and was the chairman of that council at a critical time in the history of the museum's relationship with Earlham.

My interest in Conner Prairie also could be traced to my shared ancestry with Eli Lilly. My great-great-grandfather and Eli Lilly's great-grandfather were brothers, the children of Eli and Corilla Lilly of Lexington, Kentucky. Eli's grandfather, Colonel Eli Lilly, founded Eli Lilly and Company, the Indianapolis pharmaceutical firm, in 1876. My grandfather, Berkley W. Duck, moved from Kentucky to Indianapolis in 1897, due in part, I assume, to the presence of his Lilly cousins in the city, although his career did not include employment by the drug company.

I was fortunate, as a boy growing up in Indianapolis, to have known Eli Lilly. He was a man who went quietly about his many philanthropic activities. While he might have been distressed by the very public controversy over the governance of Conner Prairie, I think he would have been satisfied with its outcome.

Berkley W. Duck III

Note

1. James H. Madison, *Eli Lilly: A Life, 1885–1977* (Indianapolis: Indiana Historical Society, 1989), and Thomas D. Hamm, *Earlham College: A History, 1847–1997* (Bloomington: Indiana University Press, 1997).

Acknowledgments

Over the four years that it has taken me to write this book, I have received help and encouragement from many people with very different skills, each of whom has contributed in important ways to the final product. I am grateful to you all. In mentioning some by name, I do not wish to slight the valuable assistance that others have provided along the way, but I need to thank Barbara Abel at Conner Prairie, for access to her understanding of the Conner Prairie archives and her willingness to allow me to tap into her personal knowledge of the people and events that made up the Conner Prairie story; Dr. J. Michael Hittle, friend, educator, and historian, for his willingness to read—twice—the entire manuscript and for teaching me the difference between a book and a recitation of facts; Dr. James H. Madison, former Conner Prairie board member and Eli Lilly biographer, for insights that he was uniquely qualified to provide and for his support and encouragement; John Herbst, for his assistance in bringing this project to completion; Dana Felton, for her help with the production of what seemed to be endless drafts of the manuscript; and Rick Beard, whose editorial skills have made all the difference.

Special thanks to my wife, Nancy, for her support during the governance crisis at Conner Prairie, for putting up with my time investment in this project, and for her thoughtful comments and insights on each question I have raised with her. She now knows the story as well as I do.

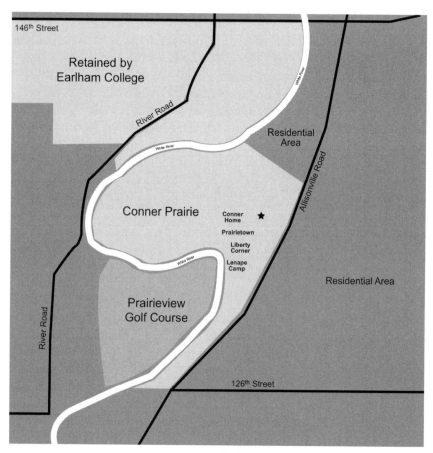

Conner Prairie

~

Introduction

In June 2003, the Conner Prairie outdoor history museum in Hamilton County, Indiana, was riding the crest of a wave of energy and innovation. It was nearing the end of a five-year plan that had brought major new attractions to the museum after a 20-year hiatus in its growth. The Museum Center had been substantially remodeled and upgraded and was functioning effectively for the first time since its construction in 1987. Award-winning programs such as *Follow the North Star* were receiving national acclaim and attention. Attendance, membership, and community support all were showing substantial year-to-year increases. The museum was led by an imaginative, dedicated professional who was popular with the staff, volunteers, and board of directors. Staff morale was soaring and people were happy and proud to be working at Conner Prairie. The museum's volunteer board of directors was actively engaged on behalf of the museum, and new members were anxious to become part of the leadership. The museum had recently renegotiated mutually beneficial arrangements under which the Indianapolis Symphony Orchestra offered the popular *Symphony on the Prairie* outdoor summer concerts. The fast-growing communities surrounding Conner Prairie had come to recognize the value that the museum's 1,300-acre complex brought to the area and were increasing their support of its operations. The annual *Spirit of the Prairie* awards dinner, a successful fund-raising event, was producing increasing revenues and favorable public attention. The Conner Prairie Alliance, a volunteer auxiliary organization, was contributing thousands of hours of time and close to $100,000 per year in support of the museum's operations.

The museum was running small operating deficits, but the gap was narrowing and it had—theoretically—an endowment of more than $150 million to draw upon as needed for its operations and capital requirements. Contributions were below expectations, for reasons that will become clear, but there was hope that a solution to this problem was at hand. Against a backdrop of declining attendance at other outdoor history museums, Conner Prairie stood out as a model for the entire industry.

But on June 11, 2003, Earlham College, which held the museum as the trustee of a public charitable trust established by Eli Lilly, fired the independent members of the museum's board of directors and its president, John Herbst, and took direct control of the museum's operations, saying that concerns about "financial integrity" required that it step in and put the museum on a different course. This was, however, a smoke screen. In authorizing the college's president to fire the board of directors and president of the museum and determining the conditions under which he could do so, the Earlham board of trustees said nothing about "financial integrity" or its absence. The real question was whether the Conner Prairie board would accept terms offered by Earlham under which the museum would have gained a measure of autonomy from Earlham's control. But, in exchange, Earlham would have secured over $75 million of the museum's endowment for its own, unrestricted, use—and Earlham needed the money. Conner Prairie refused to endorse Earlham's terms, and Earlham took over.

The Conner Prairie board of directors had been pursuing independence from Earlham College as a result of issues arising from Earlham's management of the museum and its endowment. The board had come to the conclusion that Earlham was not administering Lilly's endowment gifts in accordance with their terms, that the college had failed to deal effectively with its conflicts of interest as both the trustee and a beneficiary of the endowment, that the college was siphoning off museum resources through unwarranted fees and charges, that the college was micromanaging the museum, and that Earlham's policies were driving away public support. As a result, the board had determined that Conner Prairie should be separated from the college, but five years of efforts to resolve the issues through mediation and negotiation had not succeeded.

Earlham College's actions were particularly ominous because, as the contingent beneficiary of Lilly's gifts, Earlham stood to gain access to the entire $150 million endowment if Conner Prairie ceased to operate, and the removal of its board of directors eliminated the only watchdogs concerned solely with the museum's interests. Earlham's initial public statements following the takeover were ambiguous. College president Douglas Bennett assured the staff that there would be no immediate changes in the museum's operations. But another Earlham spokesman publicly indicated that the college viewed the museum's level of operations as excessive and unnecessary. A pall fell over the staff and volunteers. Overnight, contributions to the museum plummeted. The Conner Prairie Alliance, suspicious of Earlham's motives and offended by its tactics, suspended its efforts in support of the museum.

The ousted directors, and other supporters, formed a nonprofit corporation, Save the Prairie, Inc., to carry on a campaign of public education and advocacy in support of the removal of Earlham College as trustee of the museum, as that was the only action that could assure the continuation of Conner Prairie. Because the museum was held by the college as the trustee of a public charitable trust, Save the Prairie asked the Indiana attorney general, Steve Carter, to intervene and protect the public interest. The attorney general was charged with the enforcement of public charitable trusts, and he was the only person with the legal standing to challenge Earlham's actions. If the attorney general did not intervene, Earlham College was free to pursue whatever policies it might find to be in its best interests.

The future of Conner Prairie hung in the balance.

~

CHAPTER ONE

The Development of Conner Prairie

Conner Prairie was the result of the philanthropy and vision of Eli Lilly, the chief executive officer of the Indianapolis pharmaceutical company founded by his grandfather. Lilly was a hard-driving, intense businessman, but he also was a generous philanthropist and a knowledgeable amateur historian. The Conner Prairie property initially attracted Lilly because it was the site of a home built by William Conner, an early settler. The structure, built in 1823, is believed to be the oldest brick home in central Indiana.

Conner was an important figure in the settlement of the area and its early history. He and his brother, John, came to Indiana from the Detroit area about 1800. They were fur traders, trappers, and interpreters. Following the admission of Indiana to the Union in 1816, Conner served in the Indiana state legislature for four years, laid out the design of nearby Noblesville, was involved in the development of the state's transportation and school systems, and played a pivotal role in the negotiation of treaties with the local Delaware Indian tribe. In March 1824, on Fall Creek in nearby Madison County, six white settlers massacred a group of two men, three women, and four children from the Miami Indian tribe. Conner was asked by the U.S. Indian agent to accompany the agent on visits to the tribe intended to assure them that the killers would be put on trial and fairly prosecuted. After the trials, which resulted in convictions, death sentences, and the execution of some of the perpetrators, Conner signed a petition seeking a pardon for one of the condemned men. The governor of Indiana arrived with the pardon as the noose was being lowered over the man's head.[1]

Conner also led an intriguing private life. He married a Delaware Indian woman, Mekinges, with whom he had six children. As a result of the 1818 Treaty of St. Mary's, one of the treaties that Conner negotiated, the Delaware tribe was required to leave Indiana. Mekinges and her children went with them, headed west, but the further circumstances of their separation from Conner have been lost to history. Within a year, Conner married Elizabeth Chapman, who may have been the only single white female in the area; began a new family; and built the house that attracted Lilly's attention.

The Conner house was falling into ruin when Lilly acquired it in 1934. He stabilized and restored the structure and added several other historic buildings to the grounds.[2] Lilly eventually expanded his Hamilton County holdings to over 1,400 surrounding acres. He used the property for the operation of an experimental farm, but his primary interest was the preservation and development of the historic aspects of the site.

By the time Lilly transferred the Conner Prairie property to Earlham in 1964, he had initiated tours of the property and amassed a substantial collection of historic artifacts. Lilly's methods were somewhat unorthodox. Other than some formal technical training, he was largely self-educated, but he became an excellent researcher and writer. He read widely, and as he gathered information he wondered about the details of what he had learned. For example, what did the inside of a trapper's cabin look like? He personally researched the issue and then recreated the setting so that others could share the trapper's experience.[3] As early as 1935, Lilly was offering educational programs on the Conner Prairie grounds in the form of reenactments of historic events including, in one case, audience interaction with the presenters.[4] It was contemporaneously reported that Lilly's vision was "to create, [not] merely a museum, but [an] actual portrayal of how our Hoosier forefathers and their families lived."[5] Lilly had visited colonial Williamsburg and other historic sites. Although Conner Prairie was not the only location to benefit from Lilly's interest in and support of Indiana history, it is clear that Lilly felt that he had done something of permanent, historic value in securing, preserving, and developing the property. He wanted to provide to the people of Indiana a continuing opportunity to see what life had been like at the time of William Conner's occupancy of the premises.

～

Having nurtured Conner Prairie for three decades and seen the public's reactions to it, Lilly began in the 1960s to consider how Conner Prairie's operations might be continued without his personal involvement. Given his intense interest in the property, it seems likely that he wanted to be personally involved in selecting possible transferees, assessing their willingness and ability to carry on the museum and the experimental farm operations, and establishing terms for the use of the properties. He is believed to have approached both Purdue University, which would have been a logical choice regarding the experimental farm, and the Indiana Historical Society, which received a substantial gift from his estate. Neither institution seems to have been interested in Conner Prairie. The farm manager at the time, Tillman Bubenzer, was a Quaker. Through his involvement in a Quaker organization, Bubenzer was acquainted with an Earlham College trustee, Thomas Jones, and Bubenzer informed Jones of Lilly's interest in disposing of the property. Jones approached Lilly on the subject, and that contact led to later conversations between Lilly and Landrum Bolling, the president of Earlham College.[6]

Earlham College traced its roots to 1856, when the Indiana Yearly Meeting of the Religious Society of Friends, based in Richmond, established a "course of education in the higher branches . . . of collegiate study." In 1859, the institution adopted the name "Earlham College." The college was incorporated in 1881, as a result of a joint resolution adopted by the Indiana Yearly Meeting and the Western Yearly Meeting of the Religious Society of Friends located in Plainfield, and from that point forward the two meetings governed the college jointly.[7]

Lilly, a devout Episcopalian, became acquainted with Earlham through the writings of Elton Trueblood.[8] Trueblood was a Quaker leader, educator, and author who came to Earlham in 1945 as a member of the faculty.[9] Lilly also became acquainted with Bolling, but prior to his transfer of Conner Prairie to Earlham, Lilly had not provided any personal financial support to the college.[10]

Earlham College had a long and rich history. Although the Quaker identity of the college waxed and waned, over time it had gradually distanced itself from its origins as a religious institution and from the direct operational control of the Yearly Meetings. By the 1960s, academic freedom had taken firm hold and Earlham had become a highly respected national institution with an excellent faculty, attracting significant numbers of students from beyond the boarders of Indiana. Scholastic Aptitude Test scores of the incoming classes rose dramatically between 1959 and 1965.[11] The Earlham College that Lilly knew and dealt with in the 1960s was an ascendant institution, an intellectually vibrant school with steady growth that was the result of innovations and improvements in its academic programs. But it was Lilly's developing personal relationship with Landrum Bolling that drew him close to Earlham.[12]

⁓

In a memorandum dated October 24, 1963, Bolling provided to Bubenzer an outline of Earlham's thinking about the proposed transfer of Conner Prairie to the college, and he authorized Bubenzer to share the document with "others as you deem advisable." In discussing the "historical museum," Bolling said that Earlham would be glad to supply "a guarantee of permanent maintenance and operation." Earlham would assume the cost of maintaining the museum pending the establishment of a "more suitable means of support." To that end, Bolling proposed the organization of a museum foundation, of which a majority of the trustees would be appointed by Earlham. The foundation "might or might not" take title to the historic aspects of the site. The foundation "should have placed at its disposal, as rapidly as possible, an endowment fund of at least $200,000." That fund was to be established from any "net profits" to Earlham College from the operations of the entire property and from a "first claim" against the proceeds of any sale of the lands to be transferred to the college by Lilly. Earlham proposed to continue the farming operation, subject to the condition that it could be made to be "completely self-supporting" by shifting its focus from a research facility to a commercial operation. To give Earlham the time to complete this transition, Bolling proposed that Lilly underwrite any deficits. Otherwise, he said, the college would have to sell off portions of the land to cover operating expenses, thereby jeopardizing the availability of funding for the proposed museum foundation. As the last provision in the plan, Bolling offered Bubenzer an employment contract with Earlham on terms and conditions similar to those under which he was working for Lilly.

At this time, Earlham ran other farm operations, and it managed a museum on the college campus, so it had some experience to support its approach to Lilly regarding Conner Prairie. Lilly undoubtedly was comforted by Bolling's expressions of interest in preserving the museum operations at Conner Prairie. It is clear that, from the outset, there was no expectation on Lilly's part that Earlham would continue with the operation of the experimental farm over the long term, and both parties focused on the management of the historic aspects of the site.

On December 12, 1963, Lilly wrote to Bolling describing the terms on which he would transfer the property to Earlham. In that letter, Lilly identified a 58-acre tract that had been owned by William Conner and on which stood the Conner House and a number of outbuildings that Lilly had brought to the site. He described this tract as "one of the most important historical monuments in the State of Indiana." In a deed of trust executed by both Lilly and Earlham on January 2, 1964, the 58-acre tract was transferred to Earlham, to be held by the college "in perpetuity" as the trustee of a public charitable trust. Earlham was to keep and maintain all of the improvements in a state of good repair and make the property available for access by the public. By a separate deed, the balance of the land owned by Lilly—1,371 acres—was simultaneously transferred to the college without restriction. In his letter to Bolling, Lilly had said that the proceeds of any sale of the 1,371-acre tract could be used "to assist [the college] to maintain its educational establishments." But Lilly later wrote that he expected—consistent with Bolling's original proposal—that all of the proceeds from the sale of the land would be used to provide an endowment for what Lilly called "the public part of the program." Accordingly, Lilly provided no funding for the operations of the museum other than a small subsidy during the first three years of Earlham's management. In a letter to Lilly acknowledging the acceptance of these terms by the Earlham board of trustees, Bolling emphasized that Earlham was "keenly mindful of the trusteeship responsibility which is placed upon us in accepting this gift."[13]

A public charitable trust is similar to a private trust arrangement in that it is created by a legally enforceable instrument, executed by the person who wishes to create the relationship and by a named trustee. However, the beneficiary of a public charitable trust is the public at large and not a designated person or institution. The creator of a public charitable trust transfers property to the trustee to be held and administered according to the terms of the trust instrument, and the trustee agrees to be bound by those terms. By accepting its position, the trustee becomes legally bound by fiduciary duties of loyalty and care in its administration of the trust, and it assumes the obligation to act in the best interests of the public as the beneficiary of the trust. This is the "trusteeship responsibility" to which Bolling referred in his letter.

〜

The Conner Prairie that Earlham acquired as trustee was a nascent operation. Utilizing the historic structures and artifacts that Lilly had assembled, the museum provided tours, conferences, and other educational events on the grounds. There were about 2,800 visitors to the site during 1964, the year in which Earlham took control.[14]

As a part of the implementation of its strategy at Conner Prairie, in 1968 Earlham created an advisory council of Indianapolis-area residents, but as detailed later, the council was given no management authority. Earlham retained full financial and operational control. Using money provided by Lilly, the museum began its first major expansion in the early 1970s with the construction of Prairietown, an authentic re-creation of an 1836 Indiana community. Prairietown continued as the museum's principal attraction until 2000. The village was populated by staff and volunteer interpreters who played the first-person roles of the tradesmen, farmers, housewives, children, teachers, preachers, innkeepers, and itinerants who would have been representative of the time and the place. The townspeople worked not from scripts but from in-depth briefings on their roles and the issues and knowledge of the times. Prairietown proved enormously popular, drawing audiences from the local and regional markets and from across the country. The William Conner House was not used in the interpretation programs but served an important role as an authentic period structure and as a display area for historic furnishings and artifacts.

In 1992, Earlham incorporated the operations of the museum as a subsidiary of the college, and the advisory council became a corporate board of directors charged with management responsibility for the museum, subject to certain oversight powers retained by the college and to its continued control over financial matters. As a result of a strategic plan adopted by the board of directors in 1997, the museum embarked upon an expansion program. The board had concluded that the Prairietown experience did not provide a broad enough platform for program offerings and that, after 30 years, the museum was suffering from a "been there, done that" public perception. Two significant new attractions were added.

The first, a Lenape Indian camp, opened in 2000.[15] It recreated a small backwoods trading post and an adjacent Native American village. Because of the cultural sensitivities that might have been generated by nonnative portrayals of native peoples, the Indian camp was not presented in the first person. But it drew heavily upon the experience and expertise of current members of the Lenape tribe. The second new attraction was the more ambitious Liberty Corner project, completed in 2001. It involved the construction of an 1886 village crossroads, including a farmhouse, two important historic barn structures, fields and gardens, a Quaker meeting house, a schoolhouse, and related outbuildings. The farmhouse at Liberty Corner was presented in the first person, as the home of the next generation of the Zimmerman family, characters in Prairietown. Liberty Corner moved the historical framework of Prairietown forward another 50 years, and the facility was accessed by crossing a covered bridge that symbolically separated the two time periods. Prairietown continued as a major attraction and other programs were developed around both the 1836 and 1886 time periods.

In one popular program, on winter evenings dinner guests at the William Conner House helped prepare their meals in a working kitchen, in accordance with period menus and techniques. The museum also offered workshops ranging from historic gun making to pottery, summer camps for children, live-in weekends in the 1886 farmhouse, and "base ball" games played using 1886 rules on the meadow at Liberty Corner. One of the museum's most successful and best-known programs, *Follow the North Star*, invited visitors to play the parts of runaway slaves working their way from station to station along the Underground Railroad. In 2003, Conner Prairie attracted over 350,000 visitors and operated on a budget of over $8 million per year.

Conner Prairie's largest audience was school children. As the most logical and accessible point of contact with early Indiana history, Conner Prairie became a popular educational tool for both parents and teachers. For over 20 years, schools from all over central Indiana had used field trips to Conner Prairie as a means of fulfilling curriculum requirements. Generations of fourth graders visited Conner Prairie as a part of school programs, and more recently higher grade levels used the museum to study the creation of communities, changing technologies, and broader United States history. By the time the governance dispute erupted, the museum had been visited by hundreds of thousands of school children from central Indiana, which firmly embedded Conner Prairie in the consciousness of the community. This reservoir of memories and appreciation for the value of the Conner Prairie experience was to serve the museum well in its time of need.

The Conner Prairie staff and interpreters prided themselves on the extent and accuracy of the underlying historical research that supported their creation of the characters that populated Prairietown and Liberty Corner and shaped the development of the structures, artifacts, and clothing used in the museum's public programming. Although this background effort was not apparent to the public visitors, and much of the detail provided in the public offerings could have been omitted without anyone noticing, the staff rigorously adhered to the best scholarship and provided the most authentic experience possible. Nothing at Conner Prairie was embellished or fictive.

⌢

The development of the museum between its transfer to Earlham in 1964 and June 2003 was the result of a complex interplay between Earlham College, Eli Lilly, and interested supporters of the museum, who were largely based in the greater Indianapolis area. The initial players in this drama were the then president of Earlham, Landrum Bolling, and Lilly. Bolling's initiatives, and Lilly's reactions, culminated in a shift in Lilly's thinking about the funding of the museum's operations and led to his establishment—by way of four major gifts—of an endowment initially valued at over $30 million. The circumstances and terms of those gifts are discussed below.

After assuming responsibility for the museum, Earlham continued Lilly's educational programs on an interim basis, and it began to catalog the museum's artifacts and assemble staff. At a meeting held in September 1964, the Earlham trustees considered the potential for a housing development, gravel and timber extraction, and expansion of the museum. Bolling recommended that "inasmuch as we are trustees of a kind of public treasure . . . we should take a long look at the future of this whole 1431 acres, not singly at the 58 acres of museum area."[16] In March 1965, the trustees considered a report from a board committee that discussed the options of maintaining the museum on "little more than a minimum basis" or adding attractions and facilities with "the expectation that funds from increased admissions, sales, and services will be sufficient to finance the operation." The committee recommended the engagement of professional help in creating a master plan and reported that Lilly thought the development proposal "makes good sense."[17]

Issues related to the farm operations at Conner Prairie received most of Earlham's attention over the next three years. But even without the benefit of any significant new facilities or programs, attendance at the museum grew from about 2,800 visitors in 1964 to 26,000 in 1968. The cost of operating the museum was partially offset by admissions fees.

The first indications of Earlham's ultimate direction with respect to the future funding of the museum operations appear in 1968. The minutes of a meeting of the college trustees held on February 9 and 10 noted that the museum "is still operating at a loss" and that it needed "an endowment of about half a million dollars in order to be able to continue operation."[18] Ten days later, Harold C. Cope, Earlham's vice president for business affairs, wrote to Lilly reporting on the operations of the "Conner Prairie Farm" and the museum. He reported that the net loss on the operation of the museum since its transfer to Earlham was about $39,000. Cope noted Earlham's "commitment to the development of these resources in the most effective and socially useful ways in the years ahead," and then said, "Many individuals and companies have expressed interest in buying Conner Prairie acreage from Earlham. The temptation to sell this land is being resisted for many reasons. Our basic intent is to achieve an effective operation of the farm and museum without cost to the College."[19]

After reviewing the operations of the property over the preceding four years, Cope went on to say,

> In regard to the Conner Prairie Museum, Earlham has an important decision to make as to whether or not this would be open to the public. . . .

We initiated our museum involvements with the assumption that, even if not open to the public, we would spend not less than $12,000 per year to maintain the facility. Opening to the public would not necessarily increase this loss, we felt, and might enable us more nearly to break even on this operation.

To date, we have been unable to achieve any notable successes in this regard. We doubt that the museum can be profitably operated on a modest or "middle ground" level of activity and wonder if this is not, like so many other situations in life, one in which we must develop the resource to its fullest potential or else not keep it open at all.[20]

Cope's suggestion that Earlham might close the museum if the college could not find a way to make it profitable is curious, as that action would have violated the requirement in Lilly's original deed of trust that Earlham keep the property and buildings open for public visitation. There is no record of any reaction by Lilly to this suggestion, but Cope's letter soon was followed by a visit to Lilly by Bolling. In that meeting, held in early March 1968, Bolling discussed Earlham's plans and the funding of the Conner Prairie Farm and museum. He also solicited a gift from Lilly to Earlham's general endowment fund as "a kind of challenge starter" gift for a planned $30 million fund-raising effort by the college.[21] At their meeting, Lilly gave Bolling a check for $50,000 to subsidize the operations of the museum, but in a letter to Bolling dated March 8, 1968, he declined to support Earlham's general endowment campaign. This letter must have crossed in the mail with two follow-up letters written by Bolling to Lilly, also dated March 8. In one of those letters, Bolling expanded on the terms of the endowment funding proposal and noted that Lilly had been "extraordinarily generous" with Earlham already, for which Earlham was "exceedingly grateful." Lilly's thinking about the museum's long-term funding is revealed in Bolling's second March 8 letter, which said, in relevant part,

> You have done a great deal for Earlham already. You have provided us with an asset which we could convert to endowment funds to sustain that museum on a reasonable basis. . . .
>
> We are pleased that you take a continuing interest in the operation of the Museum and that you share our satisfaction in having it visited and enjoyed by so many thousands of people.

There were three conclusions that Earlham could have drawn from this exchange: first, Lilly was not interested in providing unrestricted support to Earlham College; second, as matters stood, Lilly was not receptive to a plea for funds to support the museum, as he viewed a sale of the 1,371-acre tract as the source of any such funding needed by the college; and third, Lilly continued to have a strong interest in Conner Prairie.

Earlham's next step was to appoint a Conner Prairie advisory council of Indianapolis-area citizens to assist in the formulation of a "master plan" for the development of the museum. The minutes of the first meeting of the advisory council held on June 20, 1968, noted Earlham's hope (consistent with Cope's analysis) that the plan would produce a course of action that would "put [the museum] in a position to be self-sustaining." The ideas presented to the meeting revolved around the construction of a historic village, the development of a visitor center, a restaurant operation, shops, and a motel. One of the Earlham representatives also expressed the view that it was Lilly's intent that the museum would be supported by the income from the farm.[22] When he read these minutes, Lilly objected to this view of his intentions, saying

> Please do not ever think that I thought the profits from the farm would pay the expense of the Museum and old house.[23]
>
> The original intent was that the College could sell the property and get about half a million dollars for it, which should yield in the neighborhood of $25,000 a year to support the public part of the program. The College authorities thought it would be better to keep the farm, and if they can do so I am all for it.[24]

Lilly's understanding that Earlham had decided to retain the farm seems to have resulted from further discussions between Lilly and Bolling in late 1968. By this time, Earlham had changed its strategy. It still sought a gift by Lilly to its general endowment, but that gift would be coupled with a commitment by the college that some part of the gift would be used for Conner Prairie, and Earlham tied that commitment to the concept of a substantial expansion of the historic museum operations on the site. Although Lilly was unwilling to provide an unrestricted gift to Earlham, if the college could interest Lilly in providing funding to support the museum, then Earlham would be relieved from that drain on its other revenues.

⁓

The concept of expanding Conner Prairie seems to have resonated with Lilly. His provision of new funding would eliminate the need to sell the 1,371-acre tract. The retention of that tract, the expansion of the museum, and the use of a new endowment fund for its development and operation could have seemed to Lilly an attractive modification of his original plans. The endowment that ultimately resulted from this shift in Lilly's thinking came in the form of four major gifts, all in shares of Eli Lilly and Company: the first made in 1969 ($3 million), the second in 1972 ($1.4 million), the largest in 1973 ($16.7 million), and a gift under Lilly's will transferred following his death in 1977 ($10 million). Each of these gifts described, in somewhat varying terms, a "fund" that was to be kept separate from the Earlham general endowment. The income from the fund, as well as its principal, was to be used for the development and operation of Conner Prairie. For its own purposes, Earlham was entitled to use any income, but no principal, left over after Conner Prairie's needs were met.[25] Initially, the 1969 gift was designated by Earlham (despite its terms) as the Earlham College Endowment Fund, Lilly's 1973 gift was called the 17/73 Fund, and the gift under his will was called the '77 Endowment Fund. Adopting terminology used by Lilly in the 1973 gift, the entire fund eventually became known at Earlham as the Eli Lilly Endowment Fund.

The first Lilly gift was made in 1969 following conversations between Bolling and Lilly regarding its terms. It is clear that Earlham was seeking terms under which it would hold the expected $3 million gift as a part of its general endowment and be permitted to use it principally for the purposes of the college. In an outline on Earlham College letterhead dated January 3, 1969, Bolling proposed to Lilly, consistent with his March 1968 request, that the forthcoming deed of gift state that Lilly's purpose was to support Earlham's general educational activities. To deal with Lilly's intentions regarding Conner Prairie, Bolling suggested that Lilly provide a side letter "to record our understanding that the gift . . . shall in the first instance be used to carry on the work of the Conner Prairie Museum and to protect the regular Earlham College budget" against expenditures at the museum.[26] But then, in a letter to Lilly dated January 4, Bolling observed that Lilly's wishes would be conveyed with "greater precision and clarity" if set forth in the deed of gift itself, and he went on to suggest that capital expenditures at Conner Prairie should be limited to $500,000 and that no more than $60,000 of annual income from the fund should be allocated to the operations of the museum "including appropriate College overhead."

In the definitive agreement setting forth the terms of this gift, Lilly rejected Bolling's terms. In the deed of gift, dated January 24, 1969, and signed by both Lilly and Earlham College, Lilly transferred $3 million in shares of Eli Lilly and Company common stock to the college. The deed of gift spoke clearly to Lilly's intent to benefit Conner Prairie and expressed no concern for "protection" of the Earlham College budget or the payment of its Conner Prairie "overhead." The "primary purpose" of the gift was to enable Earlham to maintain and operate Conner Prairie. Lilly designated up to 20 percent of the corpus of the gift ($600,000) for capital improvements at the museum and dedicated the remainder to the establishment of "a special endowment fund," the income of which was to be used to support the operations of the museum. The benefit to Earlham College resulting from this gift was limited to the use of any "remaining income" for the educational programs of the college.[27]

∿

In response to Lilly's generosity, in late January 1969 the advisory council solicited proposals for the preparation of a comprehensive feasibility study of whether "a historic village is logical and feasible" and how such a village might be integrated into the site.[28] On April 16, 1969, the advisory council recommended and the Earlham board agreed to the engagement of the Indianapolis firm of James & Berger Associates at a cost of $11,100.[29] In a letter written May 23, 1969, to a new member of the advisory council, Bolling said that "the entire project . . . is due to the creative imagination, sense of history, and generosity of Mr. Lilly. We at Earlham are grateful for the opportunity we have been given to act as the trustee for this important cultural resource for the state and nation."[30] This was one of several instances in which Earlham representatives characterized the Earlham–Conner Prairie relationship as one of "trust," the implications of which will become apparent later.

The feasibility study was completed and delivered to the advisory council on October 7, 1969. It described a comprehensive development plan that included a lodge, a motel, several exhibit areas, and support facilities in different possible configurations. The total cost of the entire project was estimated to be approximately $1,725,000.

Earlham now had to deal with the ramifications of its expansion proposal. The college had succeeded in attracting a significant gift from Lilly, but not on the hoped for terms. Lilly's generosity, the terms of his gift, and the feasibility study had created a new sense of excitement at Conner Prairie. In late February 1970, the Earlham board was cautioned by one of its members that the advisory council seemed to have "caught the vision" of what the expansion could mean for Conner Prairie, that the council would be pushing the Earlham board to approve the plans, and that the board "must find a way to respond to the expected pressure."[31]

At about the same time, Emsley Johnson, the chairman of the Conner Prairie advisory council, met with Edward Wilson, the chairman of the Earlham board, in New York City. In addition to being a history buff, Johnson was the senior partner in an Indianapolis law firm and was experienced in the structure, funding, and operation of nonprofit corporations, having served on the boards of directors of several other civic organizations. In this meeting, Johnson proposed that Earlham support the formation of a separate foundation for Conner Prairie with its own board of directors and a separate $2 million endowment, to be provided by new funding from Lilly. Johnson suggested that Earlham approach Lilly with this request. He thought it likely that Lilly would agree to this restructuring and argued that Lilly might see it as a reason to "consider more funds for Earlham." Wilson's reaction (as later reported by Johnson to the advisory council) was that he could not agree to approach Lilly with this concept unless he was convinced that the proposal "would be best for Earlham."[32]

After talking with Bolling about Johnson's suggestion, Wilson wrote to Johnson on April 11, 1970, firmly rejecting any approach to Lilly for separate funding for a restructured Conner Prairie. Doing so, he said, would be "detrimental to the interests of the Museum and Earlham." Wilson requested that, in his presentation to the Earlham trustees, Johnson not "make any recommendations, either specifically or by implication," related to an additional contribution by Lilly to the museum. As to the proposal to create a new entity for the museum, Wilson reported that, while he could see "the desirability and perhaps necessity" of doing so, he was "not clear as to how this can be accomplished with assurance that the Museum will be neither a financial or administrative burden on Earlham now or in the distant future."

In the meantime, on March 26, 1970, Wilson sent a memorandum to the members of the Earlham board enclosing a review of the James & Burger recommendations. Elaborating on the concerns at Earlham regarding the "expected pressure" from Conner Prairie, Wilson noted that, in the forthcoming meeting with the advisory council in which its recommendations were to be considered, the Earlham trustees must try "to keep [their] own priorities straight." Wilson warned that this would not be easy given the enthusiasm that Johnson and others on the advisory council had for the project. The memorandum continued,

> I believe our priorities are somewhat as follows:
> 1. Earlham is a College concerned first and foremost with the students working toward an undergraduate degree.
> 2. The Conner Prairie Farm is an asset of the College to be used in furtherance of the first objective, except that as a condition of accepting it and the gift of stock, we have a responsibility for the Museum—which we all want to carry out to the best of our ability up to the point that it does not interfere with our first priority.

3. In carrying out our obligations on the Museum, we must be prepared to spend up to $600,000 (20%) of the capital of Mr. Lilly's gift of stock for capital improvements and some part of the income of either the stock or the Farm (or re-invested proceeds from sale). In our thinking, and in order to have some perspective, I suggest that we plan in terms of $50,000 per year.

Paragraphs 2 and 3 of this memorandum reflect the link between Lilly's gifts of the 1,371-acre tract and the $3 million in Lilly stock and Earlham's commitment to develop the museum. But in paragraph 2 Wilson subordinates Earlham's "responsibility" for Conner Prairie to the "first priority" of the college, thereby reflecting Earlham's failure to recognize that it had received the museum in trust and therefore had a fiduciary duty to act in the best interests of the public as the beneficiary of the trust. Neither is paragraph 3 an accurate description of the terms of Lilly's deed of gift, under which income was to be applied "in the first instance" to operating support of the museum and only the "remaining income" could be used by the college. The terms of the gift provided no assurance that Earlham would receive any benefit, but under Wilson's proposal the $2.4 million remaining after the $600,000 investment in the museum, if invested at 8 percent per year (the then-current prime rate), would have produced income of about $190,000 per year. Of that amount, Wilson proposed to spend $50,000 on the museum, with the result that the remaining $140,000 would have gone to Earlham's bottom line. This proposal, which the trustees seem to have adopted,[33] represents the first iteration of the concept that Earlham was to share in the income of the Lilly gifts in a structured way and on a continuing basis.

Wilson's memorandum concluded with an expression of concern that, "whatever we do," the college should run no risk that the museum's operations would become "a drain on the College" or "create liabilities for the College in the future." For example, he said, the museum might construct facilities that "would cease in a few years to pay their way—let alone cast off any income for the support of the College."[34]

As Earlham was developing its position on the management of the Lilly gift, the advisory council was preparing its case in support of the expansion plan. On April 8, 1970, the council convened to discuss its presentation of the feasibility report to a meeting of the Earlham trustees to be held on April 18. At this point, Johnson had not received Wilson's April 11 letter rejecting his restructuring proposal and that proposal was reviewed in some detail at the meeting. Members of the council put forward several arguments that were thought to have possible appeal to the Earlham trustees. Earlham could name the directors of the proposed foundation. The development of the museum as a separate entity could provide an excellent public relations and fund-raising tool for Earlham, as "a donor to the College, or to the Museum, might very well contribute to both." Johnson pointed out that Earlham might not have received the $3 million gift from Lilly had it sold the 1,371-acre tract. He also speculated that if the museum succeeded in raising a new $2 million endowment, Earlham might be permitted to keep the $600,000 set aside for the development of Conner Prairie under the terms of Lilly's 1969 gift "in return for" the transfer of the current museum operations to the new entity. Johnson noted that Lilly was very pleased with the feasibility study. After reading it, he said, "Wouldn't it be wonderful if we could wave a wand and have the whole program completed?" Lilly also expressed the view that all of the land east of White River "should be in the museum."[35]

At the April 18 meeting of the Earlham trustees, Johnson presented the results of the feasibility study and requested that additional acreage be set aside for museum operations. Despite the instructions that he had received from Wilson, the minutes of the meeting report that Johnson suggested approaching "people from the Indianapolis community" for assistance in raising a $1.7 million museum endowment, to be directed to a "separate Conner Prairie Museum Foundation." In the discussion that followed, each of the board's conclusions militated against Johnson's proposal; although the minutes do not reflect that any decisions were reached. In the end, Bolling was authorized to report to Lilly that Earlham was "prepared" to set aside 230 additional acres of the Conner Prairie Farm land for the museum, but "only if and when suitable arrangements have been worked out for funding the development and providing for suitable administrative operations."[36] However, the Earlham board did not accept the James & Berger recommendations.[37]

Three days later, Cope wrote to Johnson reporting that "Landrum is going to explore with Mr. Lilly what options are open for our next steps." That letter also added the need for "the establishment of some appropriate entity which will have the responsibility for handling the enterprise" to the funding condition set out in the minutes of the trustees' meeting. Despite the Earlham trustees' discomfort with the idea, it appears that Bolling did raise Johnson's proposal with Lilly, at least insofar as it related to the creation of a new Conner Prairie entity. On June 16, 1970, Bolling reported to the advisory council that Lilly felt it was "unwise to think, at this time, of the possibility of a separate entity."[38]

As a result, Earlham's objectives remained focused on the retention of the farm land, the expansion of the museum's operations onto that land, and the attraction of Lilly gifts sufficient to fund the museum's operations. As a related objective, Earlham intended that Conner Prairie would become self-sustaining. If it was, then Earlham would not have to support the museum out of its general revenues or out of the income from the 1969 Lilly gift. Finally, Earlham intended to use a majority of the income from the gift for the college, regardless of the needs of Conner Prairie. In November 1970, Lilly sent to Earlham an apparently unsolicited check for $100,000 for the "Conner Prairie Museum Expansion Fund."[39]

∼

On March 9, 1971, Cope, Earlham's vice president, reported to Lilly that in 1970 Conner Prairie showed an operating deficit of $38,000, which was covered by "an allocation of up to $50,000" of the income from Lilly's 1969 gift. Cope's letter also informed Lilly that the new director of the museum, Myron Vourax, would be working closely with the advisory board in soliciting funds from the Indianapolis area to support the development of the museum.

In September of that year, Vourax presented a scaled-down plan for the development of the museum to the executive committee of the Earlham board of trustees, which gave it an "enthusiastic response."[40] In his presentation of this proposal to the full board at its meeting on October 21–22, Wilson, its chairman, provided a preamble in which he reviewed the history of the Lilly relationship, including Lilly's intention that "Earlham was to create a small endowment for the Museum from the sale of some of the land."[41] In January 1972, the executive committee authorized the expenditure on the construction of Prairietown of the $600,000 provided for Conner Prairie's development by Lilly's 1969 gift.[42]

∼

Lilly's second major gift, made in July 1972, consisted of 20,000 Lilly shares ($1.4 million). Under the terms of that gift, Earlham agreed that the fund was to be "kept separate from the other operating and endowment funds of Earlham College." The interest, income, and principal derived from the gift could be used for any of three designated purposes: the construction of appropriate buildings for "the Conner Prairie Pioneer Village;" the "development and operations of appropriate educational programs connected with" the village; and the "general educational program of Earlham College with particular regard for the support of [the] natural history museum and American history programs of the College." The gift expressly provided that none of the interest, income, or principal of the fund was to be used for the construction or maintenance of any building on the Earlham College campus "except in the case of some disaster which makes necessary the reconstruction or replacement of some essential educational building as determined by official action of the Board of Trustees of Earlham College."[43]

In the course of the same October 1972 meeting in which they accepted these terms, the Earlham trustees adopted a resolution approving "the dedication of 230 additional acres of Conner Prairie Farm land . . . for the purpose of expansion of" the museum, and directing the college officials to "arrange for their removal from the tax rolls of Hamilton County, Indiana."[44] There was, however, no change in the administrative structure of the museum.

At this meeting, the board also reviewed the status of Lilly's 1969 gift and determined that "half the realized income" from the $2.4 million endowment remaining after the investment of $600,000 in the museum "be applied to the Museum."[45] The other half was to go to Earlham. This division of the income from the 1969 Lilly gift into equal shares for the college and the museum appears to be the first expression by the Earlham trustees of the principle that became the fundamental basis for future allocations of the Lilly resources between the institutions. The minutes of the meeting contain no discussion of the basis for the board's action other than the statement that it was "obvious that Mr. Lilly did not favor the College over the museum." This comment suggests that Earlham may have become uncomfortable with the more aggressive policy set forth in Wilson's March 26, 1970, memorandum. The discussion concluded with the statement that, "under the circumstances," the board was accepting a recommendation to this effect from its property and finance committee. The discrepancy between the board's action and the terms of the gift instrument was not mentioned. With no further deliberation recorded, the trustees then went on to allocate one half of Lilly's 1972 gift to the museum and the other half to the college. There is no evidence that these actions were reported to Lilly.

Earlham later claimed, in its dispute with the Indiana attorney general, that the eventual fifty-fifty allocation of the entire Lilly endowment resource was the result of a "studied exercise" by the Earlham trustees. If any such exercise took place at the inception of this strategy in October 1972, there is no mention of it in the usually expansive record of the Earlham board's deliberations.

⁓

On June 4, 1973, Lilly made his third, and largest, gift to Earlham College, consisting of approximately $16 million in shares of Eli Lilly and Company. This gift coincided with the construction of Prairietown, and the terms of the gift contemplated the use of principal for that purpose and the use of income for the future support of the Prairietown operation. The terms of that gift established "a special Eli Lilly Endowment Fund" as an "entity separate" from Earlham's other endowment resources.[46] The gift created a "first charge upon the income" of the fund in favor of Conner Prairie, allowed the use of principal for development at Conner Prairie, barred the use of principal for capital improvements at Earlham, and allowed Earlham to use the "annual income" from the fund for educational programs and projects at Earlham, if and only to the extent that the income was not needed for the operation of Conner Prairie.[47]

Bolling acknowledged the gift in a letter to Lilly dated June 10, 1973. He assured Lilly of the Earlham board of trustees' "sense of responsibility to act as good trustees of this magnificent gift." He committed the college to the continued development of Conner Prairie and assured Lilly that the college would "provide what funds are needed, as they are required under our development plan, from the various gifts you have made to Earlham." The college's intent that Conner Prairie's earned revenues would eventually cover its operating expenses also seems clear from this letter.

Bolling's use of the term "trustee" in describing Earlham's relationship to this gift is significant, as Earlham later challenged the attorney general's contention that this gift (and Lilly's other gifts of stock) was held by the college in trust, claiming instead that it constituted only a "restricted" gift. Lilly was the settlor of the public charitable trust of which Earlham was trustee; that is, he established its terms and donated the property to be held in trust. Under general legal principles, a subsequent gift made by the settlor of a trust, to the trustee of that trust, and for the purposes of developing and operating the trust assets is a gift held in trust. Bolling's letter suggests that he shared this view at the time, but he left the Earlham presidency shortly after the gift was made. Earlham's subsequent failures to manage the Lilly gifts as a trust were to have far-reaching consequences.

~

Despite its assurances, Earlham did not proceed with the development of Conner Prairie as represented to Lilly. On May 6, 1974, Lilly wrote to Bolling asking for a meeting to discuss relations between Conner Prairie and Earlham. Lilly asked for a report as to the amount of income the college had received from his previous gifts and of the museum's earned income, and for the museum's 1974 budget. He said that Vourax's continuation with the museum was "vitally important" and suggested that Vourax was concerned about Earlham's commitment to the project. Lilly said that the Earlham trustees had been "a little parsimonious and/or slow in planning what the Village is to get" and noted that the "division" of his gifts was "absolutely at the mercy of the Trustees of the College." It was "high time," he said, to get together on a five-year plan and establish "an approximate and reasonable division of the funds."[48]

Earlham realized that it had a serious problem. On June 9, 1974, Wilson, the chairman of the Earlham board; Franklin Wallin, the newly named president of the college; Paul Lacey, the provost; and Hugh Ronald, the college's business manager met with Lilly at his home in Indianapolis to discuss Lilly's concerns.[49] Bolling also attended, at Lilly's request. Bolling had left the Earlham presidency to take up a position as executive vice president of Lilly Endowment, Inc., which is a measure of the regard that Lilly had for him. Lilly Endowment was created and funded by Lilly, his brother J. K. Lilly Jr., and their father, and after their deaths it became one of the largest private foundations in the United States.

Based, perhaps, on Lilly's use of the phrase "division of the funds" in his letter to Bolling, Earlham seems to have approached this meeting as an opportunity to propose to Lilly a shift from Conner Prairie to Earlham of some part of the June 4, 1973, gift, and it appears that the Earlham representatives left the meeting with the hope that Lilly might agree to a change in the terms of the gift agreement. On June 12, Wilson wrote to Lilly. He reassured Lilly of Earlham's intent to develop Conner Prairie in accordance with their prior understandings. As to the management of the 1973 gift, he proposed, "It is our intention to proceed for the foreseeable future with the division of the funds derived from your gift of stock, dated June 4, 1973, on a fifty-fifty basis between Earlham College, including the Earlham School of Religion, on the one hand, and Conner Prairie Pioneer Settlement."

Lilly responded on June 14, saying that he would study Earlham's letter.[50] It appears that Lilly's attorney, Byron Hollett, became involved at this point,[51] and that there were further conversations between the Earlham representatives and Lilly or his lawyer following the June 12 letter, as the next document in the record is a letter signed by Wilson and Wallin, dated September 9, 1974, "reporting" to Lilly on "the intentions of the [Earlham] board." This letter seems intended to preserve as much as possible of the exposition found in Wilson's June 12 letter, but the outcome was very different: Earlham abandoned its June 12 attempt to change the terms of Lilly's gift and retreated to the concepts set forth in his original gift instrument.

In relevant part, the Wilson and Wallin letter proposed that the "gift dated 4 June 1973" would be managed as follows:

1. Half of the Eli Lilly Endowment Fund shall be set aside for the needs of Conner Prairie Pioneer Settlement, including both capital and operating

purposes; with the other half to be used as an endowment fund, the income from which will be assigned for the operation of Earlham College. . . .

2. Of the portion of the gift allocated to Conner Prairie Pioneer Settlement, the Earlham Board of Trustees will assign $1,500,000 for the completion of the current phase of capital improvements, with the understanding that additional investments in capital improvements may be authorized from time to time, at the discretion of the Board, from either principal or income. In the event the income from this portion of the gift is more than sufficient for the operating needs of the Conner Prairie Pioneer Settlement in any year, such excess income may be allocated by the Earlham Board either to further capital development of the Settlement or to the general operating support of Earlham College.

The Earlham Board of Trustees reaffirms its undertaking . . . to operate Conner Prairie Pioneer Settlement as an historical site for the education and enjoyment of the public; and, notwithstanding the foregoing allocations, further commits itself to see that the first charge on the income from the entire gift shall, as necessary, be for the maintenance, support and appropriate development of the Conner Prairie Pioneer Settlement on such a scale and in such a manner as may be determined by the Earlham College Board of Trustees. Only income not required for the performance of the above commitments, with the arrangements outlined here, but none of the principal, will be used for the general support of Earlham College.[52]

This letter and Lilly's response to it, described below, provided much of the basis for Earlham's subsequent defense of its division of the Eli Lilly Endowment Fund into an Earlham share and a Conner Prairie share and its method of determining fund distributions to the college and the museum. But, on close examination, the exchange of correspondence does not support Earlham's actions. In paragraph number 1 of the letter, Earlham proposes to "set aside" half of the fund "for the needs" of Conner Prairie, for both "capital and operating purposes," with the "income" from the other half "assigned to the operation of" the college. In paragraph 2, Earlham proposes to distribute $1.5 million from the fund for capital improvements at the museum, charging that distribution against the Conner Prairie "portion" of the gift. The income on the remainder of the Conner Prairie allocation would be used for the operation of the museum, and the "excess income" not needed for that purpose could be allocated either to further capital development at Conner Prairie or to the general operating support of the college.

Although there are ambiguities in the language of these two paragraphs, standing alone they might be viewed as supporting Earlham's practice of charging the cost of capital improvements at the museum against the

Conner Prairie share. But the provisions of the numbered paragraphs related to the distribution of income and, consequently, to the accounting for capital improvements, are rendered moot by what follows. Reading on, the next paragraph of the letter overrides the wording of the numbered paragraphs by establishing the requirement that *all* of the income from the *entire gift* is subject to a "first charge" in favor of Conner Prairie's operating and capital needs, and Earlham is barred from using principal in all events. As a result, the letter does not entitle Earlham to any priority in the distribution of income from the gift, it does not support a "division" of that income between the college and the museum (as proposed by Earlham's June 12 letter), and it gives the college no proprietary interest in the principal of that half of the gift in which it had a contingent income interest.

The operative provisions of the letter, insofar as it describes any benefits accruing to Earlham College, are those set forth in the last sentence: the college may use for itself "[o]nly income not required for the performance of the above commitments" (to maintain, operate, and develop Conner Prairie). And the college could use none of the principal under any circumstances, regardless of Conner Prairie's needs or the lack thereof.

Lilly responded with a letter to Earlham dated September 18, 1974 (a copy of which he sent to his lawyer), in which he said, "It seems to me that the thoughts outlined in your letter of September 9 are perfectly satisfactory. Perhaps one simple addition might be made and that is that these paragraphs will apply to any future gifts that I might give to Earlham College."[53]

Although Lilly did not set forth his reasoning in agreeing to the terms proposed by Earlham, it seems obvious that those terms were acceptable because they were the *same* terms as those set forth in Lilly's *original* gift agreement of June 4, 1973. From Lilly's perspective, the Wilson and Wallin letter reconfirmed his original intentions and Earlham's commitment to develop Conner Prairie, put an end to Earlham's attempt to implement a different approach to the management of his gift, brought the discussions to a close, and freed up funding for the museum that Earlham had been withholding.

On September 30, 1974, Wallin sent to Lilly a letter acknowledging Lilly's response, but in the meantime, on September 19, Hollett wrote to Lilly and said,

> It is my feeling that it would be better not to include a provision with reference to future gifts in the letter of September 9, but rather to incorporate the provisions of the September 9 letter into any future gift at that time. It is conceivable that you might wish to make a gift to Earlham College in the future for some specific purpose and would not want to impose the restrictions

set forth in the September 9 letter. On the other hand, if you wish to impose such restrictions they can be incorporated by a simple statement referring to that letter in the deed of gift.

On September 23, 1974, Lilly responded by letter to Hollett, writing, "Your reasoning about the limitation on future gifts to Earlham College is sound, as usual. If I should die with my boots on, my thoughts on the subject will be available in this just-past correspondence between us."

It is clear that Earlham was not aware of this interim exchange of correspondence between Lilly and Hollett until many years later. But the end result of the Lilly-Earlham exchange was that the conditions imposed by Lilly on the use of the 1973 gift survived the 1974 negotiations, and the Lilly-Hollett exchange confirmed that Lilly had no expectation that his September 18 letter would have any effect on subsequent gifts to Earlham. Nothing in the outcome of these negotiations negated Earlham's obligation to manage the public charitable trust in the interests of the public and to apply to the museum the resources appropriate to its growth and development.

∽

Lilly knew how to make a restricted gift to Earlham College, but he did so on only one occasion. On September 5, 1972, he made a gift of $1 million in Eli Lilly and Company shares to be used for the construction of a science building on the Earlham campus.[54] This was his only gift that did not benefit Conner Prairie, and it was his only gift that did not create a fund. It is clear that Lilly viewed Earlham College as having a different relationship to Conner Prairie than it had to its science department.

∽

Prairietown opened in 1974 with six structures, and it continued to expand. In April 1975 Wallin authored a report in which he summarized the conclusions reached in two recent meetings of the task force of the advisory council charged with oversight of the museum's development. According to the report, $1,680,000 had been invested in capital improvements at the museum as of June 30, 1974, and approximately $1,200,000 would remain available for this purpose as of June 30, 1975. The total of the "capital, endowment and quasi endowment funds available" as of March 4, 1975, was $8,969,626. Excluded from this total was approximately $7,500,000, described as "50% of holdings." Although the nature of this exclusion and the manner by which the excluded amount was determined were not described, this presentation is consistent with the action of the Earlham board in October 1972 with respect to the division of Lilly's 1969 and 1972 gifts. The report concludes that the capital expansion program of Conner Prairie would have to be completed within the $1,200,000 limitation. As the funds available (under Earlham's view of the matter) were not sufficient to complete the construction project, the task force assigned priorities to the unfinished items.[55]

The task force report also described concepts for the operation of Conner Prairie introduced by a consultant, Dr. Henry Glassie. His recommendations focused on the settlement as a "sociologically accurate assemblage of the Indiana frontier presented as a 'historical novel'" and the presentation of the village as an "operating frontier community." This seems to have been the impetus for the development of the program of first-person interpretation that was subsequently implemented by Conner Prairie.

After the report was presented to the advisory council, Wallin sent a letter to one of its members responding to an inquiry from the member as to the terms of the 1969 Lilly gift, which the member described as "dedicated solely to Conner Prairie." That letter raised "several difficult questions," according to Wallin, and he pled ignorance of "the investment history" of the gift, how the income had been applied or the capital expended at Conner Prairie. However, Wallin said that he had asked Earlham's business manager to "review this matter."[56] If there was any such review, the results thereof do not appear in the Conner Prairie record.

～

Lilly closely followed the development and subsequent operation of Prairietown up to the time of his death. Consistent with his view that the details of the development and operation of the museum were up to Earlham, and possibly as a consequence of his advancing age, Lilly refused to interject his own opinions and he seems to have been content with the absence of any financial reports from the college regarding the operation of the museum or the administration of his gifts. Lilly died on January 24, 1977. His will, signed on May 29, 1973, provided for a gift to Earlham of 10 percent of the value of his residuary estate:

> [U]pon the express condition that the income and principal, if necessary, of the fund hereby given, shall be subject to a first charge in such amounts as may reasonably be required from year to year for the general maintenance, support, construction, reconstruction and restoration of the William Conner Residence and surrounding grounds and structures . . . for the construction, reconstruction, restoration, maintenance and support of any additional buildings which the College may wish to erect in the area, and for the exhibition thereof as an

historic site for the education and enjoyment of the public. Any income from such fund (but no principal) remaining after performance of the foregoing provisions . . . may be used for the general support of EARLHAM COLLEGE as its Trustees shall determine.[57]

Between 1969 and the time of his death, eight years later, Lilly had provided approximately $32 million to Earlham College to support the development and operation of the museum, including the gift under his will having a value of approximately $10 million. The operative terms of each of Lilly's gifts are summarized in appendix A.

With the minor exception of the 1972 gift ($1.4 million), which permitted the use of income both for both educational programs at Earlham College and for capital improvements and programs at Conner Prairie, without the first charge commitment to the museum, the income and principal of each of the gifts was to be used to develop and operate the museum. There was no "division" of the Eli Lilly Endowment Fund. The only interest that Earlham College had in the gifts that constituted that fund was a contingent interest in income, and that interest was limited to the income not needed for the development and operation of the museum.

Notes

1. See www.connerprairie.org.
2. Eli Lilly, letter to Landrum Bolling, December 12, 1963.
3. Tim Crumrin (Conner Prairie historian), interview with author, June 19, 2006.
4. Tim Crumrin, "Evolution of a Museum: A History of Conner Prairie," Conner Prairie, www.connerprairie.org/Learn-And-Do/Indiana-History/Conner-Prairie-History/Conner-Prairie-History.aspx.
5. "Pageant on Lilly Farm Depicts Events Leading to Settlement of Central Indiana," Indianapolis News, May 18, 1935.
6. Earlham College board of trustees, meeting minutes, meeting held December 14, 1963 (hereafter in this chapter cited as EC mins, followed by the meeting date).
7. See "A Collection of Material Related to the Origin and Legal Status of Earlham College" (compilation of documents, n.d.) and "Articles of Incorporation and Constitution of Earlham College," filed January 12, 1881, with the Indiana secretary of state.
8. Thomas D. Hamm, Earlham College: A History, 1847–1997 (Bloomington: Indiana University Press, 1997), 241.
9. Hamm, Earlham College, 187.
10. Hamm, Earlham College, 241–242.

11. Hamm, *Earlham College*, 240.

12. Hamm, *Earlham College*, 242, 243, and 254.

13. Landrum Bolling, letter to Eli Lilly, December 17, 1963.

14. Crumrin, "Evolution of a Museum."

15. The term "Lenape" is used by the tribe to describe several historic tribes including the Delaware. See www.delawaretribeofindians.nsn.us.

16. EC mins, meeting of September 25–26, 1964, p. 17.

17. EC mins, September 25–26, 1964, p. 17. It appears that nothing further was done to develop the "master plan" until 1969, as reported below.

18. EC mins, meeting of February 9–10, 1968.

19. Harold C. Cope, letter to Eli Lilly, February 19, 1968.

20. Cope, letter to Lilly.

21. See Landrum Bolling, letter to Eli Lilly, March 8, 1968.

22. Conner Prairie advisory council, meeting minutes, meeting held June 20, 1968 (hereafter in this chapter cited as AC mins, followed by the meeting date).

23. The experimental farm was never profitable and Lilly continued to subsidize the farm operations after the transfer of the land to Earlham.

24. Eli Lilly, letter to Richard Sampson, October 31, 1968.

25. The terms of the 1972 gift allowed its use for "one or more" of the purposes of construction and educational programs at Conner Prairie and "general educational programs" at Earlham. *See* p. 19.

26. Landrum Bolling, "Suggested Revisions for Deed of Gift," January 3, 1969.

27. Eli Lilly, deed of gift, January 24, 1969.

28. Emsley Johnson, letter to Thomas Speres, January 27, 1969.

29. Emsley Johnson and Richard Sampson, letter to Landrum Bolling, April 16, 1969; EC mins, meeting held April 18, 1969.

30. Landrum Bolling, letter to Guy Jones, May 23, 1969.

31. EC mins, meeting held February 27–28, 1970.

32. AC mins, meeting held April 8, 1970.

33. In 1971, Earlham mentioned to Lilly that "up to $50,000" of the income on this gift had been allocated to the museum to support its 1970 operations. See p. 19.

34. Wilson, memorandum.

35. AC mins, meeting held April 8, 1970.

36. EC mins, meeting held April 18, 1970.

37. EC mins, meeting held February 10–11, 1978, p. 4.

38. AC mins, meeting held June 16, 1970.

39. See Earlham College receipt dated November 16, 1970.

40. EC mins, meeting held September 18, 1971.

41. EC mins, meeting held October 21–22, 1971.

42. EC mins, meeting held January 22, 1972.

43. The terms of the gift can be found in EC mins, meeting held October 19, 1972.

44. EC mins, meeting held October 19–20, 1972.

45. EC mins, meeting held October 19–20, 1972.

46. Lilly's 1969 gift agreement also required the establishment of a "special endowment fund" and the gift made under his last will and testament is described as a "fund."

47. Lilly gift instrument dated June 4, 1973.

48. It would appear from this comment that Lilly was not aware of the division of his 1969 and 1972 gifts that Earlham had unilaterally adopted in October 1972, and it is noteworthy that in his June 12, 1973, letter, described later, Wilson did not disclose that action to Lilly or take the opportunity to seek Lilly's approval of it.

49. See Edward Wilson, letter to Eli Lilly, June 12, 1974.

50. Eli Lilly, letter to Edward Wilson, June 14, 1974.

51. See EC mins, meeting held August 29, 1974.

52. Edward Wilson and Franklin Wallin, letter to Eli Lilly, September 9, 1974.

53. Eli Lilly, letter to Franklin Wallin, September 18, 1974.

54. Eli Lilly, letter to Landrum Bolling, September 5, 1972. The gift transfer was completed on January 1, 1973. See Earlham College receipt dated January 12, 1973.

55. Franklin Wallin, "Summary Report," n.d. Consistent with this plan, by early 1977 Earlham's investment of Lilly's gifts in capital improvements at Conner Prairie had increased to $2,936,112. See "Review of Gifts from Eli Lilly 1964 to 1975," dated March 15, 1977.

56. Franklin Wallin, letter to Gene McCormick, May 13, 1975.

57. Eli Lilly, last will and testament, May 29, 1973.

~

CHAPTER TWO

The Development of Earlham's Endowment Management Policies

Franklin Wallin served as Earlham's president from 1974 to 1983. Financially, Wallin's years at Earlham were trying times,[1] a fact reflected in the Earlham board of trustees' management of the Eli Lilly gifts. By the time of Lilly's death in January 1977, Earlham had realized that Conner Prairie was not going to pay for itself and that there would be no additional funding from Lilly for the operation of the museum. The Eli Lilly Endowment Fund had received an infusion of $10 million, substantially increasing its value, and Earlham began to struggle with the development of policies for the future administration of the fund.

At their meeting on February 18–19, 1977, the Earlham trustees heard a report regarding the terms of the Lilly bequest and discussed its implications for the college and the museum. Landrum Bolling, who continued to serve as a member of the college's board of trustees, urged that the board develop a "comprehensive and consolidated evaluation of the total resources" that the college had received from Lilly so that it could develop an "overall policy relating to investment and spending restrictions." He cautioned that Earlham "avoid over-ambitious capital development at Conner Prairie" and advised that "firm guidelines" would be needed to "avoid misunderstandings or disappointments."[2]

The policies that Earlham would apply to the fund had their origins in a statement of "principles" adopted by the Earlham trustees on June 3, 1977, less than six months after Lilly's death.[3] These principles were to govern the application of income and principal from Lilly's 1969 gift, his 1973 gift, and the gift under his will. After acknowledging both the trustees' responsibility for administering the gifts in accordance with Lilly's intent and the pressure to expand the museum's operations that could be expected from its supporters, the statement continued,

> The Earlham Board must carefully evaluate any suggested expansion to guard against the expenditure for the museum of all the income from Mr. Lilly's bequest—and possibly more. He always indicated to us that a portion of the income (the percentage never defined) should be available for the program support of the College. Obviously, expanding the facilities at [Conner Prairie] adds to the maintenance and operating costs; if such expansion is financed by use of endowment principal, future annual endowment income will be decreased.[4]

With respect to the gift under the will, the trustees referred to Lilly's September 18, 1974, letter and said, "We know that Mr. Lilly's reference to 'future gifts' was intended to include anything left to the College under his Will." On the strength of that assertion, which the terms of the will did not support, the trustees swept that $10 million gift into the policies framed by the statement of principles. "The proceeds of this trust,"[5] the statement said, "will be governed by the principles of our correspondence with Mr. Lilly in September 1974."[6]

In reaching these conclusions, Earlham relied heavily on Lilly's deference to the college on decisions related to the size and scope of Conner Prairie, and on its view that Lilly did not want Earlham's "obligation to maintain" Conner Prairie to be "a financial drain on the College" and that "he wanted the money . . . also to support" the operations of the college. The only documents relied on by the board in making these findings were the September 9 letter from Edward Wilson and Wallin to Lilly, and Lilly's response on September 18, 1974. As a measure of the significance attached to these letters by the board in reaching its conclusions, the full text of both letters was copied into the statement.[7]

The statement then set forth the policy that the college would follow with respect to that portion of the income derived from the half of the endowment to be allocated to Conner Prairie that was not needed for the museum's operations. That income would be used "for the general operating support of the College."[8] As a result, rather than accumulating it for future use by the museum, the income earned on Conner Prairie's "share" of the endowment that was not expended on its current operations would be directed to the college, along with all of the income on the Earlham "share."

The statement concluded by recognizing that Earlham could not protect against an unforeseen disaster that might require it to use the "half of the income . . . initially assigned in any year to the College" at Conner Prairie. But, it went on, "the Earlham Board intends to exercise its control to make certain that the operation of [Conner Prairie] not be permitted to grow so large or be conducted in such manner as to necessitate use of any year of income initially included in the College budget. If this were to happen, it would, contrary to Mr. Lilly's wishes, cause severe financial distress to Earlham College."[9]

Earlham had set upon a course in which the needs of the college were to take primacy over its obligations to develop and operate Conner Prairie for the benefit of the public. The terms of Lilly's gifts and later correspondence were misstated or ignored. The "College budget" would determine the scope of development at Conner Prairie, not the trustees' judgment as to the needs and opportunities of the museum.

～

In arriving at its position on the management of the $10 million gift under Lilly's will, Earlham was unaware of the correspondence between Lilly and his lawyer in which Lilly expressed agreement with his lawyer's advice that he make no commitments regarding the application of the terms of Earlham's September 9, 1974, letter to any future gifts. However, as a matter of law, the language of Lilly's will took precedence over any other statements regarding the terms of that gift, and neither Earlham's letter nor Lilly's September 18 response were relevant to its interpretation or implementation. The applicability of this legal principle to the Lilly bequest was recognized by the advisory council when Earlham's proposal with respect to the gift was presented to a meeting of the council on February 2, 1977. In a subsequent letter to Wallin, John Rogers, a member of the council, wrote,

> Mr. Lilly's Will clearly stated what was to be done with his bequest and this cannot be changed by referring to a letter which might have indicated another idea. . . . If your interpretation has not been checked and cleared with the College's lawyer, I would strongly urge you to do so. I feel confident that he will agree with me in that this bequest must be handled as outlined in the Will and not be altered for any reason.[10]

Earlham was, therefore, on notice of the issue, but the minutes of the June 3 meeting of the trustees make no reference to any advice received from the college's legal counsel. However, the minutes of the meeting did report that both Bolling and Byron Hollett, Lilly's lawyer, "had reviewed and recommended" the adoption of the statement of principles. Given Hollett's earlier advice to Lilly that his September 18, 1974, letter should *not* be applied to future gifts to the college and Lilly's response memorializing his agreement with that advice should he "die with his boots on," it is difficult to accept at face value this report of Hollett's role in the trustees' action.

Even if Lilly's September 18 letter could have been applied to his final gift, that letter only sanctioned the application to that gift of the principles described in the Earlham letter of September 9, 1974. Those principles did not include a "division" of the gifts and did not support Earlham's subsequent policies. Lilly's will said nothing about any division of the fund and repeated his earlier phrasing subjecting the entire gift to a "first charge" in favor of the operational and development needs of the museum. The assumptions made by the Earlham trustees in adopting and applying their 1977 fund administration principles to Lilly's bequest had no basis in fact or law and were contrary to the terms of the relevant Lilly documents.

〜

Not surprisingly, the policies described in Earlham's 1977 statement of principles were not well received at Conner Prairie. In an undated report to the Earlham trustees prepared later that same year, a team of three consultants— Douglas Hough, Edward Alexander, and Darwin Kelsey—said,

> There now exists much distrust between the Conner Prairie staff, the advisory council and other segments of the Noblesville and Indianapolis communities on the one hand, and Earlham College on the other. The distrust is based, rightly or wrongly, on a perceived lack of commitment on Earlham's part to Conner Prairie's best interests. Its strongest and most concrete expression centers around disposition of the gifts and bequests of Eli Lilly which were intended primarily for the support of Conner Prairie.[11]

The most sensitive issue seems to have been Earlham's intention to apply to the college any "excess" income on the Conner Prairie share of the endowment. The report described Earlham's conflicts of interest in the administration of the Eli Lilly Endowment Fund and urged that

> for the time being at least, the Conner Prairie half of the Lilly Endowment be reserved exclusively for Conner Prairie uses. Any annual excess should be reserved for capital expenditure and for building a reserve fund to take care of any operating emergencies that might create an annual deficit. Such action . . .

seems to us a most necessary move if a difficult system of governance is to be made to work.[12]

On November 21, 1977, Warren Ruddell, who was then the chairman of the Conner Prairie advisory council, submitted a written report to the Earlham trustees covering various aspects of the museum's operations but focusing on the "fundamental importance" of the council's recommendation that the Earlham board "adopt the principle that the income from the Conner Prairie half of the Lilly gifts and bequests be reserved exclusively for Conner Prairie uses." In support of this proposal, he reported that the Conner Prairie staff felt that the college had "pulled the plug" and that, without the assurance of full access to the Conner Prairie half of the endowment, the museum would lose momentum. He noted, in addition, that "with the fifty-fifty split, Earlham College has already benefited enormously from Mr. Lilly's generosity sparked by Conner Prairie" and reported that Earlham's policy was "causing a very real public relations problem for the College" in the Indianapolis community. Ruddell urged that Earlham review the entire circumstances surrounding the Lilly gifts in order to determine whether they had been "received, allocated and administered according to the *spirit* in which they were given."[13] Ruddell accurately foresaw the problems that Earlham was creating for itself and Conner Prairie, saying, "It is a sobering thought to think that if you who knew Mr. Lilly, received the gifts, met with him and corresponded with him, do not set an appropriate pattern for the division of income, who is apt to do it in the future as the make-up of the Board changes in five, ten or twenty-five years?"[14]

In response, Earlham appointed a special committee to bring recommendations to the board of trustees with respect to its management of Conner Prairie. That report, when submitted to the trustees at a meeting held February 10–11, 1978, made a variety of recommendations regarding the governance and operation of the museum. Among them was the recommendation that if "the budgeted endowment income" for Conner Prairie is more than "is actually needed in order to achieve a balanced year-end operating statement, the remainder be held in a special fund for Conner Prairie." The Earlham trustees refused to adopt even this modest gesture toward the museum's interests. While noting agreement "in general" with the "broad principles" of the report, the meeting minutes reported that the trustees had a number of questions and that recommendations for "clarification" were made.[15] The policies ultimately adopted by Earlham mooted the troublesome issue of how to allocate the income on the Eli Lilly Endowment Fund and opened up the prospect of distributions to Earlham that would not be fettered by the limitations imposed by the Lilly gift instruments.

∽

Wallin left the Earlham presidency in 1983 and was succeeded by DeWitt Baldwin, who lasted less than one year after a clash with Gerald Mills, the chairman of the board of trustees. Baldwin's name does not appear in the Conner Prairie record. The selection of Baldwin's successor, Richard J. Wood, was the cause of some controversy within the Earlham faculty and student body due, in part, to the trustees' decision to hire Wood despite their search committee's recommendation of a different person. This decision was seen as a loss of the process of consensus so valued by the Quakers and a violation of trust and confidence.[16] Wood set about addressing the college's financial situation by initiating a series of tuition increases and launching a successful capital campaign in 1987.[17]

The policies that were to govern the administration of the Eli Lilly Endowment Fund took definitive form in the late 1970s. According to reports authored by Wood in May 1991 and September 1994,[18] Lilly's largest gift, the $16.7 million gift in 1973, "was equally divided between Conner Prairie and Earlham College." Both the college endowment and the Eli Lilly Endowment Fund were "unitized." Units of the Eli Lilly Endowment Fund were allocated equally to each of the college and its postgraduate School of Religion, on the one hand, and Conner Prairie, on the other. Earlham later characterized the fifty-fifty division of the fund as having been made pursuant to a "rule of thumb." At the same time, a spending policy was adopted and applied to the endowment, fixing distributions to "all three units" at 5 percent of the average market value of the endowment over the preceding 12 quarters. When received following Lilly's death in 1977, the gift under his will was handled in the same manner. By 1987, the "Wood Report" noted, all three institutions "had come to depend on that endowment income."

Although the college and Conner Prairie received an equal number of units of the Eli Lilly Endowment Fund in Earlham's initial allocation, the college subsequently reduced the Conner Prairie share by amounts expended on capital improvements at the museum. In doing so, rather than charging those expenditures against the entire fund, Earlham was relying on the language of the first of the two numbered paragraphs in its September 9, 1974, letter to Lilly. The first of those adjustments took place in December 1974, when the college liquidated $263,000 of endowment investments to pay for capital needs at Conner Prairie.[19] As a result, the Earlham share had a greater value than the Conner Prairie share from the outset, and in each year following the adoption of its spending policy, the college received a majority of the dollars distributed from the Eli Lilly Endowment Fund. By the time Prairietown was completed in 1976, charges against the Conner Prairie share of the endowment had mounted to $2,936,000, reducing its value to $8,425,000 compared to a value of $9,924,000 for the Earlham share.[20] According to the "Wood Supplement," subsequent capital improvements at Conner Prairie were paid for out of "endowment income" and new fund-raising, without the need for an "invasion of capital."

Earlham's investment management and distribution decisions from this point forward failed to distinguish between its own endowment and the Eli Lilly Endowment Fund. By fixing distributions at the amounts dictated by the spending policy, the income from the latter fund—the interest and dividends earned—became irrelevant, as did the need to consider the source of future distributions to the college and the museum.[21] The "Wood Report" strongly affirmed that Conner Prairie had to operate within these limitations and with a balanced budget, and said that "any further expansion, and major restoration projects such as the re-restoration of the Conner House, will require new sources of funding." Wood returned to these themes in his 1994 report ("Wood Supplement") and added the insight that because the Earlham board had "fully incorporated" the Lilly gifts "into funding current operations, . . . no contemporary Board of Trustees would regard an addition to Conner Prairie as 'appropriate development' if it required invasion of the principal of Mr. Lilly's gifts."[22] Wood also affirmed that the Earlham board "should do all in its power" to insure that the operations of the museum would not result in the need to "honor the 'first charge' provision."

In effect, after Lilly's death Earlham implemented policies that achieved the objective proposed in its June 12, 1974, letter to Lilly, even though that proposal was not accepted. As described by Wood, those policies resulted in a "division" of the Eli Lilly Endowment Fund, with Earlham and Conner Prairie each receiving distributions on its share of that fund.

The Earlham board then turned its attention to the risk that the operations of Conner Prairie might someday require access to the Earlham share under the undisputable first charge terms of the Lilly gifts. The minutes of a meeting of the trustees held February 23, 1979, refer to the spending formula and go on to report that, as the Conner Prairie staff had been unable to give the trustees "sufficient information to [determine] the optimal future size and scale of operations at Conner Prairie Pioneer Settlement," the trustees would "establish the size of operation at Conner Prairie Pioneer Settlement by resource allocation and management policies."[23] This concept—that the operations and future development of Conner Prairie would be determined by the college's fiscal policies and not by the museum's needs and opportunities as they evolved over time—was to govern Earlham's management of the museum for the next 25 years. Lilly's first charge mandate was left behind, acknowledged in principle but having no practical application to the administration of his gifts.

If the policies reflected in the minutes of the February 23 meeting were not sufficient to put an end to any further expansion of Conner Prairie, the board went on to impose a prohibition on any future increases in Conner Prairie's annual operating budget unless the museum was able to achieve annual decreases in its per-visitor expense. In establishing this condition, the Earlham board was, in effect, imposing a moratorium on the development of new programs at Conner Prairie, because data incorporated into the minutes showed that expenses on a per-visitor basis had increased dramatically in each of the past six years.

By implementing these policies, Earlham ceased to comply with the directions in the Lilly gift instruments regarding the application of the income and principal of his gifts. Under general legal principles and relevant statutory provisions, "income" and "principal" are carefully defined terms. Generally, "income" is limited to interest, dividends, and rents; all other forms of return on investment, including realized and unrealized capital gains, are part of "principal." Under the terms of the Lilly gifts, the college had a fiduciary obligation to continuously assess the needs and opportunities of Conner Prairie on the basis of its representations to Lilly regarding the museum's development and taking into account the public's response to its management of the museum. With these factors in mind, Earlham was to apply first the "income" and then the "principal" of the Eli Lilly Endowment Fund to the operation and development of the museum as needed. Earlham's needs were not relevant in making these judgments. As a contingent beneficiary of the gifts, the college was limited solely to the income from the fund left over after all of Conner Prairie's needs had been met. As a result of the adoption of its policies, Earlham abdicated its duties as the steward of the museum and of the Eli Lilly Endowment Fund. The college ceased to apply any independent judgment to the needs and opportunities of Conner Prairie, it artificially restricted the application of the endowment resources to the museum, and it ignored "income" and "principal" as separate elements of fund distributions.

Earlham continued to track the income earned on the "shares" of the Eli Lilly Endowment Fund and, to the extent that the income exceeded the amounts distributed to the college or the museum, credited that excess to separate "reserve" accounts for each institution. Earlham also seems to have recognized that the college could not invade the principal of its share of the endowment and that distributions to the college under the spending rule could not exceed the current income on that share unless there were additional funds accumulated in its reserve. One of the issues raised by the attorney general's demand for an accounting by Earlham of its management of Conner Prairie, as described in chapter 13, was whether Earlham had violated this principle. Earlham refused to provide that accounting.

Consistent with the policies described by Wood, the college severely restricted additional capital investment at Conner Prairie as a means of preserving the value of the Eli Lilly Endowment Fund and thereby protecting the amounts available for distribution to the college. Conner Prairie would have to live within the spending policy. Any new facilities or other development of the museum's operations would have to be supported by new funds raised from the Indianapolis community. Otherwise, Earlham was prepared to maintain the status quo at the museum while enjoying substantial distributions from the Eli Lilly Endowment Fund to support its own operations. As of 2003, the college was taking over $3 million per year from the Eli Lilly Endowment Fund, which constituted approximately half of the total endowment funds held by Earlham College. As noted by Wood, Earlham had become dependent on the Eli Lilly Endowment Fund.

～

Earlham's only significant departure from its endowment management policies related to the construction of the Conner Prairie Museum Center. Prior to its construction, the administrative operations of the museum were housed in an old barn on the property. The collections were held in another barn with no climate controls and dust, snow, and rain coming in through the walls. The "office barn" had been virtually condemned by the fire marshal, and it was clearly unsuited for the use to which it was being put. Given the obvious need, and with prompting from the Conner Prairie staff and the advisory council, Earlham made the decision to go forward with the construction of a new Museum Center that would house the administrative staff and the collections and provide meeting and food service facilities, exhibit areas, and ancillary space.

In accordance with its view that new facilities at the museum would have to be funded with new money, Earlham required that Conner Prairie conduct a capital campaign to raise the estimated $8.6 million cost of the facility. The campaign was to raise money for Conner Prairie, not for Earlham College.[24] By December 1986 the campaign had commitments for about $7 million. The Indianapolis-based Krannert Charitable Trust, Lilly Endowment, and

Ruth Lilly (the daughter of Eli Lilly's brother, J. K. Lilly Jr.) each pledged $1 million; Earlham provided a $3 million loan that was to be repaid from the Conner Prairie share of the Eli Lilly Endowment Fund and an additional $1 million from the Conner Prairie reserve account.[25] The balance of the funding came from other corporate and foundation grants and the general public. On the strength of those commitments, Earlham made the decision to proceed with construction in the spring of 1987.[26]

Because Earlham ran the museum as an operation of the college and not as a trust for which it was the trustee, the value of the museum's physical assets was carried on the books of the college. Consistent with this policy, when the Museum Center was completed, that asset was entered on Earlham's books, thereby shifting to the college the value—over $4 million—of the public's contributions to Conner Prairie.

⁓

All decisions regarding Conner Prairie were made by the Earlham trustees; the advisory council had no authority in the management of the museum. The Museum Center experience, however, may have served to reinforce Earlham's expectation that the Indianapolis-based members of the advisory council could be influential in raising funds for Conner Prairie. Not long after the completion of the Museum Center, discussions began regarding the organization of a separate management corporation for the museum operations. From Earlham's perspective, this was the next logical step in the attempt to position the museum as an Indianapolis institution that merited the support of Indianapolis philanthropists. Earlham had struggled for years with the problem of attracting qualified, engaged individuals as members of the advisory council (and as donors) while refusing to give them any real authority. It also had become apparent to Earlham that Conner Prairie had developed to the point where it would benefit from the oversight of a separate board of directors. The proposed restructuring addressed both issues. From the outset, however, the proposal contemplated Earlham's continued control over Conner Prairie's finances and any major decisions.[27]

The leadership of the advisory council supported this concept, despite its limitations, and participated in the design of the new management struc-ture. As a result, in 1992 Earlham College reorganized an existing, largely dormant, college subsidiary as "Conner Prairie, Inc., an Earlham Museum" and invested that corporation with responsibility for operation of the mu-seum. The college appointed a board of directors for Conner Prairie, Inc., comprised of the former members of the advisory council and four Earlham appointees, and Polly Jontz, the long-term executive director of the museum, was named as president. Conner Prairie was now positioned to appeal to the philanthropic community as directed by local, volunteer leadership and led by professional management. Earlham was careful, nonetheless, to retain fiscal control over the operations of the museum including a right of approval of all operating and capital budgets, the right to veto certain actions of the museum board, and the right to remove all of the directors, without cause.

Despite Earlham's retained powers over Conner Prairie, the restructuring of the museum's governance succeeded in instilling a sense of ownership and fiduciary responsibility among the independent members of its board of directors. Jontz retired at the end of 1995. Under the leadership of her successor, Marsha Semmel, one of the first significant projects of the new board was the development of a strategic plan for the museum. That plan, adopted in June 1997, addressed the problems inherent in having only one main attraction, Prairietown, and contemplated the expansion of the museum's programs and facilities over the next five years. As Earlham College had retained the right to approve all operating and capital budgets for the museum, all of the expenditures involved in the execution of the plan were subject to Earlham's control.

From the time of the organization of Conner Prairie, Inc., to the time of the removal of its board of directors in June 2003, that board was comprised of a blend of talents and experience. Its members included a judge of the U.S. District Court—Southern District of Indiana, the chief executive officer of one of Indianapolis's largest insurance companies, managing partners of local accounting and law firms, chief executive officers of successful small businesses and other entrepreneurs, high-echelon executives from larger area businesses, major philanthropists, knowledgeable Conner Prairie volunteers, educators in both secondary schools and universities, investment managers, and bank executives. Most of the Conner Prairie directors also served in volunteer leadership positions in other nonprofit entities. As later noted by one of the Earlham appointees to the board, the Conner Prairie directors demonstrated a high level of interest and attention to their duties as directors of the museum.[28]

～

There were two additional pieces to the Conner Prairie puzzle. In 1989, a 230-acre farm located just across White River from Prairietown and within 200 yards of its boundaries, came on the market. Conner Prairie learned that a buyer had offered to purchase the property with the apparent intention of using it for gravel extraction and an asphalt plant. With approval from the Earlham trustees, Conner Prairie used a loan from the college to purchase the property for $1.2 million.[29] Conner Prairie paid approximately $150,000 in interest on the Earlham loan between 1989 and 1992, but during that period it received some income from leasing the property for farming purposes. In 1994, discussions began regarding the development of a golf course on the property. Later that year Earlham formed a limited liability company, Earlham/Conner Prairie LLC, in which it retained a 90 percent interest and granted Conner Prairie a 10 percent interest. The land was transferred to the limited liability company, which entered into a long-term lease agreement with a golf course developer. The course opened in 1997.

Conner Prairie's interest in this land lay in protecting Prairietown from any adverse development on the adjacent property. The funding of this transaction did not involve the Eli Lilly Endowment Fund, and the land was not otherwise related to the operations of the museum. The share of the limited liability company allocated to Conner Prairie was seen by Earlham as compensation for its efforts in putting the purchase transaction together and reimbursement of the net costs it incurred in carrying the interest expense on the property for over three years.

Finally, in June 1995, the Earlham trustees allocated to Conner Prairie an additional 607 acres of land lying west of White River, to be used "for purposes related to its mission as an outdoor living history museum." Following this action, only 80 acres of the land included in Lilly's original transfers to Earlham remained outside the museum's operations. The Earlham trustees attached no conditions to this action and gave no reasons for their decision.[30] This action was reported to the Conner Prairie board in October 1995.[31]

Notes

1. See Thomas D. Hamm, *Earlham College: A History, 1847–1997* (Bloomington: Indiana University Press, 1997), 294.

2. Earlham College board of trustees, meeting minutes, meeting held February 18–19, 1977, p. 10 (hereafter in this chapter cited as EC mins, followed by the meeting date).

3. Less than a month earlier, Wallin had received a pointed inquiry from Edna B. Lacy, one of the members of the advisory council, seeking an accounting of all of Lilly's gifts for the benefit of Conner Prairie. Wallin deflected her request with a patronizing letter in which he asserted that these questions were for the Earlham trustees, not the advisory council. Lacy immediately resigned from the council. See Edna B. Lacy, letter to Franklin Wallin, May 17, 1977; Franklin Wallin, letter to Edna B. Lacy, May 27, 1977; and Edna B. Lacy, letter to Franklin Wallin, June 6, 1977.

4. "Principles for Applying the Income from and/or Principal of the Bequest from Mr. Eli Lilly, Who Died on January 24, 1977 (to Be Called the Eli Lilly '77

Endowment Fund), and References Also to Mr. Lilly's 1969 Gift (Earlham College Endowment Fund) and His 1973 Gift (17/73 Fund)," June 3, 1977 (hereafter in this chapter cited as "Principles").

5. Note the use of the word "trust" to describe the relationship of the college to the Eli Lilly Endowment Fund.

6. "Principles," 3.

7. By its terms, Earlham's September 9, 1974, letter was limited to Lilly's 1973 gift. The letter was silent as to the allocation of his 1969 and 1972 gifts.

8. "Principles," 8.

9. "Principles," 8.

10. John Rogers, letter to Franklin Wallin, February 11, 1977.

11. Douglas Hough, Edward Alexander, and Darwin Kelsey, "Report to the Board of Trustees on Conner Prairie Pioneer Settlement by the Museum Consultants" (report to the Earlham trustees, n.d.).

12. Hough, Alexander, and Kelsey, "Report to the Board of Trustees."

13. Emphasis in original.

14. Warren Ruddell, "Recommendations of Advisory Council to the Committee of the Earlham College Board of Trustees on Conner Prairie" (report to Earlham trustees, November 21, 1977), quoted in full in EC mins, meeting held February 10–11, 1978.

15. EC mins, meeting held February 10–11, 1978.

16. Hamm, *Earlham College*, 295.

17. Hamm, *Earlham College*, 297, 298.

18. Richard J. Wood, "Eli Lilly, Conner Prairie, and Earlham College: A Report on the Financial Relationship," May 1991 (hereafter in this chapter cited as "Wood Report"), and "Earlham College's Stewardship of Mr. Eli Lilly's Generous Gifts of 1973 and through His Will—a Report Supplementing [the Wood Report]," September 1, 1994 (hereafter in this chapter cited as "Wood Supplement").

19. Hugh Roland, Earlham College memorandum to Franklin Wallin, April 8, 1975.

20. "Review of Gifts from Eli Lilly 1964 to 1975," March 15, 1977.

21. In 1994, the 5 percent spending rate was reduced to 4 percent, in recognition of the fact that Earlham had only modest success in securing new endowment gifts and that if the endowment was to grow, it had to grow from within. See Conner Prairie, Inc., board of directors, meeting minutes, meetings held December 1, 1993, and April 6, 1994 (hereafter in this chapter cited as CP mins, followed by the meeting date).

22. The terms of the Lilly gift instruments expressly authorized the use of principal for the development and operations of Conner Prairie. See appendix A.

23. EC mins, meeting held February 23, 1979. Justifying this outcome on the basis of the inability of the Conner Prairie staff to foresee the future needs of the museum was particularly disingenuous, as the terms of Lilly's gifts expressly placed this responsibility in the hands of the Earlham trustees.

24. See "The Campaign for Conner Prairie" (case statement, n.d.), undated, and Wood Report.

25. See CP mins, meeting held December 4, 1996, and Wood Report.

26. Conner Prairie advisory council, meeting minutes, meeting held December 3, 1986.

27. Thomas Gottschalk, memo to Dick [Richard J.] Wood, Gwen Weaver, and Jerry [Gerald] Miles, May 27, 1992.

28. See p. 145.

29. See Doug McDonald (Conner Prairie chief financial officer), memorandum to Conner Prairie advisory council, July 24, 1989.

30. EC mins, meeting held February 17, 1996, confirming the action taken in executive session in 1995.

31. See CP mins, meeting held December 6, 1995, correcting the minutes of the October meeting.

CHAPTER THREE

~

The Origins of
the Governance Dispute

Earlham's endowment management policies as described in the Wood reports[1] went largely unchallenged following their adoption, although there was occasional tension between the museum's supporters and the college. Given the dependence of the college on distributions from its share of the Eli Lilly Endowment Fund, Earlham developed a strong aversion to any proposals that might have the effect of "spending down" the endowment. The college had secured an independent revenue stream for itself out of the distributions from the Earlham share of the endowment and thereby insulated the flow of funds to the college from the immediate demands of the museum. But Earlham was acutely aware of the first charge commitment, which it construed to mean that if the Conner Prairie share of the endowment was exhausted, the college then would be forced to dip into its share for museum purposes. Given Earlham's resistance to any changes in its fund administration policies, the issues related to the management of the endowment were sidestepped in the organization of Conner Prairie, Inc., in 1992.

Leadership changes at both Earlham College and Conner Prairie occurred within the space of a few months between mid-1997 and early 1998. In July 1997, Douglas Bennett was named president of Earlham College to succeed Richard Wood, who had retired. Bennett was a graduate of Haverford College and Yale University and had taught at the university level before becoming a vice president of Reed College in Portland, Oregon. At the time he joined Earlham, Bennett was vice president and chief operating officer of the American Council of Learned Societies in New York City. In April

1998, John Herbst was hired as the new president of Conner Prairie. Herbst's predecessor, Marsha Semmel, had resigned to take up another museum post. Herbst, a seasoned museum executive, had served as the executive director of the Historical Society of Western Pennsylvania and of the American Labor Museum in New Jersey, and had been the director of education at the New Jersey Historical Society and curator of history at the Paterson Museum in Paterson, New Jersey.

Changes also were taking place within the Conner Prairie board of directors. As the last of the former members of the advisory council retired from the board, its institutional knowledge of the terms of the Lilly gifts and understanding of the history of Earlham's management policies faded from the board's collective view. Increasingly, the museum measured its participation in the Eli Lilly Endowment Fund based on the policies described in the Wood reports.

⌒

This was the context within which Earlham addressed the first significant needs for endowment resources since the construction of the Museum Center. These arose from three separate but related sources: the costs of capital improvements, repairs, and replacements on the museum grounds; the implementation of the first phase of the recently adopted strategic plan; and a major investment in remodeling the Museum Center. The proposed renovations to the building would change the flow of traffic so that the lower level would provide visitor access from the parking lot to the museum grounds, exhibits, and gift shop, and the upper level would be dedicated to nonpublic administrative purposes.

The chain of events that ultimately led to the dismissal of the board of directors of Conner Prairie, Inc., may have had its origins in a board meeting held in December 1997. At that meeting, the board discussed the disappointing results of the museum's operations for the year just ending and its upcoming 1998 budget. Despite a strong case that investment in the strategic plan was necessary if the museum was to break out of a cycle of recurring deficits, the proposed budget included no significant outlays for the implementation of the plan. An increase in the endowment spending rate and a special draw on the endowment to fund the needed capital improvements and certain elements of the strategic plan seemed to be the only way of achieving the museum's objectives. In the discussion of these issues, however, Bennett cautioned that the Earlham trustees were unlikely to approve an increase in endowment spending. He noted that both the college and its postgraduate School of Religion also were running operating deficits, and said that the trustees needed to maintain the current spending rate in order to preserve the earning power of the endowment. Nonetheless, the Conner Prairie board adopted resolutions asking the Earlham trustees to approve a 1 percent increase in the endowment spending rate (to 5 percent) and a $2.5 million draw from the endowment to be used for the museum's general capital needs and the strategic plan investment.[2]

Following this meeting, I began to study the general background of the Lilly-Earlham relationship, using the Lilly gift instruments and related correspondence found in the Conner Prairie files to analyze the case in support of the museum's entitlement to the proposed endowment draw. In February 1998, I provided my completed analysis to Douglas D. Church, who had taken over chairmanship of the Conner Prairie board of directors a month earlier. Church was the managing partner of Church, Church, Hittle & Antrim, with a law practice in Noblesville, a few miles north of the museum in the county seat of Hamilton County. Based on my analysis, we agreed that there were substantive legal issues in Earlham's approach to the management of the Lilly gifts.

At the next board meeting, held in March 1998, Bennett reported that he had proposed to the Earlham trustees a "Repositioning Plan" that would address the needs of the college, its graduate School of Religion, and Conner Prairie. He recognized that the operating deficits of all three institutions would not be cured quickly. In his view, the solution in each case lay in enhancing the institution's "core" income stream, and he acknowledged that to do so would require additional capital investment. He was prepared, therefore, to recommend to the Earlham trustees a 1 percent increase in the spending rate and a capital draw for investment purposes at Conner Prairie. The draw was to be viewed as an "advance" against a capital campaign for Conner Prairie, the proceeds of which would be used to replenish the amount withdrawn from the Eli Lilly Endowment Fund. The Conner Prairie board viewed this as responsive to the museum's needs and undertook to develop a specific proposal within this framework.[3]

However, given our new understanding of the terms of Lilly's gifts, in particular Lilly's direction that the principal of the gifts could be used for capital improvements at Conner Prairie, Church and I set up a meeting with Bennett. At that meeting, held on April 6, Church and I outlined to Bennett our understanding of the terms of the gifts and suggested that Earlham was not giving appropriate consideration to the use of an unconditional endowment draw to fund Conner Prairie's capital investment needs. Bennett adamantly insisted that the college's endowment management policies governed the use of the Eli Lilly Endowment Fund and refused to consider any other approach to meeting the museum's needs.

In the following weeks, Bennett—perhaps unsettled by what he had heard on April 6—undertook to put to rest any uncertainties regarding Earlham's administration of the Lilly gifts and to emphasize to the Conner Prairie board of directors the nature and extent of Earlham's control over the museum's operations. At meetings of the Conner Prairie executive committee and board of directors in April and June, Bennett made comprehensive presentations addressing both issues. He distributed copies of Conner Prairie's articles of incorporation and bylaws, noting the points of Earlham's control over the museum's governance and finances. Moving on to the Lilly gifts, he reviewed the general terms of the gift instruments and reported that he had conducted an investigation into the history of the issues. In acknowledging that the situation was complex and lacking clarity, he focused on Earlham's allocation between the college and Conner Prairie of the gift under Lilly's will as the possible source of the "problems" within both the museum and the broader Indianapolis community.

Bennett then referred to the Earlham trustees' 1995 transfer to Conner Prairie the use of the 607 acres west of White River. He noted the absence of any "formal recognition" of this event and suggested that the circumstances could serve as a basis for action by the Conner Prairie board that would finally resolve the outstanding questions related to Earlham's management of the Lilly gifts. Although Bennett did not expressly state it, he seemed to be suggesting that by acquiring the right to use the 607-acre tract, Conner Prairie had received value equal to any harm it might have suffered under Earlham's endowment management policies.[4]

There were several barriers to an effective consideration of Bennett's proposal by the Conner Prairie directors. At this point, only Church and I had any exposure to the legal issues surrounding the Lilly gifts, and our understanding of those issues was incomplete. Only a few of our board colleagues had any background facts that would aid in the evaluation of the proposal, which came to our board without any discussion or negotiation with Earlham's trustees. Their action, taken three years earlier, was entirely unilateral and absent any suggestion that it was tied to concessions on the part of Conner Prairie. We found it difficult to assess the economic impact of Earlham's action. Conner Prairie's interest in the 607-acre tract was limited to a right to "use" the property, and even that right was tenuous given Earlham's control over the museum's management and resources. Moreover, the legal effect, if any, of our agreement to the proposal was unclear. Conner

Prairie had no authority to resolve questions related to Earlham's management of the Lilly gifts. In retrospect, any expectation on Bennett's part that his proposal, if accepted, would put to bed all of the issues surrounding the Lilly gifts seems wholly unrealistic.

However, Conner Prairie was in need of the funding to be provided by the still-pending "Repositioning Plan" in order to address its capital investment and operating needs, and Earlham held the purse strings. We hoped that acquiescence in Bennett's proposal would facilitate a constructive outcome on the funding issues. As a result, with little discussion, both the Conner Prairie executive committee and board of directors passed resolutions confirming the terms sought by Bennett.[5] The board of directors meeting was John Herbst's first as the new president of Conner Prairie.

The college trustees eventually approved the "Repositioning Plan" in December 1998. Conner Prairie could now apply an endowment draw of $3.7 million to the improvement of the museum's physical plant, including the remodeling of the Museum Center, and to planning for the proposed museum expansion and the anticipated capital campaign. The supplemental 1 percent draw, which was to continue for the next five years, was to support fund-raising efforts, advertising, and promotion. Earlham College used its additional funding to increase tuition revenues by supporting methods of recruiting additional students and improving student retention rates.

Unfortunately, the cost estimates for the museum's capital improvements proved to be too low. Other unanticipated capital expenditures and related expense items eventually led to a total outlay between 1998 and 2003 of approximately $4.4 million. The additional funding of $700,000 came from contributions to the project and other revenue sources, including the proceeds from the settlement of a lawsuit with the building's architect and the condemnation of some real estate for a road widening. Bennett reacted vigorously to what he viewed as a "cost overrun," even though he knew that the initial projections were only estimates. Earlham saw the circumstances as a failure by the Conner Prairie board to exercise appropriate controls over the management of the museum and sought assurances from its leadership that they would put procedures in place that would prevent any recurrence. The Conner Prairie executive committee felt that Earlham had overreacted, but they also acknowledged that there were weaknesses in the museum's internal controls and procedures. The committee subsequently designed and implemented policies to address those problems.

⁓

Instead of resolving the issues surrounding Earlham's endowment management policies and Conner Prairie's governance, events surrounding the "Repositioning Plan" and the 607-acre tract had the effect of stimulating further discussions within the museum. While framing its capital campaign, the Conner Prairie directors continued to question why, given the terms of the Lilly gifts, the museum could not draw upon the Eli Lilly Endowment Fund without a concomitant promise to replenish any endowment resources used for the development of the museum. Furthermore, since any capital improvements funded by the campaign would become assets of Earlham College, the directors struggled with the development of a case statement for the campaign that would withstand scrutiny by the philanthropic community.

In January 2000, Stan C. Hurt succeeded Church as the chair of the Conner Prairie board. Hurt was a successful local businessman and a philanthropist with considerable experience in the governance of nonprofit organizations. During the period covering the Conner Prairie dispute, he also acted as the chair of the Eiteljorg Museum of Western Art in Indianapolis and of the Arts Council of Indianapolis. Hurt served as chairman of Conner Prairie from January 2000 to December 2002, at which time I succeeded to the chair. Church and Hurt both continued as members of the Conner Prairie board following their service as chairman. During this span of time, Church, Hurt, and I had a number of conversations that led us to conclude that something had to be done to address Conner Prairie's situation. Several factors shaped our thinking: our understanding of the terms of the Lilly gifts, the fund-raising difficulties that continued to plague the museum, Earlham's endowment management policies, the burden imposed by fees and charges assessed against the museum by the college, and Earlham's attempts to extend its control over Conner Prairie's operations. These concerns began to infiltrate discussions between the institutions at several levels.

In June 2000, in conversations between Church and Howard Mills, an Earlham trustee who also was a member of the Conner Prairie board, Mills indicated that Earlham was willing to examine certain aspects of the Conner Prairie relationship, including the management of the museum's personnel functions, and they also discussed the long-term benefits to both institutions of disassociating the college from the museum. These discussions were sufficiently substantive that the Conner Prairie board appointed a governance committee, with Church as its chairman, to represent the board in further discussions with Earlham. Earlham seemed anxious to avoid any public appearance of differences of opinion between it and Conner Prairie.

On October 3, Bennett and Herbst had a meeting in which they discussed the museum's interest in another endowment draw for program and capital needs, and in other conversations between Herbst, Mills, and Mark Myers, the chairman of the Earlham board of trustees, Conner Prairie was encouraged to submit to Earlham whatever our board believed was needed by way of support from the endowment.[6]

Bennett followed up on his conversation with Herbst in an e-mail sent on October 10, 2000, in which he recited the history of the 1998 draws and reminded Herbst that Earlham's agreement to the draws "included the expectation that Conner Prairie would begin a capital campaign in 2001 or 2002 that would include an endowment goal larger than the one-time capital draw of $3.8 million." Bennett went on to express his concern that, despite the investment in new facilities and programs, the museum's operating budgets were not approaching "fiscal equilibrium" and questioned whether the museum had a "strategy for building endowment."

In subsequent meetings, the new capital draw request was refined to the amount of $1 million, but Earlham began to back away from approving endowment funds for this purpose. On October 25, 2000, Bennett wrote to Herbst setting forth "two alternative possibilities for funding the $1 million list of important needs." He argued that Conner Prairie should either build the expenditure into its operating budget, pushing aside other expense items, or finance the improvements by borrowing the money and factoring into its operating budget the resultant interest expense. He urged that Conner Prairie cost out the effect of these alternatives. The use of an endowment draw was not mentioned. Conner Prairie was well into its budgeting process for 2001, and Herbst was upset that Bennett was proposing to change the funding plan at that point. Shortly after this exchange, tension began to build regarding Earlham's administration of the museum's health insurance plan.

On December 6, 2000, Myers and Howard Mills met with Hurt, Church, and me to discuss the relationship between the institutions. In that meeting, Myers asserted that, while Earlham controlled Conner Prairie, it "supported" the efforts of the Conner Prairie board and confirmed that Earlham was prepared to review certain aspects of the relationship, but only within the parameters of the existing structure. Church responded that the Conner Prairie board and staff did not see how the museum's mission paralleled that of Earlham and urged that future discussions include the broader issues of the Earlham–Conner Prairie relationship. When Mills asked whether the real issue was the management of the Eli Lilly Endowment Fund, Church assured him that we were prepared to exclude that issue from the discussions. Mills urged Conner Prairie to raise its own endowment. We pointed out that, without a resolution of the questions raised by Earlham's role at Conner Prairie, such an effort had no prospects for success. Further, we argued that Earlham's 1992 decision to reorganize Conner Prairie, create the management corporation, and appoint its separate board of directors entailed a commitment to share the museum with the Indianapolis community, and that Earlham had to be prepared to give up its control over the museum if it expected Conner Prairie to be able to generate independent support.

In anticipation that Earlham would see these discussions as leading to negotiations over a division of the Eli Lilly Endowment Fund between the museum and the college, the Conner Prairie governance committee had debated what position it should take on this issue. While the creation of a separate endowment would have been a necessity for a truly independent Conner Prairie, at this point in the process we did not view a complete separation of the museum from the college as a possibility. Nor did it seem likely that Earlham would be willing to address any reallocation of the endowment between the college and the museum, given the college's own critical needs. Our immediate objectives were more limited, relating to management control, relief from Earlham's assessment of fees and charges against the museum, and Earlham's endowment spending policies—in particular, its resistance to funding capital improvements at the museum. We also knew that Earlham's management of the Eli Lilly Endowment Fund was so volatile an issue that calling attention to it would probably defeat any constructive discussion of the other governance issues. We therefore adopted the view that we would not press for any restructuring of the Eli Lilly Endowment Fund. But we were equally committed to the proposition that nothing in any agreement with Earlham could preclude future challenges to Earlham's endowment management policies. As it turned out, Earlham was unwilling to address the governance issues without obtaining absolution for those policies, although this did not become clear until late in the discussions.

On January 8, 2001, Hurt sent Myers a formal, detailed request from the Conner Prairie executive committee that the Earlham trustees consider a special distribution from the Eli Lilly Endowment Fund totaling $974,000 at their meeting in early February. A few weeks before that meeting, Myers, Bennett, and Richard Smith, Earlham's chief financial officer, met with Herbst, Hurt, Church, and me to discuss our request. Bennett challenged our funding request on the grounds that it did not reflect action by the full Conner Prairie board. We had considered taking the proposal to the full board, but had decided not to do so. The proposal was within the authority of the executive committee, and we were concerned that, in the context of an open board meeting, we might not be able to confine the discussion to the draw request. An open debate of the governance issues would have increased the risk that those issues would be disseminated into the broader community, which both parties were hoping to avoid. Myers also objected to what he called the "legal argument" in our request, which contained references to the terms of the Lilly gift instruments. He asserted that Earlham held the Lilly gifts "in perpetuity" and under the college's exclusive control. He urged the development of a "framework" for any future capital draws and that we consider alternatives to the use to the Eli Lilly Endowment Fund for this purpose.

Bennett circulated a draft of the framework on February 2, 2001. Five days later, Hurt responded by letter, saying that the issues deserved more consideration than we could give them before the Earlham board meeting on the following weekend. He urged that Earlham consider the "emergency" items on the needs list, totaling about $658,000, pending an opportunity for further conversation. Bennett and Myers, expressing surprise at the "emergency" characterization, deflected the request on that basis. Hurt responded by saying that the term was intended only to reflect that the items in question represented continuing programmatic and physical needs of the institution. In the end, Myers did not present the proposal to the Earlham board. We were told that he came to this decision because he was not sure it would pass and believed that it was better not to present it than to have it defeated.

In response, Herbst refined the draw request within parameters developed in consultation with the Conner Prairie governance committee for submission to the Earlham board on March 22, 2001. Four days later, Bennett wrote to Herbst reporting that the trustees had turned down the request. As an alternative to a new endowment draw, Earlham proposed that Conner Prairie "borrow against" the endowment by accepting a loan from the college's general fund. The loan would be repayable, with interest, by a one year extension of the 1 percent special endowment draw that had been instituted as part of the "Repositioning Plan" in 1998. In exchange, Bennett wanted Conner Prairie to adopt a policy of "full depreciation accounting" for all of the facilities and equipment used in the museum's operations.

As Conner Prairie's putative owner, Earlham transferred all capital improvements at the museum to the books of the college once they were completed and ready for use. Consequently, Conner Prairie carried practically no hard assets on its books and, therefore, had little depreciation expense of its own. Bennett's proposal would have increased that expense by about $350,000 per year, but only on the museum's interim statements of operations. These were modified cash-basis statements that the staff and board used for management purposes. Accounting for depreciation expense does not require the expenditure of cash and, as this charge did not relate to museum-owned assets, it would be backed out of the museum's statement of operations in the year-end audit in accordance with generally accepted accounting principles. As a result, agreement with Bennett's proposal would have had no immediate consequence for Conner Prairie other than to significantly increase its interim operating expenses. But if, as claimed by Earlham, it was the owner of the facilities in question, the depreciation expense belonged to it and not to Conner Prairie. We viewed this proposal with suspicion, as it seemed to presage a demand that the museum begin to set aside cash to fund some part of the college's depreciation expense.

The debate over the special distribution proposal had the effect of intensifying the discussions between Church and Myers on the question of autonomy for the museum, with Church taking the position that Earlham must consider the broader issues in the relationship. This, in turn, caused Church and me to renew our push for an employment contract between Conner Prairie and Herbst, who was an at-will employee and therefore without protection in the event of a blow-up. We had previously discussed this issue with Herbst. However, the attention that we were all paying to the governance issues delayed the preparation of a proposed contract until early 2003. When the proposition was put to Bennett, he aggressively rejected it. In retrospect, it is clear that by this time he was developing the strategy that removed Herbst and the Conner Prairie board of directors, and he did not want to have his freedom of action hampered by a contractual obligation to a man he intended to fire. We debated whether we should ask the Conner Prairie board to approve the contract and sign it, despite Bennett's objection. Herbst was, after all, an employee of Conner Prairie and not of Earlham College. Bennett insisted that Herbst was a "vice president" of Earlham, but this was nothing more than a paper relationship. This was not a matter on which the college had retained its "veto" power. Nonetheless, believing that we should not take any definitive action without Earlham's approval, we abandoned the idea, with Herbst's consent. Our decision turned out to be very costly to Herbst. Earlham failed to reciprocate our good faith and fired him with only three days of severance pay.

∼

Using funds provided as a part of the "Repositioning Plan," Conner Prairie began to prepare the museum for a fund-raising campaign, including preliminary assessment efforts, donor cultivation, and the development of campaign materials. However, by early 2001, the members of the Conner Prairie board had come to understand that the philanthropic community would not support the museum on the same basis as its peer institutions. Unlike other institutions supported by charitable contributions, at Conner Prairie additional facilities funded by community support did not become assets of the museum but were instead transferred to the books of Earlham College. The management of the museum was subject to budget and other controls by Earlham, and the museum's board of directors held office at the pleasure of the college. It was difficult to defend Earlham's method of determining endowment distributions for operating support and Earlham would not use the Eli Lilly Endowment Fund for capital investments in the museum unless such draws were reimbursed. The closer prospective donors came to Conner Prairie, and the greater their understanding of the museum's governance structure, the more difficult it became to move them to higher levels of support.

Woodburn, Kyle & Company, independent consultants engaged by the museum to assess its fund-raising potential, cautioned the museum board against attempting to conduct a capital campaign prior to resolving what was now being referred to at Conner Prairie as the "Earlham problem." It found that Conner Prairie's prospects were "complicated by its relationship with Earlham College. . . . We frequently heard that the resolution of the governance situation with Earlham College would improve the philanthropic appeal. . . . Many people told us that without the improvement of the governance relationship, it will probably be very difficult to raise money for Conner Prairie."[7]

These conclusions had been reflected in the museum's efforts to raise money for its Liberty Corner project, which had been constructed with interim loans provided from the Earlham general fund. A "quiet" campaign had been underway to "pay off the mortgage" on the development, but donations had not reached expected levels.

～

Despite its nationally recognized successes in instituting new programs and facilities, Conner Prairie continued to run operating deficits.[8] These deficits were in part the result of the failure of contributions to reach expected levels, but also reflected disappointing admissions and special events revenues as well as wasteful practices imposed by the college on the museum's operations. A significant part of Conner Prairie's operating expense was in the form of the assessment by Earlham of "rent" and an "administrative fee" against the museum. The administrative fee had been in place at Conner Prairie for many years. During Wallin's presidency, Earlham College had adopted the device of using the name "Earlham" to refer collectively to all three of its "parts": the college, the Earlham School of Religion, and Conner Prairie.[9] Earlham viewed the administrative fee as a means of recouping certain expenses that were common to all three of the Earlham operations, including the salary and office expenses of the college president, endowment management expenses, expenses of the Earlham trustees' meetings, and the premium for directors and officers liability insurance. Conner Prairie had no control over any of the expenses being charged to it in the form of the administrative fee and no voice in endowment management.

The administrative fee was bitterly resented by the staff and board at Conner Prairie, as they saw Earlham taking over $3 million per year in other distributions from the Eli Lilly Endowment Fund on questionable grounds. They also felt that the museum received little benefit from the expenses that Earlham associated with this fee—the largest of which was Bennett's salary—and there were persistent problems with Earlham's management of Conner Prairie's operations. For example, one of the services covered by the administrative fee was payroll and health plan administration. Health benefit claims were first processed at the museum and then transferred to Earlham for implementation, but Earlham frequently made mistakes that resulted in delays and time spent in correcting its errors.

The museum's share of the fee increased as its revenues increased in relation to those of the college, so the more successful the museum became, and the more the college struggled, the greater the amount of the funds siphoned off from the museum's endowment support. Immediate relief from the administrative fee was a high priority for us in the governance discussions.

Earlham also charged Conner Prairie "rent" for the use by the museum of its land and buildings, even though Earlham had paid nothing for those facilities and held them as the museum's trustee. By 2001, the rent and administrative fees charged to Conner Prairie had amounted to more than $2 million. Part of the museum's inability to achieve balanced budgets can be attributed to the expense that these fees represented—approximately $245,000 per year at the time.

But regardless of the revenue and expense issues resulting from Earlham's management policies at Conner Prairie, one fundamental question remained: given the terms of the Lilly gifts, how could there be any deficits at the museum, as the income and principal of the gifts were explicitly dedicated to meeting its operating needs?

Notes

1. Richard J. Wood, "Eli Lilly, Conner Prairie, and Earlham College: A Report on the Financial Relationship," May 1991, and "Earlham College's Stewardship of Mr.

Eli Lilly's Generous Gifts of 1973 and through His Will—a Report Supplementing [the Wood Report]," September 1, 1994.

2. Conner Prairie, Inc., board of directors, meeting minutes, meeting held December 3, 1997 (hereafter in this chapter cited as CP mins, followed by the meeting date).

3. CP mins, meeting held March 18, 1998.

4. This conclusion as to Earlham's rationale finds support in a file memorandum dated June 12, 1996, prepared by John Quinn, then chairman of the Conner Prairie board, reporting on a discussion between Quinn and Earlham's president, Richard Wood, regarding the background of the transfer.

5. See Conner Prairie executive committee, minutes, meeting held April 27, 1988, and CP mins, meeting held June 17, 1998. In the subsequent negotiations regarding the Lilly gifts, Earlham did not assert that this action by the Conner Prairie board acted as a bar to reconsideration of the issues, and the college was the first to propose changes in the terms of the gifts.

6. Myers was to play an important role in the events that followed. A graduate of Earlham College, he also held a PhD from Pennsylvania State University. He had recently retired as a senior vice president of Xerox Corporation and was then acting as a senior fellow at Wharton Business School of the University of Pennsylvania. He served as chairman of the Earlham board of trustees throughout the Conner Prairie dispute and was the college's chief negotiator and spokesperson in its dealings with the Indiana attorney general.

7. Woodburn, Kyle & Company, "Positioning Assessment" (report, January 24, 2001, p. 10).

8. Earlham provided any cash needed to fund the museum's operating deficits by loans to the museum from the college's general fund.

9. This device glossed over the fact that the college held the museum as trustee of a public charitable trust.

CHAPTER FOUR

~

The Governance Discussions Shift to Autonomy for the Museum

By the first quarter of 2001, it was becoming clear that Conner Prairie's future was in jeopardy. Earlham did not view the Eli Lilly Endowment Fund as a resource for the expansion of the museum's programs or the improvement of its facilities. Other, competing museums in Indianapolis, driven by the philosophy that such institutions had to either grow or die, were engaged in major construction and renovation projects. Our own experience with the development of Conner Prairie's then-current strategic plan under Marsha Semmel's administration had confirmed this with respect to Conner Prairie. But Earlham seemed alarmed by this prospect, as museum expansion could threaten the Earlham "share" of the endowment if things did not go well. Earlham president Douglas Bennett was becoming more demanding in his relations with Conner Prairie's board of directors. In his interactions with the museum, Bennett focused most of his attention on the museum's operating results while strictly adhering to Earlham's policies on the management of the Eli Lilly Endowment Fund. Bennett was a frequent visitor to Conner Prairie, but in all of his appearances before the Conner Prairie board, staff, and committees he was never supportive or congratulatory of their efforts. It also was clear to us that the college was struggling with student enrollment and retention issues. In addition to its growing frustration with Earlham's practices and policies, the Conner Prairie leadership began to question Earlham's motives, as it did not seem to have the best interests of the museum at heart.

A late March 2001 letter to John Herbst from an Indianapolis philan-thropist who was a former chairman of the Conner Prairie board of directors and a strong financial supporter of the museum brought into clear relief the difficulties that could be anticipated in attempting to fund Conner Prairie's needs through a capital campaign. The philanthropist had attended a Con-ner Prairie board meeting on March 21 and heard Douglas Church's report on our discussions with Earlham regarding the endowment draw, and Ben-nett's response. The letter expressed the writer's disappointment with Earl-ham's policies and said that as long as "Earlham continues its oversight role using what I consider a heavy hand," additional contributions will be "very hard to come by." He concluded by saying that he had taken Conner Prairie out of his estate planning, despite his admiration for all that Herbst and the board had done and were doing.[1] This letter confirmed in our minds that a capital campaign was not an option, that we had a major problem with the philanthropic community, and that we needed to squarely address the gov-ernance issues.

On April 2, 2001, Herbst, Ken Ramsey (Conner Prairie's chief financial officer), Church, Stan Hurt, and I met to discuss our situation in light of Earlham's March 25 proposal to extend the special endowment draw. We agreed that Hurt should communicate to Mark Myers that the Conner Prai-rie governance committee would reject the proposal and recommend that the executive committee do likewise. Hurt also was to report to Myers that Earlham's tactics in the governance discussions were encouraging divisive-ness between the Earlham board and the Conner Prairie board, and that it was imperative that the governance committees get to a discussion of the is-sues between the institutions. We decided to ask Ice Miller, the Indianapolis law firm in which I was a partner, to provide, on a pro bono basis, its analysis of the legal issues presented by the terms of the Lilly gifts and the available remedies. The firm agreed to our request.

Myers responded to Hurt's letter on April 11, 2001. He proposed that we meet on May 4. He urged that we reconsider our position on the Earlham funding proposal and outlined an agenda for that meeting that included the administrative fee and the broader governance issues as well as the funding request.

The May 4 meeting was held at Conner Prairie, with Myers, Howard Mills, Church, Hurt, and me in attendance. The meeting consisted primarily of Earlham defending its past practices. However, for the first time Earlham proposed a mechanism to address its concern that, given the first charge lan-guage of the Lilly gifts, the current arrangements provided no protection to the college from the invasion of "its" share of the Eli Lilly Endowment Fund in the event of a disaster at Conner Prairie. To that end, Earlham advanced the concept of a "firewall" to protect its interests; that is, a requirement that draws against the Conner Prairie share of the Eli Lilly Endowment Fund could not reduce the value of that share below a specified amount. The implementation of this proposal would have squarely contradicted the terms of the Lilly gifts.

Following this meeting, Earlham floated a proposal to restructure the administrative fee by shifting certain functions (including health plan administration) from the college to Conner Prairie and reducing the fee proportionately. We viewed this as a small step in the right direction, for we believed that we could perform the services in question better and less expensively.

By this time, the issues embedded in the draw request had become secondary to the broader structural issues between the college and Conner Prairie. We decided to accept the loan from the Earlham general fund on the basis proposed by Bennett, but without agreeing to the depreciation condition, thinking that the resolution of the governance issues would encompass the question of the loan's repayment. Between 2001 and 2003, Earlham advanced $375,000 to Conner Prairie, most of which was applied to capital projects at the museum.

In August 2001, Church, Hurt, and I developed a discussion outline that set out a proposed approach to conversations with the Earlham governance committee regarding the terms on which Conner Prairie could be separated from Earlham. The key point of that outline was that "separation . . . should be considered as a primary objective" of the continuing governance discussions. The basis for this conclusion was that, as an Earlham subsidiary, Conner Prairie would be unable to attract board members and staff in the future or to generate funding from the community at large. The outline concluded that Earlham was not administering the Lilly gifts in accordance with their terms, a point confirmed in the legal memorandum that Ice Miller had provided in the interim.

In September 2001 Conner Prairie formally notified Earlham that it would assume responsibility for all of the administrative matters that Earlham was willing to turn over to it. The implementation of this change was expected to result in an annual net savings to the museum of about $91,000.

The governance committees were scheduled to meet on November 5, and the Conner Prairie committee began to brief the members of its board on the status of the discussions and the committee's intentions as set forth in the discussion outline. Conner Prairie's board members expressed strong support for the committee's proposals. At the meeting with Earlham, discussion touched on all of the issues, with particular attention paid to why Conner

Prairie couldn't fund-raise and to the relationship between that problem and autonomy.

As to the question of separation, Earlham disclosed that it had sought legal advice on the issue, and that its lawyers had said that the museum could not be separated from the college under the terms of the Lilly gifts. If this was the advice the college had received, it clearly was wrong.

Note

1. Mel Perelman, letter to John Herbst, March 27, 2001.

~

CHAPTER FIVE

The Governance Discussions Become Confrontational

At this point, Earlham drove a stake in the ground. In early December 2001, Douglas Church and I received a memorandum from Douglas Bennett that enclosed two additional documents: a legal memorandum from Earlham's lawyers on the subject of the Lilly gifts and a "stewardship" statement that had been presented to, and adopted by, the Earlham board of trustees at its October 2001 meeting. The legal memorandum gave unqualified support to Earlham's administration of the Lilly gifts. The author of the memorandum was not identified. It was an argumentative document that contained very little analysis or citation of authority. The stewardship statement forcefully reaffirmed Earlham's control over Conner Prairie.

Unaware that Earlham was working on these documents, we were stunned and dismayed that Mark Myers and Bennett would present them to the Earlham trustees for action without advising the Conner Prairie governance committee of their intentions or giving us an opportunity to present our side of the issues. Given the existence and the purported spirit of the governance discussions, the committee viewed this as an act of bad faith on Earlham's part. It seemed to us that Myers and Bennett had decided to preempt any bi-lateral approach to Earlham trustees. This tactic set a pattern for subsequent actions by the Earlham trustees, who seemed to be operating in a vacuum regarding the facts and law of the college's relationship with Conner Prairie and to have no interest in understanding any other perspectives.

Given this development, the Conner Prairie governance committee felt that we had no alternative other than to put our position before the full

Conner Prairie board at its meeting on January 14, 2002. The committee outlined a plan that included solicitation of a "stand-still" agreement with Earlham that would preserve the status quo, including John Herbst's relationship with the museum, during the continuation of the governance discussions and the creation of an advisory group of about a dozen former board members and other key supporters of the museum (termed our "kitchen cabinet"). The stand-still agreement was confirmed by an exchange of e-mails between Stan Hurt and Myers on December 21, 2001.

On December 19, 2001, Bennett escalated the confrontation by sending to Herbst, Hurt, and Chris Cooke, the chair of the finance committee of the Conner Prairie board, a letter alluding to Earlham's veto power over the adoption of budgets for the museum and outlining "the questions and issues that I will bring to consideration of" the 2002 budget at the board meeting scheduled for January 14. The proposed budget, which reflected continuing operating deficits, was the result of several meetings of the Conner Prairie finance committee in which Richard Smith, Earlham's chief financial officer, had participated and raised no objections to the budget during the course of that process.

On January 4, 2002, Hurt invited the kitchen cabinet to a meeting with the Conner Prairie governance committee. He sent to the members of the group a package of materials that included Earlham's legal memorandum; the stewardship statement; a somewhat redacted version of the Ice Miller legal memorandum; and a draft of a position paper that the governance committee had developed setting forth the status of the matter, the issues, and a proposed procedure for reaching a resolution. The position paper proposed that "from this point forward, the Governance Committees should consider, as their primary objective, the means by which Conner Prairie, Inc. can be separated from Earlham."[1]

The paper asserted that Earlham was not administering the Lilly gifts in accordance with their terms, that Earlham had a conflict of interest in the administration of those gifts, and that its policies in managing the gifts had not insulated Conner Prairie from the consequences of that conflict. The paper called for the transfer to the museum of the real estate given by Lilly to Earlham and the "allocation to Conner Prairie, Inc. of that portion of the Earlham Endowment that is the result of Mr. Lilly's gifts to Earlham for Conner Prairie, with appropriate provision for the interests of Earlham in those gifts."[2]

When the kitchen cabinet and the governance committee met on January 9, 2002, there was unanimous support for the strategies and objectives of the committee.

The Conner Prairie board of directors met on January 14, 2002. The position paper and the Conner Prairie legal memorandum were distributed to the board meeting, as was the Earlham legal memorandum and stewardship statement. There was a sometimes intense discussion of the independence issue, with Conner Prairie board members expressing strong support for independence. The key event of the meeting was that Bennett, with Smith voting with him, vetoed the adoption of the 2002 budget. Ann Kendall, the other Earlham appointee present at the meeting, abstained from the vote. Under the Earlham-designed Articles of Incorporation of Conner Prairie, Inc., Earlham retained ultimate fiscal authority over the operations of the museum, and certain matters, including approval of budgets, could not pass without the approval of at least three of the four directors appointed by Earlham. As there were not three Earlham appointees voting in favor of its adoption, the budget proposal failed, and the board had no choice other than to instruct the Conner Prairie finance committee to come back with a modified proposal. Kendall resigned from the Conner Prairie board at the conclusion of the meeting.[3]

Hurt and I had a telephone conversation with Myers on January 17. We expressed our concerns regarding Bennett's management of the budget issue at the January 14 meeting. Myers distanced the Earlham board from the budget dispute, saying that it wasn't "structured" to consider the museum's budget issues, thereby reinforcing our impression that we were to have no direct access to the Earlham trustees with respect to Conner Prairie issues. Myers said that we should come to the next meeting of the governance committees, scheduled for January 28, prepared to discuss what we meant by "independence." He seemed willing to consider some changes in the relationship, but cautioned that consensus building takes time. We said that we were running out of time. Myers concurred with this conclusion, but from a different perspective.

Based on projections prepared by Howard Mills, an Earlham trustee emeritus, Earlham now seemed to be convinced that Conner Prairie was on a course that would exhaust the entirety of the Eli Lilly Endowment Fund including the Earlham "share." At some point, Myers said, Earlham would have to intervene to keep this from happening. We said that, if this was Earlham's concern, the solution to the problem lay in the ability of the museum to increase its contributions and the isolation of Earlham's resources from the museum's operations, both of which could occur only if Conner Prairie were wholly independent. Myers replied that some within Earlham concurred with this analysis, at least to the extent of being willing to listen to our independence proposal, but he reiterated that Earlham had received legal advice that the entities could not be separated, and he emphasized that, from Earlham's perspective, the governance discussions were focused only on improving the existing relationship, not creating a new one. When we asked why he had moved the Earlham trustees to adopt the "stewardship" statement, he replied that the action was unremarkable as the statement contained nothing new.

～

Indiana law did not provide any private redress for breach by a trustee of the terms of a public charitable trust. The attorney general, the state's principal legal officer, acting on behalf of the public interest, was the only person with standing to address such questions.[4] However, in such matters the attorney general acted like any other lawyer. When he uncovered a matter in which the public interest was involved and that required legal redress, his only option was to go to court, file a lawsuit on behalf of his client, the people of the state of Indiana, and then prove his case and seek judicial relief. Given Earlham's position on the legal issues, which to us seemed manifestly incorrect, the Conner Prairie governance committee considered setting up a unilateral meeting with the attorney general, Steve Carter, to brief him on the situation and seek his advice. That meeting was never held, for reasons described later. As the governance process went forward, we alluded to this alternative at different times. We also suggested to Earlham that we make a private, bilateral approach to the attorney general for guidance on the legal issues, which the college rejected. Earlham later claimed that the Conner Prairie board had threatened to "file suit" against the college, but as matters stood, neither Conner Prairie nor its supporters could take direct legal action against Earlham. The threat of seeking intervention by the attorney general was our only leverage.

～

On January 23, Hurt and I sent to Myers a draft of the minutes of the January 14 meeting. We outlined the views of the Conner Prairie board and said that we had lost confidence in Earlham's leadership of Conner Prairie. We questioned why Bennett seemed prepared to run the obvious risks of alienating the Indianapolis community and warned that events such as the board meeting were reducing the opportunities for a constructive solution.

The governance committees met at Earlham on January 28.[5] Earlham had received our position paper when it was distributed at the January 14 board meeting. In his opening comments, Myers asserted that Earlham understood the Lilly–Conner Prairie relationship and took great pride in what it had accomplished at the museum. He found it disturbing to have us question Earlham's discharge of its fiduciary duties and disapproved of our threats of "legal action." He reported that, in the opinion of Earlham's lawyers, our views of the issues were without merit. Myers disclosed that Earlham had retained Lee McTurnan of McTurnan & Turner, Indianapolis, as its legal counsel in connection with Conner Prairie matters, and that the firm was the author of the Earlham legal memorandum. He suggested that it might be helpful for us to talk with McTurnan. Myers concluded his opening remarks by reporting that the issues would be considered in an executive session of the Earlham board on February 22 and proposed that the governance committees should meet promptly after that date. We needed to find a way to work together, he asserted.

In response, Church laid out Conner Prairie's concerns: the elimination of Earlham's conflicts of interest, the resolution of the questions about the discharge of its fiduciary duties in its administration of the Eli Lilly Endowment Fund, and the more complete fulfillment of Lilly's intent. He challenged Earlham's view that its trusteeship was "perpetual," noting that a court of equity had the power to remove and replace a trustee. He said that representatives of the Conner Prairie governance committee would be willing to meet with McTurnan if the purpose of that exercise was to find common ground on which our objectives could be achieved. Myers replied that Earlham's instructions to McTurnan were that this was a non-adversarial relationship and that it was seeking "understanding." Church affirmed that we were not seeking a public dispute, but we wanted an outcome that was appropriate and fair and would not rule out a third-party resolution of the issues if we wound up with unalterably opposing views. The Conner Prairie representatives left the meeting with little optimism, but were anxious to see what Earlham's lawyers had to contribute.

On the following day, Church and I met with Lee McTurnan and his partner, Steve Badger. McTurnan & Turner was a "boutique" firm that specialized in lawsuits, not corporate transactions, a fact that made us wary of Earlham's professed objectives. The tagline "Concentrating in Business Litigation" appeared right under the firm's name on its letterhead. Our discussion circled around several of the substantive questions arising out of Earlham's management of the trust. The Earlham lawyers were argumentative, and the meeting seemed to have been designed to persuade us that we were wrong in our analysis of the legal issues. But at the end of the meeting, McTurnan raised the question of how, if the institutions were to be separated, we proposed to divide the endowment. That he raised this question suggested that negotiation of the terms of a separation was within the scope of McTurnan's engagement by Earlham. We said that we were open to any reasonable proposal.

We heard nothing further until March 1, 2002, when Myers and Howard Mills called Church and Hurt to report on the results of the Earlham trustees' meeting held February 22. The Conner Prairie representatives were told that the Earlham board was divided into thirds on the separation issues, with one-third in favor, one-third uncommitted but willing to pursue the issues further, and one-third opposed. Earlham's chief financial officer, Smith, was removed as an Earlham appointee to the Conner Prairie board and replaced by Thomas Fisher, an Earlham trustee who was the judge of the Indiana Tax Court, ostensibly to insulate the member's vote from Bennett's influence. Bennett had offended the Conner Prairie board by pointing out, prior to the vote on the 2002 budget, that with Smith voting with him to reject the budget, he held the power to prevent its passage. Morris Mills and Gerald Mills, both of whom opposed independence, were added to the Earlham governance committee, so as (we were told) to give them better exposure to the issues. A meeting of the two committees was scheduled for March 20, prior to the Conner Prairie board meeting that afternoon. Myers and M. Mills were frank in acknowledging the stress caused by Bennett's involvement and seemed anxious to take several small steps to relieve the tension. Things seemed to be looking up.

But we then received a letter from Myers, dated March 11, that put the issues in a very different light. The letter reported that, at the trustees' meeting,

[t]he Earlham Board of Trustees considered the request of the leadership of Conner Prairie to initiate a separation of the Museum from Earlham. After careful consideration, it was the consensus of the Board that such action would not be consistent with its responsibilities for the gifts we accepted from Eli Lilly.

We recognized that there are important issues of trust and misunderstanding affecting the governance of Conner Prairie. We request that the Earlham administration, the Earlham-approved Conner Prairie Board members, the Earlham Board leadership and the Conner Prairie Board work actively to resolve these issues. As we wish to restore a relationship of mutual trust and respect, it is recommend[ed] that we consider the services of a third party to help mediate the differences.[6]

Again, we were nonplussed. According to this letter, there was no support within the Earlham trustees for Conner Prairie's independence and no trustees on the fence. Separation was "not consistent" with Earlham's "responsibilities." We were given no explanation for the discrepancies between the information conveyed in Myers's telephone call and the action revealed by his letter. Instead of moving his board toward consideration of the independence issues, as he had represented to us, Myers now seemed to have presided over a flat-footed rejection of separation. He proposed mediation, but only with respect to the terms of the working relationship between the college and the museum.

Myers addressed the Conner Prairie board at its meeting on March 20, 2002. His comments escalated the tension by focusing on Earlham's lack of confidence in the Conner Prairie board and staff and by reiterating Earlham's concern that, left to its own devices, the museum would eventually exhaust the Eli Lilly Endowment Fund and become a drain on Earlham's tuition revenues. As a result, he concluded, Earlham needed the protection of the "firewall" beyond which no endowment draws could be made for the benefit of Conner Prairie.

Myers's comments were not well received by the Conner Prairie board. Hurt attempted to calm the waters with an e-mail to the board members stressing all that we had accomplished and noting that Earlham's concerns regarding the burden of Conner Prairie could be extinguished by making the museum independent from the college. Fisher responded to Hurt's e-mail with a letter, dated March 28, in which he expressed concern that Conner Prairie was still talking about "separation," which was "not an option." He advocated mediation, but cautioned that "we must all be entering into these negotiations and governance discussions in good faith" and that we should tell Earlham now if Conner Prairie "is only committed to separation."

Notes

1. Conner Prairie governance committee, position paper.

2. Conner Prairie governance committee, position paper.

3. On January 31, 2002, Ken Ramsey, Conner Prairie's chief financial officer, took a 30-day leave of absence, at the conclusion of which he resigned in protest over Earlham's handling of the 2002 budget issues.

4. Following the Conner Prairie dispute, the Indiana Code was amended to provide that "the settlor of a public charitable trust, among other persons, may maintain a proceeding to enforce the charitable trust." IC 30-4-2-17 (added by Public Law 238-2005, sec. 25).

5. At this meeting, Conner Prairie was represented by Hurt; Church; Conner Prairie board member Steve Holt, a Noblesville lawyer and Hamilton County Commissioner; and me. Attending for Earlham were Howard Mills; John Young, an Earlham trustee who had succeeded Kendall as one of the Earlham appointees to the Conner Prairie board; Thomas Gottschalk, a lawyer and Earlham trustee emeritus who had been instrumental in the organization of Conner Prairie, Inc.; Myers; Thomas Fisher, another Earlham trustee; and Bennett.

6. Mark Myers, letter to Douglas Church and Berkley W. Duck, March 11, 2002.

CHAPTER SIX

~

The Mediation Effort

On May 8, 2002, Mark Myers proposed to the Conner Prairie governance committee a structure for the anticipated mediation, suggesting that the issues for discussion include the following:

1. How can Conner Prairie be in a stronger position to raise money, especially in metropolitan Indianapolis?
2. How can the Earlham board and the Conner Prairie board work together in developing and carrying through a shared vision and financial strategy for Conner Prairie?
3. How should we set the endowment payout rate regarding Conner Prairie? What criteria should the Earlham board use in considering any future requests for special capital draws?
4. What should be Conner Prairie's share of the common (or overhead) expenses of Earlham as a whole? On what basis should this share be charged?
5. On matters for the Conner Prairie board requiring a majority of both the Conner Prairie board and the Earlham-appointed members, what regular procedures will serve to allow constructive and timely decisions?
6. What should be the working relationship between the Earlham president and the Conner Prairie president?
7. What administrative matters have to be worked on between Earlham staff and Conner Prairie staff, and how can we make these working relationships function smoothly?

8. How should the Earlham–Conner Prairie relationship be presented to the general public? To Conner Prairie's staff? To those at the college and ESR (Earlham School of Religion)?

While this agenda contained an accurate recitation of the questions that had prompted and sustained Conner Prairie's interest in reforming the museum's governance, it did not contemplate discussion of a separation of the institutions. Given this fact, and with Thomas Fisher having expressly taken that issue off the table, it is fair to ask why the Conner Prairie governance committee thought that it would be productive to move into mediation on the terms proposed. The answer, I believe, was that we had no alternative. We had now put four years of effort into the resolution of the "Earlham problem." The attention that had been focused on Earlham's management policies and the level of interest generated had resulted in a significant polarization of positions both at the college and at the museum. As a result, it was clear to us that the museum could never attract another leader of the quality of John Herbst. If nothing changed, Herbst's successor would most likely be an Earlham puppet, given Douglas Bennett's heavy-handed oversight of the museum. The museum's ability to recruit and retain volunteer board members able to effectively advocate and fund-raise also had been permanently compromised.

In short, we had passed the point of no return. The abandonment of the effort to reform the museum's governance would have meant reversion to a position of stagnation and total subjugation to Earlham—an outcome that, we believed, ultimately would lead to the disintegration of the museum. On several occasions, Earlham representatives had said to us that, in the college's view, its only obligation under the terms of Eli Lilly's gifts was to open the William Conner House for public visitation from time to time. All of the other elements of the museum could be extinguished if the college elected to do so. Therefore, if the museum was to avoid the risk of being dismantled and have any prospect for future growth, we believed that we had to pursue any potential avenue to a different relationship. Earlham had acknowledged that separation could address its fundamental concern that the museum might become a burden on its tuition revenues. We felt that there was the possibility that, in the hands of a capable mediator, the process might reveal to Earlham the logic of separation and condition it to the concessions that it would have to make to achieve that objective.

We had to do something, and Conner Prairie's refusal to proceed with mediation would have left us with no viable strategy other than to put the issues before the attorney general. We had no assurance that, if we approached the attorney general unilaterally, he would view these questions as having sufficient interest or public importance to warrant the investment of the time and resources of his office. There was, after all, no impending crisis at Conner Prairie. The parties were still talking to each other, and Earlham was willing to mediate at least some of the issues. The legal questions might be viewed as unclear by the attorney general. Even if he endorsed Conner Prairie's positions, if Earlham refused to accept his views, the attorney general would have no means of enforcing them other than to bring a lawsuit. A definitive third-party resolution of the issues could be years away, and the outcome was not certain.

In retrospect, it does not appear that we misled Earlham into thinking that we had accepted Myers's premises. Earlham was well aware of Conner Prairie's determination that the process should end in independence for the museum. It appeared as though Earlham itself did not view Myers's agenda as the outside parameters for the mediation. After the mediator had reviewed all of the background documents and spent one day with each of the Conner Prairie and Earlham representatives, he reported to us that, in his view, the possible outcomes of the mediation ranged from continuing with the status quo to a negotiated separation in which Conner Prairie would become completely independent of Earlham with an agreed-upon "redistribution of endowment based dollars" between the college and the museum. As will be seen, the document that resulted from the mediation process included terms that expanded upon Myers's original objectives.

Earlham selected Neil Bucklew, a professor of management and industrial relations from West Virginia University, as the mediator. The first face-to-face meeting between Bucklew and representatives of the college and the museum was held June 19, 2002. Ben Blanton, an Indianapolis lawyer familiar with the circumstances of the Earlham–Conner Prairie relationship, also attended the meeting at the request of both parties. Before discussion of the items on the mediation agenda began, Douglas Church asked the Earlham representatives about the extent of their authority to bind the college to any agreement that might result, noting that we had a prior experience (referring to the January discussions with Myers) in which the Earlham board did not back up its leadership. There was no satisfactory answer to this question, which turned out to be prophetic.

∿

Understanding the role played by the Earlham board of trustees in the subsequent developments of the Conner Prairie story requires an understanding of its constitution and processes. Earlham College, an institution with deep roots in the Quaker tradition, viewed itself as governed by Quaker-style decision making, which seeks consensus. Where committee action was involved, the committees also were expected to follow a consensus-building process in making recommendations to the board. All board members were entitled to an equal voice.[1] A single objector could thwart any action by the board of trustees. No motions were made or seconded, and no votes were taken. Action was evidenced by the entry of a "minute" reflecting the sense of the meeting, the content of which was left to the discretion of the presiding officer. Discussion ended when the presiding officer decided, based on what he had heard, that there was "unity" on the subject. The only form of disagreement with that outcome was for a dissenter to agree to "stand aside" and let the action pass without his express consent but without a "no" vote.[2] This made for a very unwieldy process in dealing with the complex, emotion-laden, and time-sensitive issues embedded in the college's relationship with Conner Prairie.

The fragmentation of the Earlham board of trustees further complicated the situation. The Indiana Yearly Meeting of Friends and the Western Yearly Meeting of Friends, the two Quaker congregational organizations that were the founders of the college, each appointed 6 trustees. The Earlham College alumni association elected an additional 4 trustees; these 16 trustees then elected another 7 "trustees-at-large," who were subject to the approval of the Yearly Meetings. The president of the college served as a member ex officio.[3] Over the years, the Yearly Meetings, which controlled 19 of the 24 seats on the board, had held different views about the proper relationship between education at Earlham and the role of the Meetings at the college. Collectively, they had been at odds with the college administration over various policies and programs of the college that were not considered to be consistent with Quaker principles.[4] Oddly, very few of the trustees resided in Indiana.

~

The mediation discussions produced a sufficient sense of agreement that Blanton was asked to draft a document incorporating terms. On July 20, Blanton circulated that draft, titled "Statement of Principles and Understanding," to Church and Fisher. Their review resulted in a redraft that was shared with the broader group of participants in the governance process, generating more questions and comments. The governance committees scheduled a second meeting with Bucklew for September 20.

Church, Hurt, Sean Skinner (a Conner Prairie board member), Herbst, and I met with Bucklew and Blanton the day prior to the September 20 meeting. Bucklew reported that Earlham continued to view as a deal breaker any demand for changes in its control of the Eli Lilly Endowment Fund, and that it continued to worry about Conner Prairie exhausting the endowment through reckless spending. Earlham's proposed solution—the "firewall"—would limit the museum's access to the Eli Lilly Endowment Fund. We considered the firewall to be inconsistent with the terms of the Lilly gifts. Bucklew added that Earlham was not going to address any of the issues we saw arising out of its past management of the fund. Although discouraged by this report, we were committed to seeing the mediation through to its conclusion.

The mediation resumed the following day at Conner Prairie. It was the mutual understanding that any agreement reached in the mediation would be presented to the Earlham board for action at a meeting scheduled for Friday, October 11. The day-long session produced two redrafts of the "Statement of Principles," the second of which, subject to some further revision, set forth a basis for further discussion. Blanton circulated a revised draft on September 30.

At Earlham's insistence, the document opened with a long set of recitals regarding the terms and circumstances of the Lilly gifts, Lilly's relationships with Earlham, and Earlham's management of the museum and the endowment. The substantive terms of that draft were as follows:

- Earlham would retain title to the 58-acre tract, but Conner Prairie would be permitted to use it as long as the museum complied with the terms of the agreement.
- Earlham would continue to manage the Eli Lilly Endowment Fund, to which the principles of the Indiana version of the Uniform Management of Institutional Funds Act (UMIFA) would be applied. There would be no change in the allocation of the fund between the college and the museum and Conner Prairie's interests would continue to consist of a specified number of "units" in the fund. UMIFA did not require that endowment distributions be accounted for as originating in "principal" or "income," and would have sanctioned Earlham's policy of making distributions from the Eli Lilly Endowment Fund based on a percentage of its market value.[5]
- The Conner Prairie share of the Eli Lilly Endowment Fund would absorb one-half of the Conner Prairie "debt" resulting from the working capital advances and funding for the construction of Liberty Corner. Earlham would absorb the other half.
- Conner Prairie would first apply any future distributions from the Eli Lilly Endowment Fund to the support of the 58-acre tract, and could use only the balance for other purposes of the museum.

- Earlham would retain four seats on the board of directors of Conner Prairie, Inc., but Conner Prairie would no longer be a subsidiary of Earlham. The draft contemplated, but did not specifically provide for, the termination of Earlham's "veto" powers over actions by the board.
- The Conner Prairie board of directors would have full control of the operations of the museum including endowment draws from the Conner Prairie share. Endowment draws, however, could not reduce the value of the Conner Prairie share to less than $75 million (its approximate value at the time) and were permissible only if the total value of the Eli Lilly Endowment Fund was in excess of $150 million. This constituted the firewall.
- Conner Prairie, Inc., would receive title to all of the real estate that Earlham had received from Lilly except for the 58-acre tract, which Earlham would continue to hold as trustee of the public charitable trust, and the 80-acre tract in the northwest corner of the property that was not dedicated to the museum's use.
- Earlham would terminate the administrative fee charged to the museum.
- Conner Prairie would construct an appropriate memorial commemorating Earlham's contributions on the museum grounds.

The terms of the draft would have given the museum operational independence from Earlham and limited control over endowment spending, but that and the termination of the administrative fee were the only clear gains for Conner Prairie. The draft would also have transferred to Conner Prairie, Inc., title to almost all of the real estate that the college had acquired from Lilly. We did not, however, view that transfer as an economic gain as the land previously had been dedicated to the museum's use, and it seemed unlikely that we would sell it. Furthermore, the terms of the arrangement failed to sever Earlham College's relationship to the museum as trustee of the 58-acre tract or to give Conner Prairie any voice in the management of the investment policies of the Eli Lilly Endowment Fund.

The legal consequences of an agreement on these terms were ambiguous. If the agreement was legally enforceable, the installation of the firewall would have substantially changed the terms of the Lilly gifts. However, the effect of the agreement was limited by its designation as the "Statement of Principles and Understanding," by the absence of the Indiana attorney general as a party, and by the lack of any court proceedings to approve it. The terms and circumstances of the agreement were tacit admissions by both parties that it would fail to resolve the historic issues surrounding Earlham's management of the Eli Lilly Endowment Fund. Despite these uncertainties, we had to assume that the agreement would be binding on both parties.

We provided comments and questions on this draft to Blanton on October 2, 2002, and again on October 4. We questioned whether UMIFA could be applied to the management of the Eli Lilly Endowment Fund and argued that Conner Prairie needed to have some degree of control over the investment management policies related to its "share" of the fund because of the possible need for investment strategies different from those adopted by the college. The "Statement of Principles," we argued, should not attempt to resolve the question of investment management strategy for all time. But our principal concerns related to the size of the firewall—the $75 million floor on the value of the Conner Prairie share of the endowment. We had expected to negotiate this amount once we had final data as to the value of the fund and anticipated that the amount would be significantly less than the current market value of the Conner Prairie share. This was a critical issue, for it defined the amount of the Eli Lilly Endowment Fund that would be available for use at the discretion of Conner Prairie. Earlham would have a stranglehold on endowment assets equal to the firewall amount. We also had questions regarding a number of other terms, including the effect of a termination of the lease arrangement. Blanton undertook to merge our comments with those he expected to receive from Earlham and produce a revised draft.

The Earlham board of trustees meeting was now just one week away, and we were anxious to place all of the outstanding issues in Blanton's hands for resolution as quickly as possible. But Blanton had heard nothing from Earlham. He inquired whether Earlham had any comments on his draft, and Bennett's only response was that the board would be discussing the matter at its Friday meeting. Blanton circulated a revised draft of the "Statement of Principles," incorporating the Conner Prairie comments but without any input from Earlham.

After the Earlham trustees' meeting, we received word that the board had taken no action with respect to the "Statement of Principles" and that the trustees had brought the college's lawyer (Lee McTurnan) into their deliberations. Church sent an e-mail to Bucklew and Blanton expressing our disappointment with this outcome. He reported that the Conner Prairie board would be meeting the following Wednesday and said that we needed to have some substantive report regarding Earlham's position in order to prevent a "genuinely angry" response from the board. Apparently oblivious to the likely reaction to news of the outcome of the trustees' meeting, on Sunday, October 13, Bennett sent an e-mail to Herbst saying nothing about the meeting, but asking for an update on the museum's capital spending and operating budgets.

Earlham's formal response to the mediated agreement came in the form of a letter from Bennett that he handed out to the Conner Prairie board at its meeting on October 16. The letter reported on the trustees' actions and said that the draft agreement "does not satisfactorily deal with the Earlham board's fiduciary obligations." In the letter, Bennett promised to unilaterally "formulate revisions of the proposal that will satisfy both parties" and said the Earlham governance committee "will be in touch soon."

We did not expect a resolution of the issues to emerge from the Earlham trustees' meeting. It was obvious from Bennett's refusal to comment on the terms of Blanton's September 30 draft that there were substantive issues to be resolved from Earlham's perspective. We also had reservations about the draft terms, including their failure to address a restructuring of the Eli Lilly Endowment Fund that more closely comported with the terms of the Lilly gifts. We hoped, however, that the full Earlham board would accept the proposed terms in principle, move the matter toward a conclusion within the general framework that the governance committees had put in place, and leave the more complicated issues relating to endowment management for another day.

In large part, the Earlham trustees' decision to reject the mediated result can be seen as turning on the failure of the agreement to resolve the question of Earlham's "fiduciary obligations," including its vulnerability to claims of breach of trust arising out of its past management of the Eli Lilly Endowment Fund and its right to continue its practices in the future. These questions were now out in the open for the first time since the advisory council objected to the fund management policies that Earlham adopted shortly after Lilly's death. Although Earlham had publicly distributed a memorandum from its lawyers that concluded that it was blameless in its administration of the Lilly gifts, the college must have realized the risks to which it was now exposed. In light of subsequent events, it is clear that the college had decided that closure on these issues was an essential element of any resolution of its relationship with Conner Prairie, and it seems likely that Earlham also realized that it might be able to use Conner Prairie's desire for independence as leverage to produce an outcome that could benefit the college financially.

The impetus, on Earlham's part, to pursue Conner Prairie's independence might have emerged out of another, initially unrelated, development. On August 30, 2002, just six weeks prior to the October meeting at which the Earlham trustees rejected the mediated agreement, a strategic planning committee of Earlham College issued a draft plan for the college for the period

2002 through 2008, for consideration by the board of trustees at that same meeting. The committee's report contained a bleak assessment of the college's prospects. According to the report, Earlham College had been plagued with "chronic budget issues." It faced serious student recruitment and retention problems. It had been unable to achieve its stated enrollment goal of 1,200 students, and it was suffering from the revenue shortfall that resulted from this condition.[6] Financial aid was inadequate. Almost every activity and program at the college was "stretched thin." Faculty salaries were not competitive. The college had deferred maintenance of its academic facilities. Student housing was "tired and shabby." There were significant gaps in important academic programs. The college had been unable to invest in the technologies and course offerings needed to remain competitive with other institutions in its peer group. The report contained a one-sentence summary of Earlham College's situation: "Our most important weaknesses and challenges . . . take financial form."[7] According to Earlham's "Factbook" for 2002, the college had accumulated deficits of $2.25 million from 1997 through 2001, and in other published reports the college had said that it was anticipating a $900,000 deficit for the 2004–2005 academic year.[8]

The circumstances of Earlham's troublesome relationship with Conner Prairie had now merged with the realities of its financial situation, offering the college an opportunity to solve two nagging problems. Earlham's next steps in the tug-of-war between the college and the museum reflected a shift in its objectives toward an outcome under which the Earlham "share" of the Eli Lilly Endowment Fund would be relieved from any obligation, under Lilly's first charge mandate, to support the operations of the museum. As a result, Earlham would have unfettered access to those funds for the purposes of the college.

Notes

1. Douglas C. Bennett, "Quaker Governance of Quaker Colleges," *Quaker Higher Education* 2, no. 1 (April 2008), www.earlham.edu/~fahe/publications/qhe2-1.pdf.

2. See generally "Essays on Earlham College Governance," collected July 2004, www.earlham.edu/policies/governance/documents/essays.pdf.

3. "Earlham By-Laws: Article I: Earlham Board of Trustees, as Amended October 20, 1989," section 2, www.earlham.edu/policies/governance/documents/bylaws.pdf.

4. See, generally, Thomas D. Hamm, *Earlham College: A History, 1847–1997* (Bloomington: Indiana University Press, 1997), 336–346.

5. The application of UMIFA to the Eli Lilly Endowment Fund is discussed in chapter 17.

6. At the time, tuition at Earlham College was the third highest of the 32 colleges and universities in Indiana ($79 less than Rose-Hulman Institute of Technology and $2,086 less than University of Notre Dame). See *Indianapolis Monthly* 26, no. 11, p. 130.

7. "Report of the Strategic Planning Committee, Earlham Campus Draft 1," August 30, 2002.

8. *Earlham Word Online* XVIII, no. 27 (May 2, 2002).

CHAPTER SEVEN

~

The Negotiations
with Earlham's Lawyers

At this point in the proceedings, Earlham transferred management of the Conner Prairie issues from its governance committee to its lawyers, reflecting recognition that a formal, binding agreement and court proceedings leading to judicial approval of that agreement would be necessary to accomplish its objectives. Talking with Douglas Church on November 22, 2002, Lee Mc-Turnan, Earlham's lead counsel, confirmed that one of the problems with the mediated agreement was that it did not release Earlham from liability with respect to its management of the public charitable trust. They discussed the possibility of a "friendly" lawsuit to resolve the issues in a binding format and the question of intervention by the Indiana attorney general in such an action. Church made it clear to McTurnan that Conner Prairie would not affirm, as a part of such an arrangement, that Earlham's conduct had been proper.

In a conversation on December 18, McTurnan told me that court approval of an agreement between the college and Conner Prairie was an essential element of any settlement, and that the scope of that approval would have to extend to the college's entire relationship with Conner Prairie. I responded that Conner Prairie was not willing to endorse the entire history of that relationship, but would support court approval of those elements of an agreement that related to Earlham divesting itself of its trust responsibilities. I pointed out that Conner Prairie had no standing or authority to approve Earlham's past conduct. McTurnan also reported that Earlham was concerned about the quality of the ongoing governance at Conner Prairie and wanted some third-party controls over the appointment of new directors at the museum as part of any settlement. I responded that this suggestion would be "politically sensitive" and that I did not understand the need for it if Conner Prairie was to be independent of Earlham. Despite the obvious gulf between our positions, McTurnan said that Earlham hoped to have a new agreement to present at its February trustees meeting and that we would receive a draft of that agreement for our review. He instructed us to deal directly with him in the future, without Ben Blanton's intermediation.

I succeeded to the chair of the Conner Prairie board on January 1, 2003. Church and I heard nothing further until January 21, when Douglas Bennett proposed a meeting of the governance committees on February 5, promising delivery of a revised proposal prior to that time. We agreed and proposed that this be a mediated session. Bennett rejected that proposal, saying that Earlham only wanted to present its revised draft for our consideration. We questioned why we needed a meeting on this basis, as we could react to the new proposal without the benefit of a meeting—unless the proposal was being presented on a "take it or leave it" basis. Bennett assured us that this was not the case, and that he hoped to go into the Earlham trustees' meeting on February 14 "with a sense of what remains problematic" and then resume mediation "with clarity and energy."[1] We expressed disappointment that Earlham did not intend to take definitive action at the trustees' meeting.

⌒

On February 3, 2003, Church and I met with McTurnan. We were given two new documents: the "Memorandum of Principles and Understanding" and the "Conner Prairie Management Agreement," which was an exhibit to the memorandum. Those documents set forth an arrangement that was similar to the relationship contemplated by the September 30, 2002, "Statement of Principles" but with a few important changes:

- Conner Prairie would no longer be an Earlham subsidiary and its board of directors would manage the museum's affairs, but Earlham would be entitled to name at least four members of the Conner Prairie board and one member of both its finance and board nominating committees.
- The lease for the 58-acre tract—now termed a "management agreement"—would be for a 30-year term, not in perpetuity. This meant, in effect, that the entire Earlham–Conner Prairie relationship would have to be renegotiated upon expiration of the agreement.
- The museum's earned revenues would have to be first applied to the operation and maintenance of the 58-acre tract.

- The parties' interests in the Eli Lilly Endowment Fund were described as the "Earlham Share" and the "Conner Prairie Share." of the fund.[2] The debt that Earlham claimed was owing to it by Conner Prairie would be repaid solely out of the Conner Prairie Share and not split between the parties.
- Earlham would receive a "conservation easement" that would restrict any development south of the existing museum improvements.
- There would be substantial requirements to be met by Conner Prairie in the appointment of any new members to its board of directors.
- The Earlham Share would be protected by a "firewall" to be applied to the Conner Prairie Share and fixed at $5 million less than the current value of the Conner Prairie Share. With this firewall in place, only $5 million of the endowment would have been available to the museum and the balance would have been locked away in the Eli Lilly Endowment Fund as a perpetual cushion against the risk that Earlham might have to tap into its share under the first charge language of the Lilly gifts.
- Conner Prairie would have to set aside $50,000 in cash from operations in each year as a depreciation fund for the William Conner House.
- The agreement would include a mutual covenant not to sue on account of any past events.
- Approval of the agreement by both the Indiana attorney general and a court would be required as a condition to its effectiveness.

The division of the real estate proposed in the September 30 "Statement of Principles" was unchanged: Conner Prairie would receive title to all of the land that Earlham had dedicated to the museum and Earlham would retain the 80-acre parcel that it had reserved for its own use. The existing arrangements with respect to the Prairie View golf course would continue in effect (90 percent share to Earlham, 10 percent share to Conner Prairie). The endowment management relationship was unchanged. Earlham would continue to manage the entire Eli Lilly Endowment Fund in accordance with UMIFA (Uniform Management of Institutional Funds Act), allocating to both Earlham and Conner Prairie a portion of that fund in accordance with Earlham's past practices. However, except for the firewall, the draft did not propose any new agreements with respect to the terms under which Earlham held and managed the Lilly gifts, and it therefore did no further violence to those terms—that was to come later—but neither did it move the college any closer to compliance with the gifts.

The Conner Prairie governance committee met on February 5, prior to the meeting with Earlham, to review the Earlham proposal and our response. We considered whether we should participate in any further discussions of this draft given its failure to address the endowment management issues, its lack of fundamental fairness, and the likelihood of an adverse community reaction against Conner Prairie if we were seen as having agreed to these terms. It seemed doubtful that the museum would be viewed as having paid a fair price for the degree of "independence" that it was achieving, and we debated whether this was the time to put the entire matter in the hands of the attorney general. Ultimately, we decided to continue with the process that was now in place to see where it led.

We were uncertain as to the scope and effect of the covenant not to sue. Under its terms, Conner Prairie, Inc., and everyone associated with it would have been barred from asserting any claims against Earlham with respect to any elements of the Earlham–Conner Prairie relationship, including Earlham's endowment management policies. That might have been acceptable, given Conner Prairie's lack of standing to raise any issues related to Earlham's administration of the public charitable trust. But it was not clear what effect that provision would have on persons not parties to the agreement—specifically, the Indiana attorney general. As the attorney general was to "approve" the agreement, there was a real possibility that this covenant would act as a bar to any other inquiries by that office. One of our fundamental tenets was to avoid such an outcome unless the terms of a final agreement could be viewed as resolving Earlham's past conduct in its management of the Eli Lilly Endowment Fund and effecting a fair disposition of that fund. The Earlham proposal failed both tests.

At the meeting of the governance committees, Bennett began with a recital of Earlham's views regarding its legal position (as set forth in the Mc-Turnan legal memorandum), the failure of the "Statement of Principles" to address Earlham's "fiduciary problems," and his expectation that the current draft would receive the approval of the Earlham trustees—assuming that any open issues were not material.[3] McTurnan emphasized the need to reconcile Earlham's fiduciary duties with Conner Prairie's autonomy, and how that action dictated the need for the management contract with respect to the 58-acre tract and the firewall concept. He also stipulated that the covenant not to sue was "fundamental" to the agreement.

Church responded by saying that we could not accept the agreement as submitted and noted that it was entirely different in tone and substance from the arrangements we had been discussing. Our efforts to this point were not designed to produce a definitive legal resolution as to the consequences of Earlham's past conduct. We were anxious to explore a new governance arrangement, and we were willing to support court approval of the forward-looking elements of a new agreement. But if Earlham was unwilling to pursue that objective without also obtaining a judicial endorsement of its prior management of the endowment, then we should take the entire matter to the Indiana attorney general for guidance.

Recognition that we had reached an impasse essentially ended the meeting, although there was some further discussion as to the import of various terms of the draft agreement. Earlham also noted that the Conner Prairie governance committee was not advised by independent legal counsel, and said that Church and I were "wearing two hats" as lawyers and as members of the committee. I was no longer practicing law, and both Church and I had been careful to make it clear to the other members of the committee that we were not acting as its lawyers but as members of the group. We did agree that Church and I would meet again with McTurnan and his partner, Steve Badger.

To facilitate that meeting, we marked up a copy of the February 3 draft documents to identify the provisions to which we objected and to suggest alternative language. We revised or deleted the more egregious of Earlham's demands. We presented the provisions relating to the management of the Eli Lilly Endowment Fund as statements of historic fact and not as covenants for the future. Under our approach, the only forward-looking provisions of the agreement were those that dealt with the future management relationship. We put a big question mark on the provision calling for "approval" by the attorney general.

Church and I met with McTurnan and Badger at Church's office on Sunday afternoon, February 9. They objected to and argued with almost every one of our changes in the draft and wanted further concessions favoring Earlham on several new issues that emerged. It was an adversarial meeting, not one in which lawyers talked candidly about their positions.

Of course, neither Earlham nor Conner Prairie had the power, acting either unilaterally or in concert, to effect a change in the terms of Lilly's gifts. Nor could Conner Prairie effectively absolve Earlham from any claims arising from its management of the Eli Lilly Endowment Fund. Achievement of these objectives required court approval. The most that Conner Prairie was willing or able to do, had we been satisfied with all of the other terms proposed by Earlham, was to acknowledge the existence of Earlham's policies and agree (for whatever it was worth) that those policies could continue to govern Earlham's management of the Eli Lilly Endowment Fund.

Given these circumstances, Conner Prairie's strategy was to attempt to eliminate or revise the most troublesome terms of the Earlham proposal and to arrive at an agreement under which the Eli Lilly Endowment Fund would remain intact, the terms of the Lilly gifts would be preserved and Conner Prairie would achieve operational and structural independence from Earlham. We recognized that this outcome would have left the question of the museum's participation in future endowment distributions at risk, but Earlham's role then would have been reduced to that of a custodian of a trust fund held for the museum's benefit. This was a less-than-ideal resolution of the issues, but it would have significantly improved the museum's operational situation and would have opened the door to future discussions about Earlham's endowment management policies that would have been grounded in the new reality of Conner Prairie's independence. Under this sharper focus on the relationship between the college and the museum, Conner Prairie could have attempted, over time, to shift Earlham's actions as trustee into closer conformity to the terms of the Lilly gifts. But the inclusion of a covenant not to sue in an agreement "approved" by the attorney general and a court remained problematic for us if Conner Prairie was to walk away with any hope of future reformation of Earlham's endowment management policies. We understood we had no leverage other than the seemingly obvious need for an outcome that would allow both parties to end the dispute with their core objectives intact and without a public showdown. Earlham's continued willingness to engage in the process indicated that it shared this concern. But a significant gap remained between our positions.

The Conner Prairie executive committee met on February 10, 2003, the day following our session with the Earlham lawyers. Church reported on the developments. The executive committee passed a resolution requesting the prompt resumption of the mediation process "in the expectation" that, given the progress that had been made, an agreement could be ready for approval at the Earlham trustees' meeting in May. The resolution said that, absent Earlham's agreement to this process, the executive committee would consider "other options." This resolution was sent to the members of the Earlham governance committee.

On February 14, in my capacity as chairman of the Conner Prairie board, I attended the meeting of the Conner Prairie committee of the Earlham board of trustees in Richmond. I reported that the meeting with McTurnan had not been productive and distributed copies of the resolution adopted by the Conner Prairie executive committee. There was no reaction from the Earlham members of the board committee.

McTurnan called me five days later. He reported that the board of trustees had discussed our response to his draft agreement and that we would be receiving a revised draft. Notwithstanding the objective of further mediation that Bennett had laid down when he turned the issues over to his lawyers, McTurnan now stipulated that there would be no further mediation and that the matter was to be resolved in "lawyer-to-lawyer" negotiations. Church and I received the new draft on February 27.

The revised document McTurnan delivered left intact the provisions related to Conner Prairie's future governance and the economic terms found in Earlham's February 3 proposal, but it made significant changes in the terms related to the Eli Lilly Endowment Fund. The draft included new provisions expressly separating the Earlham Share and the Conner Prairie Share into two different funds. It went on to provide that the Earlham Share "will be used only to support the educational programs and projects of Earlham College" and that the Earlham Share was to be held by the college free and clear of any demands of Conner Prairie. The provisions relating to "approval" of the agreement by the attorney general now spoke of his "consent" to court approval, thereby making him a party to the contract. This was the first time that Earlham had explicitly set out terms upon which the college would be forever insulated from the demands of Conner Prairie under the first charge provision of the Lilly gifts. The Earlham Share would become part of Earlham's general endowment fund.

After several conversations with the Conner Prairie governance committee as to how we should respond, Church and I delivered a marked-up copy of the draft to McTurnan's office on March 14. In an accompanying memorandum, we observed that, contrary to our understanding of the context of our discussions, the draft seemed to reflect a movement toward a definitive resolution of the issues surrounding the Lilly gifts. We went on to provide comments and questions on the terms of the draft, and we again revised the language relating to management of the Eli Lilly Endowment Fund to reaffirm our earlier approach, under which the agreement would not have attempted to resolve these issues.

Church and I again met with Earlham's lawyers on March 17. We were told that the Earlham trustees had given "full authority" to their governance committee to agree to the terms of the revised draft, but that only "some elements" of the draft were negotiable. When we pressed for an explanation of why we should support Earlham's proposal to transfer the Earlham Share from the Eli Lilly Endowment Fund to the college, we were told that the quid pro quo lay in the transfer to Conner Prairie of the land west of White River that had been part of the original grant to Earlham by Lilly.

In linking the conveyance of this parcel to Conner Prairie's approval of a transfer of the Earlham Share to the unrestricted control of the college, Earlham was breaking new ground. Of the approximately 400 acres contained in this tract, Earlham previously had committed all but 80 acres to the purposes of the museum. This fact was reflected in the audited financial statements that Earlham's accountants had produced for Conner Prairie, Inc., and in the prior drafts of the agreement itself. Until this time, both parties had been operating on the assumption that all of the land previously assigned to the operations of the museum would remain with Conner Prairie in any restructuring of the relationship. The terms of the document that emerged from the previous fall's mediation would have given that land to Conner Prairie without the necessity of any concession to Earlham regarding ownership of the Eli Lilly Endowment Fund. Therefore, we did not see that Conner Prairie was gaining anything of value in the exchange being offered to us. Earlham's position seemed to be that, since it had never divested itself of the legal title to the land, it was free to revoke its prior actions designating the land for the uses of the museum.

We inquired as to how the process of getting the attorney general's consent to the agreement would work, noting the material changes proposed in the terms of the Lilly gifts and the reservations that we had expressed regarding Earlham's prior management of those gifts. McTurnan's response was that the attorney general would be given no information other than that contained within the four corners of the agreement, and that Conner Prairie and Earlham would present a "united front." We made it clear that this condition would present extremely difficult issues of fiduciary duty for the directors of Conner Prairie, Inc. At the conclusion of the meeting, the Earlham lawyers agreed to complete their review of the redraft we had given them, and we agreed that we would meet again two days later.

At the March 19 meeting, Church and I were told that our proposed revisions to the February 27 draft had been rejected by Earlham. McTurnan expressly acknowledged that Earlham intended, by the language of the agreement, to amend the terms of the Lilly gifts to eliminate the first charge commitment with respect to the Earlham Share. The "split" percentages were not negotiable and the firewall amount was not negotiable. However, each side indicated that it was willing to make some minor concessions on other points. McTurnan agreed to provide another draft reflecting those changes, understanding that we did not have a meeting of the minds on the substantive terms of an agreement.

The Conner Prairie board met later that same day, and Church reported to the directors on the status of the negotiations. If we did not reach agreement in the lawyer-to-lawyer discussions, and if Earlham was not willing to consider other dispute resolution mechanisms—either a return to mediation or private bilateral consultation with the attorney general—then we saw no alternative other than to take the issues to the attorney general ourselves, with whatever consequences that might have for the museum and the college.

The revised documents we received on April 1 conceded a few of our minor points, but retained the proposed split of the Eli Lilly Endowment Fund, the elimination of the first charge commitment with respect to the Earlham Share, the firewall, the insulation of the college from any accounting for its management of the fund, and our participation in what seemed to be a whitewash before the Indiana attorney general and a court. McTurnan asked if we could meet again the following week.

⌒

At this point, we began to focus our attention on the development of a rationale supporting a counterproposal to Earlham within the framework of a division of the Eli Lilly Endowment Fund between the college and the museum. If there was to be a formal split of the endowment and a bar to any future inquiry regarding Earlham's management of the fund, we believed that the terms of the agreement should provide for a transfer of greater value to the museum in recognition of what we believed to have been Lilly's priorities and intent. The question was how to arrive at a proposed division of the fund that would be consistent with this objective.

Lilly had made four major gifts to Earlham for the benefit of the museum: the 1969 gift ($3 million), the 1972 gift ($1.4 million), the 1973 gift ($16 million), and the gift under his will ($10 million). Our somewhat crude methodology began with the assumption that Earlham had divided each of those gifts equally in arriving at its position as to the value of the Earlham Share and the Conner Prairie Share of the fund. Working without the benefit of any accounting from Earlham or sophisticated tools for financial analysis, we came up with a rough estimate of the present value of each of the Lilly gifts. Given the need to leave Earlham with a substantial portion of the Eli Lilly Endowment Fund if there was to be any hope of getting an agreement, and adopting Earlham's view as to the outcome of the 1974 negotiations with Lilly regarding the management of the 1973 gift, we set aside the split of that gift and assumed that its present value would remain with Earlham. One-half of the present value of the 1969 and 1972 gifts and of the gift under the will would be transferred to Conner Prairie. These calculations arrived at a rough estimate of $95 million for the Conner Prairie Share, contrasted with the value of approximately $65 million to be assigned to Conner Prairie under the Earlham proposal, or a shortfall equivalent to $30 million.

On April 15, 2003, Church and I wrote to McTurnan accepting his offer to meet. However, we pointed out that the terms of the latest drafts "would pose serious issues for the Conner Prairie Board of Directors" arising out of two related concerns. We noted that the directors of Conner Prairie had fiduciary duties that must be met in making decisions that affect the museum and that we also had to be able to support the outcome of the negotiations within the broader community as a fair and reasonable disposition of the Lilly gifts. We did not believe that the proposal on the table met these standards. While acknowledging that the circumstances that brought Earlham and Conner Prairie to their present relationship were complex and that each party had its own view of the facts, we observed that the first-charge commitment was at the heart of the relationship and that we could find no justification in the record for Earlham's division of the gifts made by Lilly in 1969, in 1972, and in his will. The Conner Prairie board's endorsement of the terms of Earlham's proposal, as a means of achieving its governance objectives, would be questionable from a fiduciary duty perspective and would not produce a fair and equitable outcome.

We went on to say that, given the complexity of the facts, the passage of time, and changes in the circumstances since the dates of the Lilly gifts, and anticipating the benefits to Conner Prairie that would flow from a resolution of this matter, we would support—and we believed that the Conner Prairie board of directors, the Indiana attorney general, and a court would approve—an agreement that compromised some of Lilly's objectives. We enclosed a summary of terms that we believed to be consistent with our fiduciary duties and that would be perceived as fair. We explained that, in our proposal, we had attempted to recognize Earlham's interests in eliminating the contingencies surrounding the first charge obligation, to provide for the disposition of the Lilly gifts on a basis consistent with his intentions, to repay the Conner Prairie debt to Earlham on a reasonable and equitable basis, and to meet Earlham's other legitimate needs in the restructuring of the relationship.

Our summary of terms provided the following:

- The Conner Prairie endowment share would be equal to the current value of one-half of Lilly's 1969 and 1972 gifts, and of one-half of the gift under his will. Earlham would provide a reasonably detailed accounting of the determination of this amount.

- Conner Prairie would agree that $2,035,907 of its current debt would be repaid to Earlham by a charge against the Conner Prairie endowment share.
- Earlham would agree to forgive an amount of the debt equal to the administrative fees paid by Conner Prairie to Earlham ($2,185,835 as of December 31, 2002, to be adjusted to date of closing), and Conner Prairie would agree that the balance of the account ($538,281 as of March 25, 2003, to be adjusted to date of closing) would be repaid to Earlham by a charge against the Conner Prairie endowment share.
- The firewall would apply to the Conner Prairie share, but the amount would be $5 million.
- The "conservation easement" would be eliminated.
- The land west of White River to be transferred to Conner Prairie would include the 80-acre tract in the northwest corner of the property.
- The management agreement would continue until terminated by mutual agreement.

We arrived at the proposed firewall amount by estimating the cost of maintaining the William Conner House as a stand-alone facility and then backing into the endowment amount that would be needed to provide that level of support. Earlham's latest proposal had fixed the firewall amount at about $58 million, with the result that only $7 million of the Conner Prairie Share would have been available for use at Conner Prairie. Proposing an indefinite term for the management agreement under which Conner Prairie would occupy and operate the 58-acre tract was necessary if we were to avoid the need to renegotiate the entire Earlham–Conner Prairie relationship in 30 years.

McTurnan responded by asking for an analysis of our calculation of the amount described in the first bullet point in the summary, and of the firewall amount. On April 23, we sent to him a memorandum in which we said that, as to the firewall, an endowment of $5 million should produce approximately $250,000 per year to maintain the William Conner House, an amount that would be more than adequate based upon the results of operations of comparable historic home facilities in the Indianapolis area. As to the proposal described in the first bullet point, we reported that, based upon our calculations, the shift in endowment value would result in the addition of approximately $30 million to the Conner Prairie Share.

We received no response. The silence masked a major shift in Earlham's tactics. The college had gone to work on a plan that would end the governance discussions and advance its broader strategic objectives by firing the board of directors and president of the museum and taking direct control of its operations. Earlham was done negotiating, although we were not told of this decision until June 11, when all of the planning for its takeover was in place.

Notes

1. Douglas Bennett, e-mail to Douglas Church, February 2, 2003.

2. In this chapter, the word "Share" is capitalized in *Earlham Share* and *Conner Prairie Share* in reference to usage in the legal document "Memorandum of Principles," September 30, 2002.

3. The Earlham attendees at the February 5 meeting were Douglas Bennett, Thomas Fisher, John Young, and Morris Mills, and Earlham's lawyers, Lee McTurnan and Steve Badger. Conner Prairie was represented by Douglas Church, Stan Hurt, Sean Skinner, Pat Garrett Rooney, and William Neale (Conner Prairie board members); John Herbst; and me.

CHAPTER EIGHT

~

The Sun Goes Down
over Conner Prairie

Almost immediately after the delivery of our counterproposal to Earlham in late April 2003, the president's office at Conner Prairie received a call from Sease, Gerig & Associates (SGA), an Indianapolis public relations firm, seeking information on the members of the Conner Prairie board. The firm wanted to do some background reading before a scheduled meeting with Earlham president Douglas Bennett to discuss the Conner Prairie directors. Apparently the caller from Earlham had neglected to inform SGA that the college had designs on the board, and that the engagement should be kept confidential from the museum.

In retrospect, it seems obvious that Earlham intended to seek SGA's assessment of the public reaction to the firing of the board and enlist its help in developing a story line as to why it had done so. But the full import of this news was not clear at the time. We were sufficiently alarmed by this development, however, to send an e-mail to Mark Myers, the chairman of the Earlham board, reporting that we had received the call from SGA. We reminded Myers of his commitment that Earlham would not exercise its power to remove the board or management of the museum in the course of the governance negotiations, and said that we intended to continue to rely on that commitment unless Earlham gave us adequate notice that it intended to withdraw it. Five days later, Myers provided a carefully worded response, but he did not deny having made the commitment nor did he withdraw it.

The Earlham trustees met on May 15 and adopted a resolution authorizing Bennett to remove the independent members of the board of directors of Conner Prairie, Inc., and its president, John Herbst, unless the museum directors approved the terms of Earlham's proposal of March 31. No news of this action reached Conner Prairie. All of the pieces were now in place.

It is not surprising that the Earlham trustees would decide upon a course of action that would necessarily result in a confrontation with the Conner Prairie constituents, who, after all, had no legal standing in the matter. Under the terms of Lilly's gifts, if Conner Prairie were to cease operations, the income from the entire amount of the Eli Lilly Endowment Fund—valued at over $150 million—would become available for use by Earlham College. In Earlham's view, its only obligation was to maintain the William Conner House. The college seems to have been convinced that the museum, left to its own devices, would exhaust the endowment and then become a drain on the college's other revenues. The termination of the museum's operations would eliminate this risk and would benefit the college financially. The college trustees did not see themselves as standing in a trust relationship with Conner Prairie. They had been told that the college "owned" Conner Prairie, that the museum was "part" of Earlham, that Earlham could deal with the museum as it saw fit, and that the college's only legal obligation was to maintain and provide occasional public access to the William Conner House.

As the logical result of these views, the Earlham trustees saw their duties as owing to the college and not to a museum, 70 miles away, the operations of which bore no relationship to the core mission of the college. The college trustees also may have believed that the museum was badly managed and that Earlham could, and would, preserve the museum and improve its financial performance. But underlying whatever rationale the trustees considered in support of their strategy, the fact remained that with the Conner Prairie board out of the way, Earlham would wind up with unfettered control of the operations of the museum, an endowment worth more than $150 million, and unrestricted ownership of almost 1,400 acres of prime Hamilton County real estate.

Notwithstanding the compelling nature of this logic, Earlham's trustees failed to foresee the public relations consequences of their proposed actions. In addition, the trustees' refusal to listen to Conner Prairie's views, their chosen objectives, their confrontational tactics, and their failure to make a careful inquiry into the law and the facts of the Conner Prairie relationship were wholly at odds with the principles of open inquiry, conciliation, and consensus that purportedly governed their decision making. For a college steeped in the Quaker tradition, the Earlham trustees' actions represented a systemic failure to adhere to the fundamental principles of their institution.

～

On May 14, Myers asked for a meeting between the governance committees in which Landrum Bolling would be a participant. Unaware of the Earlham trustees' actions, we remained willing to engage in any discussions that might lead to an agreement on the governance issues, particularly if Bolling would be in attendance. After leaving Lilly Endowment, Bolling had been involved in foundation work at the national level before becoming a college professor. For the past 20 years, he had been deeply involved in international diplomatic efforts and had particular expertise with respect to the problems in the Middle East. In recognition of this work, Bolling had been awarded honorary degrees by more than 25 institutions of higher education.[1] It was difficult for us to believe that the Earlham leadership would seek an open confrontation with Conner Prairie, and we hoped that Bolling's judgment, perspective, and experience with dispute resolution would prove to be of value. We were even cautiously optimistic that cooler heads had intervened at Earlham, and that the meeting might lead to a breakthrough. In the meantime, heedful of Earlham's sensitivity to the lack of legal representation for the Conner Prairie governance committee, we contacted the Indianapolis firm of Krieg DeVault, one of whose partners, William Neale, was a Conner Prairie board member. The governance committee negotiated terms of engagement that permitted the firm's lawyers to get up to speed and be in a position to advise the committee and board of directors in their management of any further proposals that Earlham might make without a significant investment in legal fees. Given our lack of standing to do so, we did not ask for Krieg DeVault's assistance in filing a lawsuit against Earlham.

The meeting of the Earlham and Conner Prairie governance committees convened in the council room at Conner Prairie at noon on June 11, 2003. Earlham was represented by Bennett, Morris Mills, Earlham trustees Thomas Fisher and John Young, and Lee McTurnan (along with two other members of his firm). Contrary to our expectations, Bolling was not in attendance. Conner Prairie was represented by Douglas Church, Stan Hurt, Pat Garrett Rooney, Neale, Herbst, Tony Momert, a Krieg DeVault partner, and me. We had sandwiches and small talk, but Bennett seemed edgy and anxious to get down to business. He shuffled his papers and called the meeting to order. Speaking from a script, he began by characterizing our latest settlement proposal as a "nice try" and, without further discussion of that proposal, announced that Earlham could not accept our position. He said that Earlham was resubmitting its March 31 offer, which he thought met Conner Prairie's needs, and asserted that Earlham was "legally and morally bound" by the terms of the Lilly gifts.

Church responded by saying that Earlham's March 31 proposal was, in fact, outside the framework of the Lilly gifts and inconsistent with their terms, and he went on to briefly outline our objections to the proposal and the rationale of our counteroffer. Bennett replied by saying that Earlham's offer was not negotiable, but it would drop its demand for the "conservation easement" if we accepted all of its other terms. Otherwise, he said, Earlham would have to do what was best for Earlham.

We had previously agreed among ourselves that we would make no substantive response to whatever Earlham put on the table without a caucus of our group. Church reported that fact, but as we got up from the table, Bennett interrupted and demanded that we agree not to "file suit" while we were out of the room. This surprised us. We had no standing to file any lawsuit that addressed Earlham's management of the public charitable trust, which Bennett should have known, and therefore had no intention to do so. Up to this point, Earlham had taken no other action that could form the basis for a lawsuit against it. We had no lawsuit prepared for filing. So we freely gave that promise and adjourned to Herbst's office.

Once settled, we quickly agreed that we could not accept the Earlham proposal, notwithstanding the obvious threat. The negotiations with Earlham's lawyers had failed to achieve any significant concessions in favor of Conner Prairie on the endowment management issues. Although the Earlham proposal incorporated many of our governance objectives, we could not, in good conscience, agree to support a modification of the terms of the Lilly gifts in the manner proposed by the college as a means of achieving those objectives. And even if we could get past that hurdle, we could not participate in a proceeding before the Indiana attorney general and a court in which there would have been less-than-full disclosure of the facts relevant to an understanding of the agreement, its effect on the Lilly gifts, and Earlham's potential liability for breach of trust. In rejecting Earlham's terms, our only option was to urge further discussions even though we were not sure what we could do to move Earlham off of its position nor did we know what Bennett had in mind if we rejected his demand. Reflecting on the SGA engagement, we had, of course, considered the possibility that Earlham might exercise its power to remove the Conner Prairie board and what our response to that action might be, but the public relations fallout from that action seemed so unacceptable that we did not believe that Earlham would run the risk. Moreover, we had Myers's assurance that Earlham would not do so without prior notice. Even if removal of the Conner Prairie board was what Earlham had in mind, it seemed to us that some further process was needed before the college could take that step.

Back in the council room, Church announced that we could not recommend Earlham's proposal to the full Conner Prairie board, and he provided a comprehensive and straightforward explanation of our position. He reviewed the course of the mediation and subsequent negotiation leading up to Earlham's March 31 proposal, summarized the issues of equity and fairness raised by that proposal, and explained how our counterproposal attempted to better reflect the terms of the Lilly gifts. He questioned whether the philanthropic community would approve of Conner Prairie's acceptance of the Earlham proposal and said that a settlement on these terms would not accomplish the goal of improving our fund-raising capability. In conclusion, Church reaffirmed our lack of intent or ability to litigate the issues, assured Earlham of our willingness to continue to work on a resolution in any productive format, and asked how we could go forward given the grave risks to both institutions of our failure to reach agreement.

Bennett's response was that Earlham's offer was "take it or leave it," and that we had elected to leave it. Earlham had not changed its mind on the legal questions. The governance discussions were not working. He then pulled several papers from his file, signed them, and handed them across the table, saying that the Earlham board had concluded that, absent our agreement to its terms, it would "dissolve" the Conner Prairie board. All of the non-Earlham members of the board were fired. Herbst was fired and Bennett was now the president of the museum. Young whipped out his cell phone and placed a call. Earlham personnel poured into the building, where they began to ride herd on each of the members of Conner Prairie's senior staff. An Earlham press release soon appeared in the media outlets.

The Conner Prairie representatives retreated to Herbst's office, followed by Young and Fisher, where we were told that we must immediately leave the building, which we did. We reconvened at the branch office of Church's law firm in nearby Fishers and began to organize a response. Back at Conner Prairie, Bennett called a meeting of the staff to explain what had happened. He said that Earlham's actions had been taken because of "increasing concerns about rising deficits" and that Earlham was "determined to restore the museum's fiscal integrity."[2] The staff was stunned and outraged. Some were in tears. Bennett assured them that nothing had changed, that their jobs would not be affected, and that a new board of directors would be quickly selected. An SGA representative told members of the Conner Prairie staff that the press and the public would forget about the firing in a couple of days.

～

The Earlham press release followed the narrative Bennett had laid out for the staff. In it, Bennett cited "a significant increase in the museum's debt" as the primary reason for the board's dismissal, together with the breakdown in the governance discussions. He said, "[W]e are concerned that the museum has made significant capital expenditures in recent years and has not raised sufficient funds or grants to support them. Also, the museum has incurred significant operating deficits over the last five years that, along with the capital expenditures, have now reached $4.5 million. This has given us concerns about the financial integrity of an institution for which we remain responsible."

A form letter from Myers was hand delivered that afternoon to each of the former members of the Conner Prairie board. In that letter, Myers thanked us for our service to Conner Prairie. The letter described Earlham's "disappointment that the leadership of Conner Prairie has been unable to achieve fiscal equilibrium" and deplored the museum's "significant budget deficits" and unfunded capital expenditures, which Myers implied stemmed from a lack of attention to "long-term financial stability." He concluded by saying that "with improved financial stability, we can better ensure that the museum will continue long into the future."[3]

Earlham hoped, therefore, to convince the public that we had been bad directors and that it had been forced to remove us because of our incompetence and its greater skill at achieving financial success for Conner Prairie. Of course, that was not the reason for our dismissal and financial stability—or lack thereof—was not what drove Earlham to do what it did. Final control over all financial matters relating to Conner Prairie was, and always had been, in the hands of Earlham College. If there were financial issues at Conner Prairie, they were issues that resulted from policies that Earlham had adopted and pursued. As set forth in the resolution approved at their meeting on May 13, 2003, the Earlham trustees had authorized Bennett to take the action that he did "unless Conner Prairie's Governance Committee and the Conner Prairie Board of Directors accept the terms of Earlham College's proposed Memorandum of Principles and Understanding dated March 31, 2003."

Therefore, the trustees' action rested solely on the question of whether the Conner Prairie board would support Earlham's proposal to allocate over $75 million of the Eli Lilly Endowment Fund to the college, free and clear of the first charge language of the Lilly gifts, and allow the college to walk away from any inquiry into its management of those gifts. The benefits that Conner Prairie would receive in return were freedom from Earlham's veto powers and legal title to land that Earlham previously had dedicated to the museum's use. The museum's "share" of the Eli Lilly Endowment Fund would continue to be at the mercy of Earlham's endowment management policies. If we did not accept these terms, we were to be fired, and Earlham then would be in a position to manage the museum in a manner that better served Earlham's interests.

The terms of Bennett's June 11 ultimatum precluded any opportunity for the full board of directors of Conner Prairie, Inc., to consider and act on Earlham's proposal. A board meeting had been called for the following week, and it was at least possible that the full board might have reached a conclusion different from that reached by its governance committee, overruled the committee's recommendation, and accepted Earlham's offer. But Earlham fired the board before that meeting could be held.

Conner Prairie's very existence was now threatened by the actions and conflicts of interest of its trustee, Earlham College. The governance discussions and negotiations had taken place against the backdrop of questions surrounding Earlham's decisions regarding the allocation of the Lilly gifts, its imposition of the spending rule, its management interference, its reluctance to use the Eli Lilly Endowment Fund for the purposes for which it was intended, the assessment of the administrative fee, and Earlham-related problems with the museum's fund-raising. These issues were troublesome to the Conner Prairie constituents and, in our view, required rectification, but they were not life threatening. Suddenly, we confronted the very real possibility that Earlham would terminate the museum's operations given the college's view that its legal obligations under the Lilly gifts were limited to the maintenance of the William Conner House. Earlham did not view the Prairietown operation, the Lenape Indian camp and trading post, Liberty Corner, the 1886 farm, or any of the other attractions and programs of the museum as part of its responsibilities as trustee of the public charitable trust. The implications of this position were that Earlham, without violating its fiduciary duties, could shut down all of the programmatic elements and most of the properties that made up the Conner Prairie experience, terminate nearly all of the staff, and reduce the museum to a skeleton operation.

Earlham later would assert that it had no such designs on Conner Prairie. But Earlham College was the contingent beneficiary of the Lilly gifts. If Conner Prairie ceased operations, the museum's demands upon the income of the Eli Lilly Endowment Fund would drop to almost nothing, thereby freeing up the entire fund—not just the Earlham share—for use by the college. And Earlham had just eliminated the Conner Prairie board, who were the only persons in a position to exercise some independent oversight of

Earlham's management and look after the public interest in the operation of the museum.

Notes

1. See "Engaging the World: The Landrum Bolling Center," www.earlham.edu/landrumbollingcenter/.

2. Douglas Bennett, letter to the employees of Conner Prairie, June 11, 2003.

3. Mark Myers, letter to former Conner Prairie board members, June 11, 2003.

CHAPTER NINE

~

Retreat and Reorganization

Arriving at Douglas Church's law office after leaving Conner Prairie on the afternoon of June 11, 2003, the refugees from the confrontation in the council room set about organizing a response. There was never any suggestion that we should acquiesce in Earlham's actions: the premise was that we would carry on. We agreed to form a new nonprofit corporation, to be named Save the Prairie, Inc., as a vehicle for fund-raising and the management of what we intended to be a comprehensive effort to bring the circumstances into full public view. Our immediate goal was to persuade the Indiana attorney general, Steve Carter, to investigate Earlham's management of Conner Prairie, as he was the only person with the authority to address the core issues.

Anticipating the possibility of a breakdown in the negotiations with Earlham, the Conner Prairie governance committee previously had contacted Hetrick Communications, Inc., the museum's public relations firm, and informed it of the possibility that we might be in need of its services. With help from Hetrick, we crafted a press release that addressed the claims made in the earlier Earlham release. By going public with its version of the board firing, Earlham had eliminated any constraints that we otherwise might have felt as to our tactics. Issued that afternoon, our release announced that the former Conner Prairie board members would call on the attorney general to investigate and intervene. Earlham had not followed the terms of Lilly's gifts, we claimed, and we pointed out its inherent conflict of interest in the gifts' administration.

By personal contacts, we urged the senior staff members to stay on the job and continue to work for the good of the museum. We also agreed on a number of other actions and informed our board of directors about what had happened.

⌒

The Conner Prairie governance committee had considered the possibility of taking legal action seeking the reinstatement of the board of directors if Earlham exercised its power to discharge them. If successful, that action would preserve the status quo pending a review of the issues by the attorney general. We decided to go forward with that strategy. Earlham might make immediate cutbacks in the staff and programs of the museum. If we lost the staff, we knew that rebuilding the museum would be a Herculean effort. We believed that the individual members of the board had standing to bring this action, even though we could not enforce compliance by Earlham with the terms of the public charitable trust.

The next morning, June 12, the former directors filed a motion for a temporary restraining order in Hamilton County Superior Court seeking their reinstatement as the Conner Prairie board of directors as well as John Herbst's reinstatement as president. Argument on the motion was heard that afternoon but, in an order issued the next day, the court refused to intervene, citing our failure to establish that the public would suffer "irreparable harm" if the order was not granted or that there was a "reasonable likelihood of success at trial" on the merits of our case. Both findings were necessary conditions to the granting of a temporary restraining order. Earlham later filed responsive pleadings and moved for summary judgment in its favor. But in the meantime, public opinion had deterred Earlham from taking any action against the staff, the attorney general decided to take up the matter, and, in our view, the superior court action had become moot. Accordingly, we ultimately agreed to dismiss the action with prejudice.

Earlham claimed that the filing of this lawsuit was proof that the Conner Prairie directors harbored the intent to "sue Earlham" and that its action in terminating the board therefore was justified. It also characterized the court's order as a finding that Earlham had done nothing wrong in its administration of the trust, although neither our claims in this suit nor the court's ruling addressed those issues. This characterization of the events may have influenced the Earlham trustees and others who were not paying close attention, and the adverse outcome momentarily shifted the balance of the dispute in Earlham's favor. But, in retrospect, it was beneficial to our cause not to have prevailed in this action. The initial public reaction tended to view the dispute as one over operational control of the museum. Had the former directors succeeded with this action and regained that control, the larger issues of Earlham's management of the public charitable trust might have faded into the background and remained unresolved for another 40 years.

⌒

The events of June 11, 12, and 13 attracted a great deal of media attention in central Indiana and in Richmond. The filing of the former directors' lawsuit propelled the dispute into the headlines in both the print and electronic media. With advice from Pam Klein of Hetrick Communications, Save the Prairie developed a media strategy and honed its approach to the telling, in plain language, of what was a complicated and somewhat arcane story. We assembled a package of background documents for distribution to the media. Klein also provided valuable expertise in developing the Save the Prairie website and in editing the many letters to the editor that formed the backbone of Save the Prairie's public education efforts. Her untimely death in March 2005 deprived us of a friend and trusted advisor. Supportive messages began pouring in from all quarters, many from people whom we did not know but who knew Conner Prairie and understood Earlham's intentions.

It seems probable that Earlham's plans for Conner Prairie were disrupted by the media attention that was generated in the days following the board's discharge. It did not blow over in 48 hours, as Earlham's advisers had predicted it would. Instead, it became a major Indiana news story. Within a week following the events of June 11, 2003, the press was reporting that Earlham was projecting losses of over $300,000 at Conner Prairie in the form of withdrawn sponsorships, grants, and contributions and revenues from events that were cancelled because there were no board members to lead them.

The Conner Prairie board had been scheduled to meet on June 18, one week after it was fired. The former directors met instead that day for the purpose of completing the organization of Save the Prairie, Inc., which had been incorporated in the meantime as an Indiana not-for-profit corporation. Each of the discharged members of the Conner Prairie board agreed to serve as a director of Save the Prairie, and we added to our number a few former museum directors and other friends of the museum. Financial contributions began to come in to underwrite our expenses, which included fees for both legal and public relations services. We also established a consulting relationship with Herbst that provided him with an income stream and allowed us to tap in to his knowledge and expertise in the museum field.

Herbst, who had played an important role during the governance discussions, mediation, and negotiation, had been in a very delicate situation. He had no employment contract, as mentioned previously, and Earlham viewed him as an instigator of the governance crisis. While it was true that Herbst had pushed back against Earlham's attempts to expand its management control over the museum and had supported the efforts of the Conner Prairie board and sympathized with its objectives, the governance issues predated Herbst's involvement by decades, and the impetus for the actions taken by the board lay in Earlham's management policies and not in his personal views. It would have been far safer for Herbst to have wished the board well and retreated to the sidelines, but to his credit he played a visible role in support of the board's efforts. He paid for that involvement with his job. In the early days following the board's discharge, Save the Prairie hoped that intervention from the attorney general would be swift and decisive and that the board and Herbst would find themselves back in charge of an independent Conner Prairie within the space of a few weeks or months.

The assault on the reputations of Herbst and the former board members of Conner Prairie created an immediate backlash against Earlham's tactics both in central Indiana and in the broader world of museum professionals and professional organizations. Even people with no understanding of Conner Prairie's operations or of Earlham's role at the museum were not prepared to accept Earlham's assertions that board members who they knew to be knowledgeable, responsible, and civic-minded had been guilty of mismanagement. The media reaction, as well, seemed to be driven by suspicion of Earlham's objectives. The summary discharge of the entire board of directors of a major nonprofit organization was unprecedented in Indianapolis. Things were just not handled that way. If, in furtherance of its objectives, Earlham was seeking to alienate the people who supported the museum and to secure a high-visibility platform from which to launch its designs on Conner Prairie, it could not have chosen a better strategy.

The Conner Prairie board of directors now consisted of Earlham trustee John Young as chairman, Bennett, Morris Mills, and Thomas Fisher. Earlham belatedly realized that, under the bylaws of the museum, the president of the Conner Prairie Alliance was an ex officio member of the Conner Prairie board and it thereafter included her in formal board meetings, but all substantive decisions with respect to Conner Prairie were made by the Earlham representatives on that board.

On June 12, Young wrote a letter, on Conner Prairie letterhead, to each of the members of the William Conner Society. The society was comprised of all persons giving more than $1,000 per year to the museum. The letter said that Earlham's "regrettable action was necessary to ensure the museum's fiscal health going forward" and went on to claim that Conner Prairie had run up a "$4.5 million deficit for which Earlham—as owners [sic] of the museum—is financially liable." Young promised no changes in museum programs or staff and encouraged continued financial support of Conner Prairie.

As Earlham rolled out its arguments, it clarified how it had arrived at the $4.5 million number. Of that amount, $1.8 million related to capital improvements at the museum that Earlham had funded in the form of "bridge" loans to Conner Prairie from the Earlham general fund, mostly for the development of Liberty Corner. These loans were to have been repaid out of contributions in support of the project. The use of the loan device, instead of a draw on the endowment, allowed Earlham to keep the Eli Lilly Endowment Fund intact and to protect Earlham's interest in the continuing distributions from the Earlham share of the fund. At the time the board was fired, Conner Prairie had generated contributions sufficient to repay about half of the original advance.

The balance of the $4.5 million, or approximately $2.7 million, was claimed by Earlham to be the result of six years of accumulated operating deficits. The audited financial statements of Conner Prairie, Inc., certified by Earlham's auditors, fixed this amount at less than $534,000. The difference lay in the accounting methodology used to produce these reports. The number used by Earlham in its press release was derived from modified cash-basis statements used by the museum board for certain management purposes, while the audited number reflected the application of generally accepted accounting principles and usually would be considered as the final word on the subject. Both numbers reflected the results of operations of the museum, but in different ways and for different purposes. In any event, Earlham held final authority over all financial matters at Conner Prairie, and the results of its operations, however measured, were the product of Earlham's policies.

In Save the Prairie's response to Young's letter, copies of which were sent to all of the Earlham trustees, we suggested that Earlham's true purpose in terminating the board was to *discourage* further support of Conner Prairie by its traditional patrons. Young's letter told them, in effect, that Conner Prairie was nothing more than a financial pipeline to Earlham and that any new contributions to Conner Prairie would go to reducing the $4.5 million "liability." There was no such liability, and Earlham was not the "owner" of the museum. And since Conner Prairie could have achieved its budget objectives only by maintaining its development revenues (which Young knew, as a member of the museum's finance committee), there was no way that Earlham could keep its commitments to make no changes in staff or programs without those revenues. We pointed out that, if there were no Conner Prairie, Earlham would be awash in distributions from the Eli Lilly Endowment Fund and the college's looming deficits would be extinguished. Several irate members of the William Conner Society responded to Young's letter. One wrote, "You and your Earlham cohorts are an embarrassment to the values and integrity of the true Conner Prairie board." Another wrote that Earlham's actions were "suicidal" and "not ethically or morally acceptable."

⌒

At its first meeting, on June 18, 2003, the board of directors of Save the Prairie heard a detailed report from Church on the events that led up to Earlham's June 11 actions. Church and I outlined the proposed objectives and strategies of the corporation, including our intention to seek a determination from the Internal Revenue Service that the corporation was a tax-exempt organization and eligible for tax-deductible contributions. We elected a full board of directors and officers, all of whom were to serve without compensation. I was to serve as chairman and president. We discussed our media strategy and broader action plan and authorized the retention of Herbst as a consultant to our group. All of the directors signed a 38-page memorandum to the attorney general that outlined the history of the Lilly–Earlham–Conner Prairie relationship and our analysis of the legal implications of that relationship. After the meeting, I held a press conference to outline our plans and positions.

The memorandum was delivered to the attorney general the next day, along with a binder containing copies of about 30 of the documents that we considered to be important to an understanding of the issues. Save the Prairie's first objective was to convince Carter that he should conduct a full review of the matter. In our request for action, we focused not on Earlham's past management of the Eli Lilly Endowment Fund but on the risks Earlham's actions in firing the board presented to Conner Prairie. We emphasized the public policy reasons—rooted in Earlham's conflicts of interest—why the museum should be separated from the college. Since there was no statutory law that spelled out the attorney general's responsibilities in a case such as the one now before him, he had complete discretion in deciding whether and how to intervene.[1] The attorney general would bring to the Conner Prairie crisis his moral authority and his access to the judicial system, but not the power to impose a solution.

Carter called on June 23 to advise that he would conduct a formal review, and he issued a press release to that effect the following day. Carter also reported that he had engaged Mark Mutz as a consultant to his office, and that Mutz would be primarily responsible for the initial review of the documents. Carter had been elected as attorney general of Indiana in 2000, having previously served as chief city attorney for the city of Indianapolis and as legislative counsel for the Indiana State Senate. He was an honors graduate from Harvard University, where he earned a bachelor's degree in economics, and held both a law degree and an MBA from Indiana University. Carter was to demonstrate great skill in his management of the Conner Prairie dispute. Slow to anger, thoughtful, patient, and resourceful, he resisted the temptation to take short cuts and instead built the state's position step-by-step, always keeping open his lines of communication to both Earlham and Save the Prairie. Mutz was a lawyer who had been in private practice for several years, but was then the owner of a business consulting firm in Indianapolis. Intelligent, inquisitive, and analytical, Mutz also had substantial experience in issues relating to the governance of nonprofit corporations, and Save the Prairie viewed his involvement in the Conner Prairie matter as a positive development.

～

On June 25, Herbst, Pat Garrett Rooney, and I met with the leadership of the Conner Prairie Alliance. Rooney was a member of the Save the Prairie board. A well-known civic leader, she had been a staff member at Conner Prairie, was a member of the alliance, and had served as the interim president of the museum during the period between Marsha Semmel's resignation and Herbst's employment. The alliance ran a well-organized and energetic program of volunteer support and fund-raising on behalf of Conner Prairie and was contributing approximately $100,000 per year to the museum's operations in addition to thousands of hours of time and effort. Members of the alliance were well-known to the Conner Prairie staff. The leadership of the alliance was alarmed and confused by Earlham's action in firing the board. But before taking any action, they wanted to hear explanations of what had happened from both Save the Prairie and Bennett.

We outlined the objectives of Save the Prairie, the background of Earlham's actions, and the potential adverse effects of those actions on the museum. We acknowledged that the alliance faced the same dilemma that all other supporters of Conner Prairie faced: whether to withdraw their support of the museum and thereby further damage its ability to effectively carry on its programs, or continue that support under the new Earlham regime. We made clear our suspicions regarding Earlham's objectives and our lack of confidence in Earlham's management, and said that we all had to focus on what was in the long-term best interests of Conner Prairie. But each supporter of Conner Prairie had to decide individually whether to continue to provide financial support to the museum. Save the Prairie subsequently was accused by Earlham of engaging in a concerted effort to discourage contributions to

Conner Prairie, but in none of our public statements or private conversations did we urge supporters to withhold contributions from the museum. Some Save the Prairie directors continued to provide funding to Conner Prairie throughout the dispute.

The Conner Prairie Alliance leaders previously had met with Bennett, and we had the impression that they had not been satisfied with his explanations of Earlham's actions or the plans the college had made to deal with the crisis it had created. Several times, Bennett had described the relationship between Earlham and Conner Prairie as that of "parent and child," and the alliance leaders were particularly interested in understanding Earlham's responsibilities as trustee of the public charitable trust.

On June 30, the membership of the Conner Prairie Alliance voted unanimously to put all of its fund-raising activities on hold. This important step positioned Conner Prairie's most active and dedicated volunteer support group behind the objectives of Save the Prairie. Throughout the remainder of the dispute, the alliance continued to meet, to follow developments, and to do what it could to maintain staff morale at the museum, and it was back at work at Conner Prairie before the ink had dried on the settlement agreement a little over two years later.

Others with long-term relationships with Lilly, including his personal secretary and two former executive directors of Conner Prairie, called to express their reactions and their impressions of what Lilly had intended in his relationships with the museum. Each of them had heard Lilly talk about his interest in Conner Prairie and about his intentions regarding Earlham's involvement in the museum, and they strongly supported our views of the issues and the objectives of Save the Prairie. The mayors of Indianapolis and of Carmel, Indiana, the city limits of which abutted the Conner Prairie property, called to express their support for our efforts.

~

By the end of June, the staff at the museum had stabilized somewhat under the leadership provided by Ellen Rosenthal, who had been named by Bennett as acting executive director of the museum. Rosenthal, a museum professional who had worked with Herbst during his prior employment in Pittsburgh, had been vice president for internal affairs and planning at Conner Prairie and was well-respected by the former board of directors. Her continued presence was viewed by Save the Prairie as a positive influence. We knew that she had the interests of the museum at heart and would do her best to continue its programs and policies. Within a few weeks, the museum's director of development resigned, which was not surprising given the impossible task of doing any significant fund-raising under the circumstances. With but one other exception, the remainder of the senior staff stayed on the job throughout the next two and a half years, until the ultimate rescue of the museum. Staff at all levels retained an intense interest in the development of the dispute and supported the objective of independence for the museum. However, throughout the ordeal staff morale was one of Save the Prairie's major concerns. Had they left their jobs, Earlham would have been presented with an opportunity to significantly curtail the museum's programs.

Save the Prairie believed that it was positioned to carry on the fight. With help from Hetrick Communications, we had developed a website in which we outlined the history of the museum's relationship with Earlham and the issues in the dispute. Earlham had posted its version of the events on both its and Conner Prairie's websites. We had created a workable organizational structure and had defined our goals and begun to develop our strategies. We had support from the Conner Prairie Alliance and key political leadership. The staff seemed to be willing to hold on and see what happened next. We had established contacts within the media outlets. We could now present our full case to the public. And, most important, we had the attention of the Indiana attorney general. We had crossed the first threshold toward independence for Conner Prairie.

Note

1. Carter later reported that, upon hearing of Earlham's actions at Conner Prairie, he immediately asked his staff to review the issues and make a recommendation to him. Subsequent to the Conner Prairie dispute, Indiana law was amended to codify certain powers of the attorney general. See IC 30-4-5.5-1 (P.L. 245-2005, sec. 8, as amended by P.L. 61-2008, sec. 15).

William Conner was a trader, trapper, and interpreter who settled on what is now the Conner Prairie property in the early 1800s. Conner married an Indian woman, played an important role in the relations between the early settlers and the Delaware Indians, and became a major figure in area politics and government. The house he built for his second wife became the cornerstone for Eli Lilly's efforts to preserve and develop Conner Prairie.

The Golden Eagle Inn in Prairietown. Opened in 1974, Prairietown, a re-creation of an 1836 Indiana community populated by first-person interpreters, was the first major attraction to open under Earlham's stewardship.

The covered bridge between Prairietown and Liberty Corner, Conner Prairie's 1886 village crossroads community. Visiting children were encouraged to play the games and use the toys that were common to the time and place.

Lenape wigwam and trading post. Conner Prairie's third major attraction, a re-creation of a Native American village adjacent to a trading post. Visitors could experience economic and cultural interactions between the white and native populations.

Hearthside supper in the Conner House. Winter evening dinner guests were invited to share in the preparation of their meals according to period recipes and cooking techniques.

The Conner Prairie Museum Center, completed in 1988. Issues that arose during a major remodeling of the building in 1999 became a source of tension between Earlham College and the Conner Prairie board of directors.

Symphony on the Prairie concert. One of the most popular offerings on the Conner Prairie grounds were the outdoor summer evening concerts by the Indianapolis Symphony Orchestra.

John Herbst was named as president of Conner Prairie in April 1998 and became a supporter of the board of directors in its emerging governance dispute with Earlham College. He was fired when Earlham removed the board on June 11, 2003. He subsequently served as chief executive of two other large history organizations in Indianapolis.

Douglas Bennett was elected president of Earlham College in July 1997 and managed Earlham's role in the governance dispute at Conner Prairie.

Ellen Rosenthal was a vice president of Conner Prairie under Herbst and was named by Earlham as acting executive director of the museum following Herbst's removal. When the museum became independent in 2005 she was elected as its president and chief executive officer.

Mark Myers, left, chairman of the Earlham College board of trustees, and Indiana Attorney General Steve Carter, right. Myers and Carter sign the agreement giving Conner Prairie its independence from Earlham, under the watchful supervision of three Conner Prairie interpreters. July 5, 2005.

Berkley Duck, left, and Indiana Attorney General Steve Carter, right. Carter presents Duck with a certificate memorializing his appointment by Indiana Governor Mitch Daniels as a "Sagamore of the Wabash," one of the state's highest honors.

CHAPTER TEN

~

The Issues Take Shape

With our organizational matters behind us, we at Save the Prairie shifted our attention to the development of the arguments supporting intervention by the attorney general and to the pursuit of our media campaign. The immediate challenges were to put our best case before the attorney general's representative, Mark Mutz, and to attempt to determine the approach that Earlham would take in responding to the attorney general's inquiry. We agreed with Mutz that he could send to Earlham's lawyer, Lee McTurnan, the memorandum we had given to Steve Carter on June 19, on the condition that he would provide to us a copy of any response Earlham might have. Thereafter, each of the further legal memoranda submitted to Mutz by Save the Prairie and by Earlham was provided to the other party. It turned out that McTurnan did not produce Earlham's initial response until August 5, thereby setting a pattern for its lack of responsiveness to the attorney general's initiatives that would persist throughout the dispute.

Save the Prairie had several conversations with Mutz regarding the role that the attorney general might play in the litigation filed by the former directors in Hamilton County, which was still pending. Despite the court's denial of a temporary restraining order for their reinstatement, the plaintiffs could have continued to press for a hearing on a preliminary injunction that would provide the same result. There were, however, several procedural issues presented by this strategy, and it would have had the effect of aligning the attorney general with Save the Prairie at a point in time at which his review of the facts and the law was incomplete. With the staff appearing to have adjusted to their new relationships with Earlham and Earlham deterred by media attention and public opinion from making any additional changes at the museum, the need for immediate court intervention was less pressing. As reported previously, the plaintiffs later dismissed the lawsuit voluntarily, and Conner Prairie's supporters thereafter were dependent upon the attorney general for any judicial resolution of the museum's situation.

By July 3 Save the Prairie had provided to Mutz an analytical framework within which the attorney general could consider the issues related to the Lilly gifts and Earlham's management. Our analysis, which focused on the trust aspects of the relationship, discussed Earlham's conflicts of interest in the administration of the public charitable trust, the competing interests in how the Eli Lilly Endowment Fund was administered, and the effects of Earlham's policies on the operations of the museum. We also argued that Earlham's actions in terminating the museum's board and president breached its fiduciary duties to the museum, and that the separation of Conner Prairie from Earlham on terms that would assure its continued presence and its future development best served the public interest.

⁓

We realized that an effective campaign of public education and advocacy would be important in shaping the attorney general's response. For its part, Earlham also seemed willing to use the media to advance its interests, and a spirited debate quickly developed in an attempt to sway public opinion.

Understandably, the media had many questions regarding the events at Conner Prairie. John Herbst and I met with a reporter from the *Indianapolis Business Journal* and traveled to Richmond, Indiana, Earlham's hometown, to meet with the editorial board of the *Palladium-Item*, the local newspaper. Our group also met with the editorial board of the *Indianapolis Star*. On June 13, the *Palladium-Item* published an editorial that took the Earlham line, saying that "since the college owns the museum, Bennett was within rights" in firing the Conner Prairie board as a method of dealing with what it erroneously described as "an operating deficit of about $4.5 million." On June 18, the *Indianapolis Star* lamented the loss of the "operational expertise and institutional memory" embodied in the former museum board, and described Save the Prairie's claims regarding Earlham's use of the Eli Lilly Endowment Fund for its own purposes. The *Star* also noted the dangers presented by a loss of donations and a decline in staff morale and urged mediation and an investigation of Earlham's endowment management by the attorney general. "Ideally," the *Star* concluded, "Conner Prairie's finances and operations would be independent of the college's. . . . Conner Prairie . . . must not be allowed to fade into history."

A full page of letters and opinions ran in the June 19 issue of the *Indianapolis Star*. Ignoring the college's recurring deficits, Earlham spokesman Morris Mills was quoted as saying that the "accusations that Earlham needs the [Eli Lilly Endowment Fund] dollars for its use are completely false. . . . Please remember," he added, "Conner Prairie was a gift by Lilly to Earlham College."[1] In counterpoint, Elizabeth Kryder-Reid, the director of the museum studies program at Indiana University–Purdue University Indianapolis, wrote, "Conner Prairie is a vital cultural resource to the central Indiana community and beyond. . . . It is unconscionable that Earlham has treated the museum as a private fiscal asset."[2] The *Star* editorialized again on June 21, urging "swift action to ensure the future" of the museum.

In its June 23–29 issue, the *Indianapolis Business Journal*, a weekly, ran the first of what turned out to be a number of thoughtful, well-researched articles on the dispute by Andrea Muirragui Davis. The paper's coverage of the Conner Prairie story was very important in shaping public understanding of the issues, despite Earlham's subsequent refusal to talk with the reporter. For its part, Save the Prairie's media policy was to talk with any reporter who called. In those interviews, we attempted to be open and candid, provided each interviewer with a useable quote, and urged the reporter to call back if he or she had any further questions or needed additional information.

News of the decision by the Conner Prairie Alliance to withdraw its support of the museum appeared in the *Indianapolis Star* on July 2, along with the report that the museum had sustained a loss of nearly $250,000 in sponsorships and contributions. The following day's paper reported on Earlham's opposition to a proposed rezoning by the city of Carmel of approximately 700 acres of land at the museum that lay within the Carmel city limits. The city had moved to protect the land in response to what it saw as threats presented by Earlham's takeover. The mayor of Carmel, Jim Brainard, was quoted as saying, "The instability that we see in the way that Earlham College is serving as trustee for Conner Prairie and its assets at this time lead me to believe that the undeveloped land Earlham owns on [the west] side of [White] river might be in jeopardy."[3] The dispute ultimately became the subject of a standstill agreement between the college and the city. This tract of land was to figure prominently in the final resolution of the Conner Prairie issues.

On July 3, the *Chronicle of Higher Education*, a national publication, ran a story reporting on the attorney general's investigation of Earlham's management of the Lilly gifts. Although Douglas Bennett had refused to talk to the reporter, the story contained Earlham's version of the events and a report on Save the Prairie's contentions. It closed with a quote in which we said, "It's not lost on Earlham that, if Conner Prairie went away, there would be a huge amount of money to spend out of this trust. The fact of the matter is that [Earlham] would stand to benefit substantially if Conner Prairie were to fail."[4]

Without explaining why it was backing away from its earlier position in support of independence for Conner Prairie, in its July 5 edition the *Indianapolis Star* ran an editorial in which it castigated the "well meaning folks" seeking to protect Conner Prairie. Citing the story of King Solomon and the baby claimed by two women, the paper said that Conner Prairie's defenders were hurting the museum, not protecting it. We responded with a letter to the editor that appeared in the July 9 edition, in which we observed that "Conner Prairie is not being torn apart by those who love it. The risk it faces is a steady dismantling by the only entity that stands to benefit from its demise: Earlham College."

On July 13, the *Star* reported that the estimated losses at Conner Prairie had grown to $400,000 for the current year. In its July 21–27 edition, the *Indianapolis Business Journal* carried a letter from Earlham trustee and Conner Prairie board member Thomas Fisher in which he claimed that "as administrator of the public trust . . ., [Earlham] is free to use [the Conner Prairie] land however it chooses" and that "public statements claiming that Conner Prairie is a 'community' asset may be an interesting metaphor, but they have no basis in law." Fisher, a former practicing lawyer, was the judge of the Indiana Tax Court.

But the most candid views on Earlham's relationship to Conner Prairie, and the most ominous, were those of Earlham trustee and Conner Prairie board member Morris Mills. In the June 23 edition of the *Indianapolis Business Journal*, Mills was quoted as saying, "I hope we find citizens interested in helping. If not, the museum might just have to do what Mr. Lilly had in mind in the first place—preserve the [Conner] house. It doesn't have to advertise on the radio or try to make itself a national attraction."[5]

And in a television interview with WTHR on July 17, addressing Earlham's future plans for the museum, Mills said, "Earlham is not a philanthropic institute. It has a hard enough time running a college. . . . You may not be able to have all those interpreters around. I mean, those are very expensive. You may not be able to do as much historic research as you did."

The handwriting was on the wall for all to see. The public trust of which Earlham was the "administrator" was only an "interesting metaphor." Earlham was not a "philanthropic" organization. It was free to use Conner Prairie "however it chooses." The college had little interest in preserving, and no interest in expanding, Conner Prairie's operations. Indeed, it was prepared to shut down everything at the museum except for the William Conner House. Earlham's management of the museum as its trustee would not be driven by its fiduciary responsibility to act in the best interests of the public, who were the beneficiaries of its trust, but by Earlham's judgments as to what was best for Earlham.

⁓

On July 7, Landrum Bolling called me, apparently in reaction to the media attention to the Conner Prairie story, to lament the way in which Earlham's positions were being characterized. In his view, the dispute was over control of Conner Prairie. The money, he said, was irrelevant. The college was in excellent financial condition and not dependent on income from the Eli Lilly Endowment Fund. He knew what Lilly meant by "first charge," and anyone challenging Earlham's interpretation had not a leg to stand on. Why, he asked, could not reasonable people sit down and resolve this matter? I pointed out that we were not the ones who broke off the discussions, and that it was Earlham's tactics that had led to confrontation and public examination of the issues. I assured Bolling that we remained open to any process—I again suggested mediation—that might lead to a prompt resolution of the matter. This was one of several instances in which Bolling directly interacted with participants on the Conner Prairie side of the dispute, but he supported Earlham's positions in statements to the press and on the Earlham website, and he provided an affidavit as to his relationships with Lilly for Earlham's use.

Mutz called on July 9 to discuss the analytical framework that we had sent to him six days earlier. He raised relevant questions relating to our approach to the issues and asked Save the Prairie to focus its attention on whether Conner Prairie was a part of or separate from the mission of Earlham College. Apparently, Earlham's legal arguments to the attorney general were based largely on the view that the museum and the college were one and the same. As a result, it asserted that the gifts that created the Eli Lilly Endowment Fund were not held as part of the public charitable trust. This question—whether or not the fund was held in trust—was to become the central issue in the subsequent litigation between the attorney general and Earlham.

In the response that Save the Prairie provided to Mutz on July 14, we pointed out that the museum and the college were not the same thing, either operationally or legally. There was no overlap between the missions of the two institutions, and Earlham's decisions regarding the structure and management of the museum had been premised on the expectation that it could be made to be self-supporting. We noted that the organization of Conner Prairie, Inc., was intended to separate both the strategic policy making and the day-to-day management of the museum from that of the college. We also pointed out that Lilly's gifts contemplated different funding mechanisms for the two institutions by setting up the Eli Lilly Endowment Fund as a separate fund from Earlham's general endowment. Earlham had invested none of its own money in Conner Prairie. There had been direct continuity in the operation of the museum from its founding by Lilly to its transfer to Earlham as trustee and its subsequent development by Earlham, and none of Earlham's policies had linked Conner Prairie's programs to the internal operations of the college.

In response to the question whether the Lilly stock gifts were held in trust, we pointed out that, under Indiana law, "trust property" included property transferred to a trustee for purposes of the trust, whether or not the property was titled in the name of the trust. We argued that the terms Lilly used in his gift instruments—"corpus" to be held "in perpetuity" in a "special endowment fund" and to be "managed" (not "owned") by Earlham in order "to maintain and operate" Conner Prairie—were consistent with trust concepts. Moreover, on several occasions Earlham College had characterized its relationship to the Lilly gifts as one of "trust." In acknowledging Lilly's 1973 gift, Bolling used the term "trustee" to describe Earlham's relationship to the fund that Lilly had created. The "principles" adopted by the Earlham trustees on June 3, 1977, referred to the gift under Lilly's will as a trust. As recently as 1994, then-president of Earlham Richard Wood had characterized Lilly's monetary gifts to Earlham as a trust and the college as "a very good steward of that trust."[6]

On July 15, Bennett sent a memo to the Conner Prairie staff in which he announced that Earlham had engaged a consultant "to help us with financial questions" and to "look at the museum's business model in the larger context of its mission and vision." He also announced that Earlham had begun a search for a new president for Conner Prairie. The college, he wrote, would increase the distributions from the Eli Lilly Endowment Fund "to cover recent losses in income from gifts and special events" so as to "allow us to sustain all current programs and current staff." He reported on Mutz's engagement by the attorney general and asserted that Earlham was "cooperating fully in this review." "We anticipate," he said, that "the attorney general will find no problems in the way the Earlham Board of Trustees has discharged its responsibilities with regard to the gifts from Mr. Lilly." In a cover letter, Bennett thanked the staff for its efforts since June 11. Alluding to media speculation that Earlham would "dismantle" Conner Prairie, Bennett asserted that "nothing could be farther from the truth." But, he continued, the vision for Conner Prairie had to be implemented "in a manner that restores and sustains fiscal stability." Similar statements were made in letters Bennett sent to members of the Conner Prairie Alliance on August 5 and to members of the William Conner Society on August 7.

Bennett's persistence in pursuing Earlham's tactics and story line in the face of the initial public response to the crisis led us to wonder whether the Earlham trustees understood what was going on. Only a few of the trustees lived in central Indiana, and there was no assurance that the other members of the board were aware of the media coverage that had followed June 11 and the damage that coverage was doing to Earlham's reputation. Save the Prairie decided that we should reach out directly to the trustees, individually, and on July 21 we mailed a letter to each of them and sent a copy to each Quaker pastor in Indiana. That letter recited the facts surrounding the events of June 11 and noted the adverse publicity that Earlham had received as a result of its actions. We also observed that, if Earlham's objective was fiscal stability for Conner Prairie, its actions had produced the opposite effect, citing the increased endowment draws needed to support the museum's operations. We asked the trustees to consider whether the college's actions had been appropriate, given its own needs, and questioned whether Bennett's tactics would extinguish the 25-year history of questions regarding Earlham's administration of the Lilly gifts.

Morris Mills called on July 23. He had received our letter. Earlham "did not want to run a museum," he said, and urged that we resolve the dispute. I agreed. The Earlham representatives were meeting on August 8, he reported, and would be in contact with us. His allusion to a possible settlement encouraged us. Rumors of other developments seemed to reinforce this conclusion. But Save the Prairie also received a response from Earlham trustee Thomas Gottschalk in which he took a hard line regarding Earlham's discharge of its duties as trustee. We received no other response to our letter, and we heard nothing further about the August 8 meeting.

On August 5, Earlham gave the attorney general a memorandum setting forth its view of the law applicable to the administration of the Lilly gifts. Earlham's memorandum also provided its version of the events leading up to June 11, which posited a scheme on the part of Conner Prairie to gain unreasonable concessions from Earlham by threatening litigation. Earlham charged that the subsequent damage to Conner Prairie's finances was the result of Save the Prairie "advocating a boycott" of contributions to the museum. The memorandum argued that the Lilly gifts gave Earlham the "discretion" to determine the size and scope of the museum, which had been "sufficiently funded." The fifty-fifty allocation of the Eli Lilly Endowment Fund between the college and the museum was "a reasonable exercise" of Earlham's "discretion." The use of the spending rule was permitted by the Indiana version of the Uniform Management of Institutional Funds Act, as it "applies to the stock gifts." The gifts "do not reflect any intention to create a trust." The 1,371-acre tract was Earlham's to use as it saw fit, under the terms of the original deed, and nothing that Lilly or Earlham had said or done after the transfer changed that fact. And most important, Earlham could have no conflict of interest in the management of the Eli Lilly Endowment Fund because Earlham College and Conner Prairie were one and the same thing. What Save the Prairie saw as a conflict between a trustee and the beneficiaries of its trust was "merely the tension between the three parts of Earlham regarding budgeting and allocation of endowment."

At Mutz's request, on August 8 Douglas Church, Stan Hurt, and I met with him at Church's offices in Noblesville. Mutz reported that the attorney general had asked Earlham to provide an accounting of its management of the Eli Lilly Endowment Fund, not as a formal legal response but as an aid to his understanding of the facts. Mutz asked us a number of questions that were designed to test our counterarguments to Earlham's view of the issues. He particularly challenged our views that the entirety of the museum operation should be viewed as part of the public charitable trust and that Lilly's stock gifts were part of that trust. We talked at length about the "discretion" Lilly gave to Earlham and the standards that applied to Earlham's exercise of that discretion. We argued that the standard was that of a fiduciary charged with the development and maintenance of a trust asset for the benefit of the public, and that the process Earlham had followed in arbitrarily dividing the Eli Lilly Endowment Fund into two "shares" and making distributions from the fund based on an automatic spending rule, instead of continually assessing the museum's needs and opportunities, was flawed.

On August 18, Save the Prairie sent to Mutz a 38-page response, with several attachments, in support of our points. In our response we

- detailed the history of the Lilly-Earlham relationship, the governance discussions, and the removal of the museum board;
- discussed the effects of Earlham's actions on the museum;
- argued that the public charitable trust included the subsequent Lilly gifts, that Earlham had misused its "discretion" in its management of the Eli Lilly Endowment Fund, that UMIFA did not apply to the Eli Lilly Endowment Fund because Earlham College and Conner Prairie

were not the same thing, and that Earlham, by its actions before and after Lilly's death, had assigned all but the 80-acre tract of the Conner Prairie land to the uses of the museum and had presented the museum to the public on that basis;

- pointed out Earlham's various conflicts of interest and how those conflicts had been aggravated by its endowment management policies;
- provided an outline of Earlham's breaches of its fiduciary duties; and
- identified seven specific violations of the Indiana Trust Code and listed the remedies available to the attorney general, which included the forced removal of Earlham as trustee and restitution to the trust of any amounts found to have been distributed to the college in violation of the terms of the Lilly gifts.

Mutz said it would be several weeks before we would have any reaction from the attorney general's office.

We also decided to talk with the first managers of Conner Prairie about the development of the museum and Lilly's role in it. Myron Vourax, the executive director of Conner Prairie from 1971 to 1976, had supervised the construction of much of Prairietown. After talking with Vourax, we asked him to meet with Mutz, which he did on August 26. According to Vourax, during his tenure at Conner Prairie he had weekly meetings with Lilly in which they discussed the development of the museum and its funding needs. Vourax's view was that Earlham saw no connection between the missions of the museum and the college, and that it never took advantage of the opportunity to integrate museum programs into the curriculum of the college. Earlham's principal objective in its relationship with Conner Prairie, in Vourax's view, was as a point of access to Lilly. Earlham never revealed to Vourax how it was managing the Lilly gifts.

From Vourax's perspective, the development of the museum went along successfully during Bolling's presidency. But when Bolling was succeeded by Franklin Wallin, Vourax said that Wallin "made my life hell" by insisting that every action at the museum receive his personal approval. Frustrated by the refusal of the Earlham trustees to make any decisions regarding the development of Prairietown, Vourax began to undertake initiatives that Wallin had not approved. Vourax speculated that Wallin blamed him for Lilly's letter of May 6, 1974, in which Lilly complained to Bolling about Earlham's "parsimonious" failure to proceed with the development of Prairietown in accordance with its previous representations to him. That letter was the genesis of the discussions that resulted in Earlham's failed attempt to reform the terms of Lilly's 1973 gift.

We also met with Richard Sampson, Vourax's predecessor at Conner Prairie. During Sampson's tenure from 1967 to 1971, programming at Conner Prairie was informal, consisting largely of school tours. From his contacts with Lilly, he was aware of the philanthropist's interest in sharing Conner Prairie with the public by expanding its programming, particularly for school-age children. A wave of school consolidations at this time led to the wide use of school busses and provided a means of transporting students to venues such as Conner Prairie. Sampson attributed the first expansion—Earlham's 1972 dedication of 230 additional acres to the uses of the museum—to Lilly's view that Conner Prairie needed room to grow.

In the meantime, the legal arguments continued. On August 26, a 17-page "Supplemental Memorandum" advanced two new arguments. Earlham now contended that the original 58-acre trust could not be expanded without the college's consent, and that Lilly had "waived" any conflicts of interest in creating the Eli Lilly Endowment Fund. Responding to a question from Mutz, Earlham also asserted that its failure to differentiate between the 58-acre tract and the balance of the museum in its reporting on the museum's operations was not an admission that the entire museum operation was held in trust. The college defended its management of the museum by claiming that it had given specific consideration to the operating needs of Conner Prairie, just as it had to those of the undergraduate college and the Earlham School of Religion, and contended that limiting Conner Prairie's participation in endowment distributions to "about 50% of the income" pursuant to its "rule of thumb" was not an abuse of Earlham's "discretion." Earlham further asserted that it would not be in the museum's best interests to be separated from the college because the college had done a good job with the endowment fund's investments and that, even in light of all that had become public in the recent past, Earlham's role at Conner Prairie would not—at least in the long term—diminish volunteer support and financial contributions. In selecting Earlham as the subject of his largess, the college asserted, Lilly had made a "good choice." Earlham vowed to "rebuild" the museum's board of directors, and it blamed Save the Prairie for all of the damage sustained by the museum since June 11.

On August 28, Bennett announced that, as a result of the demands that Conner Prairie matters were making on his time, he was postponing a six-month sabbatical planned to extend from October 2003 to March 2004, and would be away instead during the spring semester. Things obviously were not going as smoothly for Earlham as Bennett had assumed they would.

Save the Prairie provided a response to Earlham's "Supplemental Memorandum" on September 5. In our view, Earlham's management of the entire museum complex as a single entity was, in fact, an admission that all of Conner Prairie was part of the public charitable trust. Created as an express public charitable trust, the museum was not "part of Earlham." The college's conflicts of interest were not limited to those inherent in the terms of the Lilly gifts but extended to broader conflicts created solely by its own doing. The law imposed upon Earlham the burden of proof that its actions had been proper, and the division of the endowment into "shares" and the adoption of the spending rule did not constitute an appropriate discharge of Earlham's fiduciary obligations with respect to the museum. With respect to Earlham's claim that the original trust could not have been expanded without its consent, we pointed out that Earlham had expressly agreed, in writing, to the terms of Lilly's 1969, 1972, and 1973 gifts and had accepted the fourth gift under the provisions of his will. As Earlham's endowment management policies were not adopted until after Lilly's death, he obviously had not "waived" any management obligations created by the original terms of his gifts.

Responding to Earlham's claims regarding its management of the endowment, Save the Prairie pointed out that the college's board of trustees had never reexamined the "rule of thumb" or questioned whether the division of the Eli Lilly Endowment Fund into an Earlham share and a Conner Prairie share was an appropriate discharge of its fiduciary duty. It had never considered any other method of allocating the fund between the institutions. The college had become wedded to the distributions received under its policies and was dedicated to maintaining that revenue stream regardless of the needs and opportunities of the museum. We argued that the policies and motives of the college were clearly evident in how it accounted for those few endowment draws that it did approve for the needs of the museum: Earlham charged those draws not against the entire Eli Lilly Endowment Fund, but against the Conner Prairie share of the fund. This device preserved the full amount of the revenue stream on which Earlham had become dependent. There was nothing in the language of the Lilly gifts that suggested that Earlham College's limited interest in income distributions from the Eli Lilly Endowment Fund entitled it to this priority over the legitimate needs of the museum. In fact, Lilly made it clear that the *museum's* needs were paramount, under the first charge language of the gift instruments.

We argued that simply because Lilly assumed that the college would be a good steward of his gifts did not make it so, and that the validity of that assumption had to be examined in light of the current facts and circumstances. Earlham had created conflicts of interest in discharging its duties as trustee of the public charitable trust, had breached its duties as a fiduciary, and had violated the Indiana Trust Code in several respects. Viewed in nonlegal terms,

Earlham's management of the museum had alienated its core constituents, destabilized its staff, produced large operating deficits, alarmed the surrounding communities, attracted a great deal of adverse publicity, and diverted the attention of the college's top management from its own urgent needs. In retrospect, we contended, Lilly had not made a "good choice."

Finally, Save the Prairie argued that it was unlikely that Earlham College would succeed in "rebuilding" the board of directors of Conner Prairie, Inc., if by that term it meant recruiting a board with the broad community involvement, independent thought, expertise, and interest demonstrated by the board it removed on June 11. It was not easy to find people to serve on a volunteer board of directors with the responsibility for managing a complex institution with an $8 million–plus budget. There were many demands on the time of qualified people, and there was stiff competition for persons having the skills and interest needed to be of value as directors of an institution such as the museum. Earlham had demonstrated that it was prepared not only to disregard the opinions of any board members who questioned its decisions, but also to discharge them and accuse them of fiscal irresponsibility. It also was clear that future members of the board would have little or no authority. Earlham obviously intended to run Conner Prairie from Richmond. Who would want to serve the museum under these conditions?

September 5 was the deadline for Earlham's submission of the accounting of how the college had applied the Eli Lilly Endowment Fund to itself and to Conner Prairie that the attorney general had requested. The legal briefing that had gone back and forth between Save the Prairie, Earlham, and Mutz was over, and Mutz was ready to deliver his analysis and recommendations to the attorney general.

⌒

The exchange of arguments between Earlham and Save the Prairie and the public debate of the issues presented the attorney general with a blend of legal and public policy questions. From a legal perspective, the root question was the scope of the public charitable trust. Should Lilly's subsequent gifts of stock be considered a part of that trust? If not, what was their character in the hands of Earlham? How should the physical boundaries of Conner Prairie be determined? Was the museum limited to the 58-acre tract? Did it include the 230-acre addition? Or did it extend to encompass the improvements and exhibits that had been constructed outside the boundaries of that property? What about the open land, both east and west of White River, that had been treated by Earlham as part of Conner Prairie? Were Earlham and Conner Prairie one and the same, or was Conner Prairie something more than a figment of Earlham's imagination? Could Earlham sidestep any further inquiry into its management of the Lilly gifts by pointing to Conner Prairie's successes? What was the proper scope of Earlham's "discretion" in determining its rights under the Lilly gifts? In response to these questions, Earlham urged a restrictive, narrow view of the trust-related issues and relied heavily on its discretion. Save the Prairie advocated a broader view of the trust issues and argued that, as a trustee, Earlham should be held to the high standards of conduct applicable to a fiduciary in its management of Conner Prairie.

From a public policy perspective, the question was whether it was in the long-term best interests of a valued cultural institution to leave its future in the hands of an entity that had a fundamental and substantial conflict of interest in deciding questions related to its operation, maintenance, and development. The attorney general also had to consider the public's willingness to continue its support of Conner Prairie under the circumstances that had come to light regarding its governance.

Although there was no dramatic event signaling the conclusion of this phase of our efforts, Save the Prairie believed that by the end of September 2003, we had accomplished a great deal. We had put into Mutz's hands all of the available documents bearing on the issues.[7] We seemed to be winning the public relations war, and the flow of information to the public had not subsided. In late September, *Indianapolis Monthly* magazine carried a major feature article about the dispute, and in its September 22–28 edition, the *Indianapolis Business Journal* carried a story about the financial situation at Conner Prairie, reporting that the 2003 deficit could reach $800,000. We had refined and honed our legal arguments into what seemed to be an effective and persuasive form. In our review of the materials submitted to the attorney general by Earlham, we had found nothing that undermined our positions, and we were encouraged by Earlham's failure to come up with any new legal arguments. If we had seen Earlham's best case, we had reason to believe that the attorney general would intervene on behalf of the museum. Save the Prairie had submitted its application for tax-exempt status to the Internal Revenue Service, which it later granted and thereby assured us of an adequate stream of contributions to continue our efforts. We had received a great deal of interest and encouragement from community leaders. The press had exposed the problems that Earlham was having with its management of the Conner Prairie operations and fund-raising. It was apparent that the attorney general's inquiry was going to continue, and Earlham had received no assurance that it would remain in control at Conner Prairie. The museum staff had recovered from its initial shock and seemed to be encouraged that help was on the way in the form of intervention by the attorney general.

Notes

1. Morris Mills, letter to the editor, *Indianapolis Star*, June 19, 2003.

2. Elizabeth Kryder-Reid, letter to the editor, *Indianapolis Star*, June 19, 2003.

3. William J. Booher, "Rezoning Attempt Riles Earlham," *Indianapolis Star*, July 3, 2003, p. B7.

4. John L. Pulley, "Earlham College Is Investigated for Its Management of a Museum's Assets," *Chronicle of Higher Education*, July 3, 2003.

5. Andrea Muirragui Davis, "Battle Drenched in History," *Indianapolis Business Journal*, June 23–29, 2003.

6. Richard J. Wood, "Earlham College's Stewardship of Mr. Eli Lilly's Generous Gifts of 1973 and through His Will—a Report Supplementing [the Wood Report]," September 1, 1994.

7. At this time, Save the Prairie did not have access to many of the documents in the Conner Prairie archives that were later reviewed for purposes of this book, so the case before the attorney general was not as complete as that recited here.

CHAPTER ELEVEN

~

Waiting and Thinking

Save the Prairie had no idea when the attorney general might announce his findings or what he might decide to do. Neither did we know whether Earlham had responded to the attorney general's request for an informal accounting of its management of the Eli Lilly Endowment Fund. More than three months would pass before the attorney general made his findings public. In the hope that we might be able to have some influence over the outcome of the attorney general's investigation, we turned our thoughts toward the possible outcomes.

On October 22, 2003, Save the Prairie sent Mark Mutz the first in a series of memoranda related to the post-Earlham financial and governance structure for Conner Prairie. The removal of Earlham as trustee of the museum was the cornerstone of our position. We argued that Conner Prairie could not survive under Earlham's continuing trusteeship, because institutions such as Conner Prairie, which rely on the support of the community for funding, for volunteer labor, for leadership, and for patronage, were delicate entities. People did not have to support Conner Prairie with their money, time, or skills. The museum must earn individuals' respect and their affection or it ultimately would fail. Even the museum's ability to attract and retain paid staff depended, in part, on employees' esprit de corps and sense of identity with the mission of the institution. Conner Prairie was irrelevant to the college's core mission. Earlham had no incentive to make the museum a success. Furthermore, the college would benefit substantially from reductions in museum programs and staff, and even more substantially from its closure.

We noted that Earlham could kill the museum even if that was not its intention. Subtle changes in programs, gentle shifts in leadership attitudes, even slightly waning enthusiasm on the part of management could all ripple through the staff and the volunteers and change the culture of the institution. Program changes and cuts could lead to reductions in staff. Recruiting new people with the necessary skills would become more and more difficult. These attitudes could feed on themselves and begin a downward spiral for the museum. Conner Prairie could disappear, not with a bang, but with a whimper.

This process had already begun at Conner Prairie, we asserted, but it was muted by the staff's hope that the prior management would be restored. For these reasons, we argued that the attorney general must act to remove Earlham as trustee of the museum. Without this step, all other remedies for Conner Prairie's situation ultimately would be in vain. The museum must be independent. If Earlham College continued to have the ultimate responsibility for Conner Prairie, even with safeguards in place, the institution would lose the support of the people who cared about it and, absent that support, would cease to exist.

Our views notwithstanding, Save the Prairie's leadership assumed that whatever action the attorney general decided upon, he would be seeking a strategy that did no further harm to Earlham's public image and allowed the college both to save face and to survive as a viable institution. Obviously Earlham was unhappy that it had received so much public attention as a result of its discharge of the Conner Prairie board. More importantly, unless it quickly could raise new funds for its endowment, the college might well face the prospect of cutbacks in its operations if any significant part of the Eli Lilly Endowment Fund were to be allocated to Conner Prairie. Given our treatment at Earlham's hands, the former directors of Conner Prairie had little sympathy for these considerations.

Save the Prairie reminded the attorney general that the dispute was Earlham's doing. Conner Prairie had not sought a partition of the Eli Lilly Endowment Fund; that was a term insisted upon by Earlham. Conner Prairie did not take the dispute public; that also was Earlham's decision. We asserted that Earlham had exercised very bad judgment in setting self-interested goals for the outcome of the governance discussions and in the tactics it chose to employ, and we urged that Earlham not be allowed to forestall an equitable outcome based upon its needs and wants. If Earlham was forced to restructure its operations, or to find new capital, as a result of the resolution of the matter, those were risks that it had elected to run. Had it managed the Eli Lilly Endowment Fund according to the terms laid down by Lilly, the college would have had to take those actions long ago. The museum should not suffer, we concluded, because of the mismanagement of its trustee. Little could be done to reverse the damage that Earlham had sustained. If Earlham's removal as trustee—the only outcome that could assure the museum's future—proved detrimental to the college, we argued that it had only itself to blame.

Save the Prairie proposed a complete restructuring of the museum. Conner Prairie, Inc., should be dissolved and a new not-for-profit corporation created to act as trustee of the public charitable trust. We assumed that the trust would include all of the museum operations, the 58-acre tract, some part of the additional 1,371 acres given to Earlham by Lilly, and some or all of the Eli Lilly Endowment Fund. The reformed trust should be designed to preserve and advance Lilly's intentions as expressed in his gift instruments, and the governance structure of the new corporation should protect the interests of the public as the beneficiary of the trust. We advocated simplicity, transparency, and accountability in the management of the museum.

We also considered the nature and extent of any continuing interest that Earlham might have in the Eli Lilly Endowment Fund and how to recognize that interest. One possibility would be to transfer the entire fund to Conner Prairie. In that case, we suggested an arrangement, based upon the language of the Lilly gifts, under which Earlham would annually receive any income on the fund not needed for the support of the museum. The museum could charge its capital expenditures against the principal of the fund, but the museum, and not Earlham, would make the decisions regarding the museum's development activities and manage the fund's investments. The other possibility was a complete separation of the institutions. Both the Eli Lilly Endowment Fund and the real estate could be divided between the college and the museum, with some part of the endowment assets being allocated to Earlham in settlement of its contingent interests in the Lilly gifts. We recognized that the calculation of that amount would be problematic, but suggested that a starting point might be the present value of the future income stream that Earlham could expect from the Eli Lilly Endowment Fund on the assumption that the fund was managed under the terms of the Lilly gifts. As we will see, this was the framework within which the dispute ultimately was resolved.

~

On October 26, 2003, Douglas Bennett and John Young sent a letter to the Conner Prairie staff in which they reported that the Earlham trustees had decided to distribute $4.1 million to the museum from the Eli Lilly Endowment Fund for 2004, which they described as "a 5% draw plus $700,000." The letter did not include a projection of the museum's operating deficit.

Bennett and Young went on to update the staff on "various legal matters." They characterized the dismissal of the former directors' Hamilton County lawsuit as having "effectively ended any possibility that a judge would order the reinstatement of any of the former directors." This was untrue, for that could have been the result of a lawsuit brought by the attorney general for that purpose. While the statement may have assured the staff Earlham had stabilized the museum's governance, it could also have been intended to stamp out any lingering hope that the court would force Earlham to go away. The letter also revealed the terms of a settlement offer that Earlham had made to John Herbst, who had retained a lawyer to pursue his claims for wrongful termination of his employment, while acknowledging that the issues were still in negotiation. This inappropriate disclosure seemed to have been intended to convince the staff that Earlham was being more than generous with Herbst, so as to temper any remaining sympathy generated by Earlham's treatment of him.

Bennett and Young also outlined three possible outcomes for the attorney general's investigation: (1) he could take no action; (2) he could "make recommendations to Earlham to change some practices and Earlham agrees to do so," or (3) "he could sue Earlham in court" if Earlham does not agree with his opinion. The letter concluded by saying that "we continue to be optimistic that the attorney general will not find significant problems with Earlham's stewardship."

October 30, 2003, was a busy day. Save the Prairie sent a letter to the Conner Prairie staff responding to the letter from Bennett and Young. It seemed to us that the Earlham letter had been designed to discourage the staff members and undermine their hopes for a prompt resolution of the matter on terms that the staff would find acceptable. After expressing our gratitude for all that the staff had done for Conner Prairie since June 11, we outlined the actions we had taken to bring the matter to the attention of the attorney general and our conclusions that Earlham had violated both the terms of the Lilly gifts and the Indiana Trust Code. We expressed hope that the issues could be resolved without the litigation that Earlham foresaw and we explained that the dismissal of the Hamilton County lawsuit had no bearing on the issues before the attorney general or on his ability to seek reinstatement of the former board. We noted that, had Earlham agreed to the level of endowment support for 2003 outlined in the Bennett and Young letter, Conner Prairie would have been operating with a balanced budget. In closing, we encouraged the staff to keep up their good work and assured them that we would continue working for an independent Conner Prairie.

That same day, Herbst met with the attorney general. Steve Carter told Herbst that each side of the dispute—Save the Prairie and Earlham—had adopted a position that left little room for compromise, but that the investigatory phase of his involvement was over and he was working on an action plan.

⌒

At the same time, Earlham was ramping up its public relations campaign. On October 31, Bennett sent a letter to a wide audience of Earlham constituents in which he referred to the recent media attention to "governance" at Conner Prairie "and the success of new programs at the museum" each of which, it turned out, was in place prior to June 11. He said that he wanted to "emphasize how much Conner Prairie means to Earlham." He enclosed copies of articles that were to appear in the Earlham alumni magazine and a six-page brochure with color pictures and graphics describing "Earlham's Conner Prairie Museum." The brochure generally described the Lilly gifts as "for Conner Prairie and Earlham College," as though the two institutions were to share equally in Lilly's largess. Bennett attributed the discharge of the Conner Prairie board to its failure to raise "sufficient gifts or grants" to support the "significant capital expenditures in recent years." He assured his readers that "Earlham has fully cooperated with the Attorney General's review" and asserted that Lilly had "agreed" to Earlham's fifty-fifty allocation of his gifts. The brochure acknowledged the "serious financial implication because of the management changes" and, in an appeal for financial support for what Earlham had done, said, "Supporting Conner Prairie supports Earlham" because Conner Prairie was "one of the three basic parts, along with the College and the graduate School of Religion, that comprise Earlham."

Earlham's attempts to assure the staff and the public that nothing had changed at Conner Prairie were diminished by a report in the November 5 edition of the *Indianapolis Star* that Earlham would shut Conner Prairie down for the first quarter of 2004. Historically, the museum had not operated during the winter quarter, but two years earlier the former board and management had decided that it would be helpful, in maintaining staff interest and public awareness, if there could be some level of programming during the winter, and had initiated year-round operations on a limited basis. The decision to reverse this policy was not, in and of itself, significant to the museum's total operations, but it contradicted Bennett's representations that there would be no cutbacks in Conner Prairie's programs.

On November 11, Save the Prairie received a letter from Lee McTurnan, Earlham's lawyer, castigating us for sending our October 31 letter to the

Conner Prairie staff. McTurnan, with an eye toward some broader audience, claimed that "Earlham has built, supported and sustained Conner Prairie for 40 years" and "devoted tremendous resources, including money and the use of its own land, to ensure Conner Prairie's success." He stated that our letter was "designed to undermine the staff's loyalty and generate uncertainty," and he ordered that Save the Prairie "cease and desist" from communicating directly with the Conner Prairie staff. McTurnan did not ask for a response, and we did not provide one.

If any evidence of the staff's views of the matter was needed, on November 19 several staff members visited the attorney general's office. Although they had no appointment, they waited until Carter was able to see them, so that they could describe their concerns about their job security under Earlham, their lack of trust in Earlham, and the effect of its actions on programs and morale.

～

On December 6, 2003, the *Indianapolis Star* carried a story reporting that Lilly Endowment, Inc., had announced grants totaling $38.9 million, to be allocated among Indiana colleges and universities in order to fund programs developed by the grantees to combat the "brain drain." The article included this one-sentence paragraph: "Only Earlham College did not receive a grant."[1] Every other Indiana college and university had participated. Lilly Endowment, an institution with enormous influence in Indiana and the nation and one that paid particular attention to education issues, had signaled its views on Earlham's management of Conner Prairie. Lilly Endowment was, at this time, the second-largest private foundation in the United States and had been one of Earlham's largest sources of annual support.

～

At our request, the leadership of Save the Prairie met with the attorney general and Mutz on December 8, in order to discuss our concerns, inquire about the progress of the attorney general's investigation, and propose strategies for dealing with the situation. We outlined what we believed to be the necessary conclusions of a review of the facts and law surrounding the Lilly gifts and their management by Earlham. We argued that the only chance for a private resolution of the issues lay in Earlham understanding that, without a settlement, it faced a lawsuit seeking its removal as trustee of the public charitable trust and the transfer of the Eli Lilly Endowment Fund and the museum real estate to a new trustee. The attorney general could pursue other available remedies including restitution of any amounts wrongfully withdrawn from the endowment fund over the past 25 years. We urged that a firm deadline be set for such an agreement. The circumstances, we said, presented important questions of public policy, and the outcome had to be fair and equitable and consistent with Lilly's intent.

In mid-December Herbst and Earlham settled his employment claims. The terms of that settlement barred Herbst from providing any further assistance to Save the Prairie, so we terminated our consulting relationship.

As 2003 came to a close without any action by the attorney general, Save the Prairie and the community in general felt a great deal of concern over the possible reasons for his lack of action. The *Indianapolis Business Journal* named the Conner Prairie story as one of the year's top three local news stories. An article in the paper's January 5–11, 2004, edition said that the museum "was running out of time," citing the financial reverses and declining staff morale at Conner Prairie. A statement by Earlham's public relations firm indicated that Earlham finally had realized that it was not going to be able to rebuild the museum until the attorney general had made a decision: "Until that happens, there's no sense moving forward," the Earlham spokesman said. Save the Prairie's Stan Hurt was quoted as saying, "The attorney general is the only one who can give us a time line. But it has to come soon. The longer it drags on, the harder it is going to be to rebuild."[2]

Young, the Earlham-appointed chairman of the reconstituted board of directors at Conner Prairie, responded to this story with a letter to the editor lauding Earlham's operation of the museum. He cited the strategic plan that "continues to guide the museum's path," its "excellent, experienced" management team and rising attendance in 2003. He claimed that Earlham had "cooperated fully" with the attorney general's investigation and chastised Save the Prairie for doing "all that they can to harm Conner Prairie." Young alleged that we had "urged donors not to contribute to the museum" and "defamed Earlham's intentions with regard to Conner Prairie."[3]

In the January 19–25 edition of the *Indianapolis Business Journal*, Save the Prairie responded to Young's letter by pointing out that the fired board of directors had developed the strategic plan and John Herbst had recruited and trained the management team. Why, if these were the persons responsible for the museum's success, did Earlham see fit to depose them? Since Earlham controlled the purse strings, it was not fiscal irresponsibility. And why, if Earlham was fully cooperating with the attorney general, was Carter still waiting for the delivery of basic financial information he had requested in August 2003?

At this point, we wondered whether Earlham was acting in good faith in its dealings with the attorney general. Carter had not disclosed whether

Earlham had responded to his August request. We felt certain that, if the college possessed exculpatory accounting records, it would have produced them by now; but it had no reason to provide anything that did not support its actions. Absent any deadlines or sanctions for noncompliance with the attorney general's request, Earlham had no reason to tell the attorney general that it was not going to comply. In expressing our concerns to Mutz, we pointed out that the information sought by the attorney general should have been readily available if Earlham had been properly discharging its duties as trustee. Its failure, or inability, to produce an accounting was, to our minds, prima facie evidence of a breach of trust.

As it turned out, Earlham had responded to the attorney general's request. But it took an escalation of the dispute by the attorney general to move the matter along.

Notes

1. Barb Berggoetz, "'Brain Drain' Grants Awarded," *Indianapolis Star*, sec. B, p.1.

2. Andrea Muirragui Davis, "Museum on Hold, Awaiting Decision," *Indianapolis Business Journal*, January 5–11, 2004.

3. John Young, "Differing Views of Conner Prairie" (letter to the editor), *Indianapolis Business Journal*, January 12–18, 2004.

CHAPTER TWELVE

~

The Attorney General
Rolls Out His Strategy

Earlham's submissions to the attorney general failed to resolve his questions. The *Indianapolis Business Journal* later reported that the college's financial data ran to thousands of pages and posited at least four different explanations of how it had used the Eli Lilly Endowment Fund. Without a complete and satisfactory accounting of Earlham's administration of the fund, the attorney general had two options open to him. He could decide that the data available to him—fragmentary though it may be—did not support any further expenditure of the public's funds, and close his file. Or he could go to court. In filing a lawsuit against Earlham, the attorney general could elect between two tactical approaches: he could charge Earlham with breach of trust, based on the documentary record before him, or he could seek the production of a court-ordered accounting that conformed to the requirements of the Indiana Trust Code and then decide upon a further course of action once that accounting had been produced. Steve Carter chose the latter alternative.

On January 17, 2004, the attorney general filed a lawsuit in the Hamilton County Superior Court seeking a formal accounting of Earlham's management of Lilly's gifts. In a press release announcing his action, Carter said that he was "not entirely satisfied with the quality of [Earlham's] information or the timeliness of its presentation to us." He also outlined his concerns regarding Earlham's distributions from the Eli Lilly Endowment Fund, contrasting the college's actions with the "intended cash flow" desired by Lilly. He went on to say that he was calling for the appointment of a new trustee for Conner Prairie as "the best long term solution to resolve the recurring conflicts of financial management involving Earlham College and the living history museum," and he invited Earlham to meet with him to move toward the goal of a "final resolution."

Save the Prairie saw these actions as evidence that the attorney general accepted the positions we had advocated, and from this point forward we were confident that our views aligned with those of the attorney general. However, throughout the dispute the attorney general's team was careful to keep us at arm's length and to avoid any appearance of collaboration. Earlham supporters had suggested that the attorney general was "in the pocket" of Save the Prairie and scoured the reports of his campaign contributions for evidence of that fact, finding nothing to support that conclusion.

We were confident that the attorney general would not have filed suit unless he was convinced of the merits of the case against Earlham for breach of trust and was prepared to make those claims if necessary. Apparently Carter had adopted the strategy of using both a carrot, in the form of an invitation to negotiate a settlement, and a stick, in the form of his willingness to take the first step toward a judicial resolution of the issues. He had not publicly charged Earlham with breach of trust, thereby respecting its sensitivities and improving prospects for a negotiated settlement. He based his call for an independent Conner Prairie on public policy grounds, citing Earlham's conflict of interest as both the trustee and beneficiary of Lilly's gifts. By moving the dispute into a judicial forum, Carter had laid the groundwork for raising the breach-of-trust issues. In setting the appointment of a new trustee as his ultimate objective, the attorney general had eschewed half measures that would have left Earlham in control of the museum under some different accounting or fund management strictures. The questions now were how Earlham would respond and how aggressive Carter would be in following up this initiative. Save the Prairie was to be disappointed on both counts, for Earlham threw everything it had into the defense of the attorney general's lawsuit, and ultimate resolution was still more than a year and a half away.

Carter called a press conference for Sunday, January 18, to discuss his actions. Interestingly, Landrum Bolling was in attendance, having been alerted to the event by a friend as he was passing through town. The press quoted Bolling as being in agreement with Carter's call for a change in governance for Conner Prairie. Pam Klein of Hetrick Communications, who was an experienced reporter, was at the attorney general's press conference and she reported Bolling's statement to us: "The central point that [Carter] makes is that there needs to be a change in the governance structure. I think the Earlham College board would agree, too. Some kind of separate entity with a new governance structure is absolutely needed and it has been needed for a long time. I think that can be done, and to the benefit of both Conner Prairie and Earlham College."[1]

But if Bolling appeared to have sided with the attorney general on the question of independence for Conner Prairie, Earlham's current president did not. In a January 19 midnight e-mail sent to the Conner Prairie staff, Douglas Bennett said that the appointment of a new trustee "would override Mr. Lilly's clear intentions." He denied that Earlham had any conflict of interest in the administration of the Lilly gifts and said that Earlham's "legal case and public policy positions are very strong." On January 19, Bennett sent a letter to Indiana Quakers in which he reported on Carter's action. He promised that he would let Carter know, "firmly but respectfully, that we will oppose" the appointment of an independent trustee. He went on to expound on Earlham's high moral principles and its expectation that "the college itself [will] manifest high standards of moral conduct in its behavior as an organization." He concluded by saying that "those who go to Earlham are drawn into a learning community where issues of 'right conduct' are front and center every day. There is no better way, I believe, for students to learn moral responsibility."

At Carter's request, Douglas Church, Stan Hurt, and I met with him on January 20. He confirmed that in order to facilitate a settlement he intended to avoid condemnation of Earlham and focus on the future of Conner Prairie. He proposed first to get an agreement on a new governance structure, and then to deal with the split of the endowment between the college and the museum. He was, in any event, committed to complete independence for the museum.

In a letter published in the January 21 edition of the *Indianapolis Star*, Bolling dashed our hopes that he had intervened with the intention of effecting a change of direction in Earlham's policies by denying having endorsed independence for the museum. Conner Prairie was "the property of Earlham College," Bolling wrote, and the "change" he had in mind was one that would eliminate challenges to Earlham's authority such as that launched by the former directors of the museum.

In the same January 21 edition, the *Star* had also editorialized in favor of "Carter's call for an independent management corporation to oversee the museum and the trust." Public opinion was now squarely aligned in support of independence for Conner Prairie. Even the Richmond *Palladium-Item* said, in an editorial published January 20, 2004, under the lead-in "Separation Must Occur," that "[i]f Conner Prairie and Earlham are split, each receiving an agreed-upon portion of Lilly's bequest, then each could manage its own affairs. Neither could covet the money the other group was receiving. Earlham College and Conner Prairie need to be split."

Save the Prairie responded with a January 25 letter to the *Star* in which we characterized Earlham's rejection of Carter's public policy position as "regrettable," and we pointed out that nothing in Earlham's agreements with Lilly prohibited the removal of Earlham as trustee of the public charitable trust.

Bennett and Carter met in late January. Prior to that meeting, Bennett repeated his view that separation was contrary to Lilly's intentions and suggested (consistent with what he was telling his Earlham constituents) that Earlham's purpose in having such a meeting would be to "shed light on [Carter's] concerns" and not to discuss the terms for independence.[2] Earlham's persistence in its refusal to consider independence for Conner Prairie seemed, to Save the Prairie, to be increasingly at odds with the flow of events.

The Earlham trustees met at the end of the week of February 2, 2004. Almost simultaneously, the *Indianapolis Business Journal*'s January 26–February 1 edition carried an extensive story covering the circumstances of the dismissal of the Conner Prairie board of directors and the subsequent events. Given the attorney general's action and the continued adverse publicity and editorial opinion, Save the Prairie was hopeful that the Earlham trustees would give some constructive direction to their representatives. Instead, the minutes of the trustees' meeting said that "the Board is comfortable in its deep certainty that we have fully abided by the terms of Mr. Lilly's gifts and that under our stewardship Conner Prairie has thrived. We will continue to steer by these stars."[3]

These sentiments were conveyed to the Conner Prairie staff in a letter from Bennett dated February 9, which he concluded by saying, "We expect we will have further discussions with the attorney general as his review draws to a close." The letter was not well received when it was read to a staff meeting. The staff perceived that this message, like Bennett's earlier reports, was designed to demoralize and discourage them. If that was Bennett's objective, his tactics were not persuasive. By now, even the most casual observer could see that the attorney general was not about to draw his "review" to a close.

A report from Mark Mutz that Earlham had made a "public records" request of the attorney general's office for copies of all of the letters that Carter had received from people on the Conner Prairie staff heightened Save the Prairie's concerns for staff morale. If this was a prelude to some sort of retaliation by Earlham, it was averted by the attorney general's insistence that the college agree to accept copies of those letters that had been redacted to eliminate the names of the writers and other identifying information.

Bolling spoke to a large crowd, including representatives from Save the Prairie, Earlham, and the attorney general's office, at a public issues forum in Second Presbyterian Church, Indianapolis, on Sunday, February 8. Save the Prairie had previously addressed the group on the Conner Prairie issues, and Bolling's appearance was intended to give the Earlham side of the story. He indicated that the Earlham trustees had spent time during their meeting the previous day designing a new management structure for Conner Prairie, presumably one under which Earlham remained in full control, rather than discussing the terms of a separation. It later became clear that this was in fact the case. Bolling noted that there were ambiguities in the terms of the Lilly gifts and acknowledged that there were questions whether Earlham had properly administered the gift under his will. He claimed that he tried to persuade Lilly to be more explicit in the terms of his gifts, "but he was a handshake guy and he trusted me and Earlham College." He acknowledged that Conner Prairie would not regain the support of the community until the role of Earlham was resolved.

The Conner Prairie staff met again with Carter on February 18, and came away with the impression that he anticipated a long course of negotiation. The staff members were, nonetheless, encouraged by what they heard. The subject of Conner Prairie's accreditation by the American Association of Museums came up. The national body had extended the museum's accredited status, but the staff anticipated that they would have to initiate the re-accreditation process by March 2004. The development of a new strategic plan would be an essential element in the museum's application, but this could not happen until its governance situation was resolved. The loss of the accreditation would have been a serious blow to Conner Prairie's credibility and its recruitment and fund-raising capabilities. The association, however, understood the museum's situation, and Conner Prairie was able to obtain further extensions of the submission deadline.

On February 24, the Indiana State Museum announced that John Herbst had accepted employment as its president and chief executive officer. This was a position of considerable prestige and responsibility, as the museum's management was responsible not only for the operation of an extensive new complex in downtown Indianapolis but also for the oversight of 12 historic sites owned by the state. Save the Prairie had hoped that circumstances would permit Herbst's return to Conner Prairie, but this obviously was not going to happen any time soon. We therefore urged Herbst to accept this offer and counseled that he had to do what was in his best interests. He was the only person whose paid employment had been disrupted by Earlham's actions. This was, after all, not his fight, and he had his career to consider. Chief executive officer positions in Indianapolis museum operations were limited, and Herbst was committed to staying in the community. We were concerned that this news might trigger resignations at Conner Prairie, and we took steps to assure the staff and the community that we intended to carry on, regardless of Herbst's decision.

Earlham's efforts to placate the Conner Prairie staff were meeting with little success. Bennett and Young met with the staff on March 25, 2004, and again faced a hostile and suspicious audience. The staff felt that Young had not been forthcoming in answering questions put to him at the meeting in June 2003. Bennett was asked a number of questions regarding Earlham's position and its tactics, and from his reactions it appeared to the staff that he was angry and frustrated.

At the attorney general's invitation, 18 members of the board of directors of Save the Prairie met with him on March 19, to assist him in getting a better understanding of the museum's current and future needs. Carter said that his goal was to create a structure in which Conner Prairie could survive into the future and that he viewed his position as rooted in public policy, not legal argument. Earlham's position as both a beneficiary and trustee of the trust was not good public policy. The language used by Lilly in his gift instruments needed clarification, for a relationship that was founded largely on personal contacts was no longer reliable. Conner Prairie needed a change in corporate governance and the endowment provided by Lilly should be divided between Conner Prairie and Earlham. His lawsuit against Earlham was necessary because the college had provided incomplete and inconsistent information in response to his request for an informal accounting. What role, he asked, did we think Lilly intended for Earlham to play? In our view, what assets were part of the public charitable trust? What would Conner Prairie do with the land outside of the 58-acre tract, if the museum received it in a settlement? What were the museum's needs for endowment support of its operations? We had an extended discussion of these questions.

Carter also reported that he had held two meetings with Earlham and that he and the Earlham representatives had agreed to continue to meet. His strategy was to first get agreement on a governance structure for the museum and then discuss the endowment split. Carter noted that he had told Earlham that this would be a public process and that he intended to seek public reaction to his governance proposals. We pressed for more information about the timetable and pointed out that, since Earlham continued to draw over $10,000 per day from the Eli Lilly Endowment Fund while this process was going on, it had little incentive to bring matters to a conclusion. Carter responded that it was not wise, in his judgment, to set deadlines, and that he believed, from his conversations with the staff of the museum, that it had a reservoir of energy and dedication that was not in danger of being exhausted.

We left the meeting convinced of Carter's resolve but unconvinced by his tactics. The dynamics of the situation were becoming clear, and we were not comfortable with the attorney general's lack of urgency or his assessment of the staff's resiliency. Earlham had no incentive to settle the dispute and would continue to draw substantial distributions from the Eli Lilly Endowment Fund for as long as the matter remained unresolved. The attorney general was not likely to seek restitution for any past misappropriations as a part of any settlement, and Earlham had the leverage of holding the museum hostage to an outcome that favored the college financially. Except for its value as a bargaining chip and a desire to avoid additional damage to its reputation, Earlham had no reason to avoid a collapse in the museum's operations. The demise of Conner Prairie would benefit Earlham financially as the residuary beneficiary of the trust, and a breakdown in operations at Conner Prairie might actually take some of the steam out of the attorney general's case. If there were no Conner Prairie to save, the impetus to do so might evaporate; and if a damaged Conner Prairie survived, it was not likely that Earlham would bear any financial responsibility for rebuilding it. All we could do was attempt to keep up the pressure.

In its March 15–21 edition, the *Indianapolis Business Journal* ran two stories on the Conner Prairie situation, one reporting that the museum expected a $700,000 deficit for 2004 despite a $194,000 boost in endowment distributions resulting from an increase in the spending rate to 6 percent. That story reported that Bennett had refused to answer the reporter's questions about the museum's operating results for 2003 and Save the Prairie was quoted as noting that, if Earlham had agreed to a 6 percent draw in 2003, Conner Prairie would have been running a surplus. The story also reported that the attorney general had received dozens of letters on the subject, including one from the chairman of the Outdoor Living History Museum Forum, who wrote, "Conner Prairie has served as a model museum for others around the country to follow. I am afraid, however, that the more recent action taken is a cautionary tale of how *not* to run a museum."[4]

Earlham battled back with a series of paid advertisements featuring college graduates talking about how valuable their Earlham education had been. Earlham's media advertising for Conner Prairie began to carry the tagline "Conner Prairie—Made possible by generous gifts from Eli Lilly and others; developed under Earlham's stewardship since 1964." But the student newspaper, the *Earlham Word*, had earlier carried a story on March 5 noting that Earlham had been passed over in another round of Lilly Endowment grants, and an editorial speculated on whether Earlham could afford to give up future financial support from the Endowment.

Save the Prairie continued to supply arguments and analysis to the attorney general's team. During the first three weeks in April we sent to Mutz a series of additional memoranda elaborating certain of the points that we had made in our initial submittals. We felt that these memoranda could substantially strengthen the attorney general's arguments regarding the accounting requirements of the Indiana Trust Code; the status of the Lilly stock gifts and the Conner Prairie real estate as part of the public charitable trust; the impropriety of the split of the Eli Lilly Endowment Fund; and the failure of Earlham's spending rule to satisfy its fiduciary duties to Conner Prairie.

In mid-April Mutz reported to Save the Prairie that there seemed to be little progress in the discussions with Earlham. We said that it seemed obvious from its public relations campaign that Earlham was conditioning the Indianapolis community to its long-term presence rather than withdrawal from Conner Prairie. We reported that the Conner Prairie constituents were losing patience, and that there was not much confidence that Carter's tactics would be successful. Earlham was still running Conner Prairie and nothing visible was happening. We argued that the strength of the attorney general's legal position offered the probability of success in the event of litigation. Although we understood the risks that would flow to the museum from lengthy court proceedings, the inability of the staff and the public to see that any progress was being made was as great a danger to the museum as was extended litigation. The threat of removal and restitution might stimulate a settlement. We again suggested adoption of the strategy we had advocated in December: put in front of Earlham a draft of an amended complaint in which the state would seek Earlham's removal as trustee, based on breach of trust, and restitution of all amounts improperly withdrawn from the Eli Lilly Endowment Fund. Then set a firm deadline for the filing of that complaint in the pending Hamilton County litigation unless the parties reached an agreement. Mutz said that the time was not ripe to escalate the dispute and that Carter was trying to accelerate the discussions and test Earlham's intentions.

We also pointed out to Mutz that Bennett's postponed sabbatical was now scheduled to begin on July 1 and extend to December 31, 2004. Given the role that Bennett had played thus far in the Conner Prairie story and his interest in its outcome, it was difficult to imagine any progress in the matter without his active involvement. We argued that the Earlham trustees had to consider a settlement agreement at their June meeting if there was any hope of bringing the matter to a conclusion during 2004. If the trustees did not approve an agreement at that meeting, we argued that the attorney general should then file his amended complaint.

As his next step, the attorney general did return to court, but remained focused on his initial strategy. On April 29, he filed a motion in his pending Hamilton County lawsuit seeking a partial summary judgment (as discussed more fully in the next chapter). The attorney general's motion pointed out that it was undisputed that Earlham held the 58-acre tract in trust, regardless of the college's position on the other Lilly gifts, and on that basis asked the court to compel Earlham to account for its management of that property. In so doing, the attorney general expressly reserved the right to follow up on his demand for an accounting of the entirety of the Lilly gifts. At a minimum, Earlham had admitted that the 58 acres was part of the public charitable trust, and the attorney general was entitled by law to an accounting for that trust.

This was not all Save the Prairie had hoped for, but the order sought by the attorney general would have required Earlham to publicly file a document that it obviously did not want to produce. Earlham responded with a press release that recited its provision of "thousands of pages of financial and accounting records" to the attorney general and its belief that "an amicable approach to all the issues should be preferred."

At this point, the Richmond *Palladium-Item* editorialized to the effect that it was time for Earlham to "provide leadership" in resolving the Conner Prairie issues by furnishing the accounting, giving the museum its independence from the college and coming up with a "fair" division of the endowment. "Earlham . . . should have known its responsibilities as a trustee," the paper said. The *Palladium-Item* also reported that Earlham had graduated 228 seniors in the class of 2004. This was three fewer graduates than the previous year, suggesting that Earlham, which was attempting to maintain a total enrollment of 1,200 students, was a long way from solving its retention issues.[5]

The attorney general's actions and the media's continued support for his objectives led us to believe that our strategy of combining private advocacy with public pressure was having a positive effect. Save the Prairie pressed forward with a letter to the *Indianapolis Business Journal*, noting that Earlham was refusing to provide an accounting of its trust and asking, "[I]f Earlham has discharged its fiduciary duties at Conner Prairie in accordance with the law, what does it have to hide?"[6]

We talked again with Mutz on May 10. We urged that Carter take the opportunity of the upcoming Earlham trustees meeting to contact each of the trustees individually, as there was no assurance that his positions were being adequately conveyed to them. Again, we advocated that he take a hard line. We were told that additional meetings with the Earlham representatives were scheduled.

In early May Save the Prairie became aware that the Hamilton County Convention and Visitors Bureau (HCCVB) was in the process of soliciting local business support for a paid newspaper advertisement supporting the attorney general's efforts and calling upon Earlham to resolve the Conner Prairie dispute. We understood that Bennett had heard the same thing and was not happy with the prospect. The ad was scheduled to run on May 22. Three days before that date, a fax on plain paper arrived at the *Indianapolis Star*, sent by Earlham's public relations firm and consisting of a single paragraph that reported that Earlham had made a "comprehensive proposal" to the attorney general in March "that would satisfy both his and Earlham's objectives." The proposal included the "creation of an independent Conner Prairie and a division of the endowment gifts . . . as well as a division of the land." The statement said that "Earlham is awaiting the attorney general's response to its March proposal." The *Star* reporter verified that it was, in fact, from Earlham and sent it on the attorney general, who had not been given a copy by Earlham.

This appeared to be a hurried and clumsy attempt to mitigate the adverse reaction Earlham anticipated from the publication of the HCCVB advertisement and to shift the blame to the attorney general for the delay in the settlement process. When the full text of the Earlham proposal became public on June 9, it was apparent that its economic terms essentially reflected Earlham's last offer to the former Conner Prairie board, made almost one year earlier. However, instead of Earlham backing away from its role in the management of the museum, the college would dictate the makeup of the board of directors of "New Conner Prairie." Obviously, this was not a proposal to which the attorney general would have given any serious attention, and he was well aware of Earlham's willingness to withdraw from Conner Prairie on the terms it had offered to the museum in 2003.

Based on the Earlham press release, the *Star* reported on May 20 that Earlham had, for the first time, publicly said that it could agree to "a form of independent oversight for Conner Prairie" and quoted Carter as saying, "That's progress. . . . We need to work on the details of this for a truly independent Conner Prairie." The article noted that the issues surrounding the Eli Lilly Endowment Fund remained unresolved and that the Earlham statement came two days before the HCCVB advertisement was set to appear.[7] The following day, the paper again editorialized that Conner Prairie needed its independence as the best path toward Lilly's goal of "developing a world-class living-history museum that will teach and inspire Hoosiers for generations to come."

On May 20, the attorney general invited Save the Prairie directors Church, Hurt, Steve Holt, Walt Kelley, and me to a meeting with members of his team. Holt was a Hamilton County commissioner and Kelley was a former president of the town council of Fishers, and both were members of the former Conner Prairie board. The subject of the meeting was to be post-Earlham governance of Conner Prairie, and it was apparent that there would be a political element to the discussion. At the meeting on May 24, we received a draft outline for the governance of the museum that reflected the creation of two entities—a foundation and an operating company. The foundation would hold the museum's endowment and real and personal property, and the operating company would run the museum on a day-to-day basis, including all hiring and other management decisions as well as fund-raising. The foundation's board of directors would determine the endowment distributions to be provided to the operating company for capital improvements and operations.

The outline contained detailed provisions regarding the structure of the boards of directors of both entities, and it described the selection process for the individuals who would serve on those boards. Earlham would be represented permanently on both boards, but it would not have any control over either entity and under no circumstances could any endowment funds be transferred to Earlham. The foundation's board of directors would have seven members. The governor, the chief justice of the Indiana Supreme Court, and the Hamilton County judiciary each would appoint one director. The attorney general and Earlham each would appoint two directors, but the attorney general's appointees could be replaced after their first year in office by persons appointed by the museum board. Nine different public officials and agencies would nominate the initial directors of the museum board, who would then be appointed by the board of the foundation. Earlham would appoint one person. Once the initial board was seated, it could then determine its own size and constitution, although Earlham was always guaranteed one seat.

Although the attorney general's representatives argued that this structure provided various benefits and safeguards by separating the responsibility for endowment management from the operations of the museum, it seemed to us that the desire to find a permanent, visible role for Earlham to play in the future governance of the museum also had influenced the plan. Carter unquestionably enhanced his chances of reaching an agreement with Earlham by publicly reinforcing Earlham's opinion that it was in no way to blame for anything that had happened at Conner Prairie and that Lilly had intended for the college to have a continuing role at the museum.

Save the Prairie expressed some reservations about this design, having previously argued to Mutz that the museum should continue to be governed by a single, self-perpetuating board. We saw no reason for the added layer of complexity involved in a two-board structure. The attorney general's proposal also inserted a perpetual political element into the museum's governance, with all of the uncertainties and risks that entailed. We argued that, at a minimum, all the directors should be volunteers and prohibited from receiving any compensation for their services. We saw a risk in giving Earlham so prominent a role in the museum's continued management and contended that Conner Prairie's ability to successfully fund-raise in the future would be dependent, in large part, on the public perception that any Earlham influence over the museum's operations had been eliminated.

Carter, we learned, intended to announce this proposal publicly prior to the next Earlham trustees' meeting, which was scheduled for June 4, 2004, and request that the trustees consider and endorse this structure at that meeting. He also intended to hold public meetings in both Fishers and Richmond to solicit comments. Then, with the governance issues on the table, and hopefully resolved, the discussions with the Earlham negotiators could move on to the question of the endowment split. While we were doubtful that this strategy would be successful, we were eager for any forward movement.

The Fishers public meeting was to be held on June 10. On May 25, Bennett and his public relations advisers met with representatives of the Fishers Town Council in the first of a round of visits with leaders of the communities adjacent to Conner Prairie. These meetings seemed to have been designed to convince those leaders that Earlham had been a good steward of Conner Prairie and to sell the settlement proposal that Earlham had made back in March.

On May 27, Bennett continued his public relations offensive by sending out a form letter to the presidents of each of the colleges and universities in Indiana arguing Earlham's case for removing the Conner Prairie board and criticizing the attorney general for his management of the issues. He lamented both the failure of the attorney general to respond to Earlham's March proposal, which "would meet his objectives," and his lawsuit seeking a trust accounting, which Earlham "will continue to defend." He then went on to suggest that if the attorney general were to prevail in his lawsuit, "other institutions" would become subject to public accounting requirements and "could find themselves pressed to violate donor intent to satisfy a government official's view of the public interest." Bennett obviously hoped to generate peer support for Earlham's positions by suggesting that the attorney general's tactics were putting at risk the management by other colleges of their endowments.

Save the Prairie believed that Bennett's scare tactics were misleading. After drafting a response to his allegations, we decided not to send it. It turned out that this was the right decision, as we later found a more advantageous context within which to argue our case to this audience.

As a part of Bennett's pitch, he distributed a slick brochure titled *A Report on Earlham's Stewardship of Conner Prairie, an Eli Lilly Legacy*. The report contained the standard claim that the museum was "a part" of "Earlham," but it took a new tack in trumpeting Earlham's investment management of what the report called "Conner Prairie's endowment," charting the growth of the value of that endowment from $14 million in 1979 to $65 million in 2003. The use of $14 million as the beginning value of the endowment reflected Earlham's decision to allocate half of Lilly's gifts to itself. The report also charted the growth in the endowment's contribution to the museum's operating income. It said that these endowment distributions represented "an unusually high percentage" of the museum's revenues (48 percent for 2003). "No major living history museum in the United States gets more than 30 percent of its operating income from endowment," the report continued, nor did any other major museum in Indianapolis—"Not the Indianapolis Museum of Art. . . . Not the Children's Museum of Indianapolis." The argument suggested that Earlham had been overly generous with Conner Prairie, or that the museum had been badly run, or both. In its May 31–June 6 edition, the *Indianapolis Business Journal* noted that Earlham's data were inaccurate, as the Children's Museum and the Indianapolis Museum of Art derived 48 percent and 78 percent, respectively, of their support from endowment distributions.

For several weeks Save the Prairie had been engaged in the preparation of what we called a "white paper" in which we assembled the facts, refined the legal analysis that we had previously provided to Mutz, and addressed the critical issues that were emerging in the Conner Prairie debate. Once we completed this project, we began to disseminate the document to selected community leaders and media as a counterpoint to Earlham's public relations efforts.

Carter went public with his governance proposal on May 27. Predictably, Bennett responded that he wanted all issues resolved before Earlham would present any proposal to its trustees. He was not going to release his grip on Conner Prairie without an agreement on the economics of the separation.

Bennett's focus on the money issues was undoubtedly rooted in the perception that Earlham could not run the college without continued access to all of its distributions from the Eli Lilly Endowment Fund. In Earlham's March 2003 proposal to the Conner Prairie board, the museum's share of the Eli Lilly Endowment Fund would have continued at the level of approximately $65 million—the amount that Earlham previously had allocated to the uses of the museum. The Conner Prairie representatives were seeking approximately $100 million. At a spending rate of 5 percent, the loss of that additional $35 million from the Earlham share—whether as the result of an agreement either with Conner Prairie or with the attorney general—would have meant a $1.75 million reduction in annual revenues for the college. The question was whether the college somehow could replace endowment dollars shifted to Conner Prairie in any settlement. Other Indiana colleges and universities were, at the time, engaged in capital and major gift campaigns that were raising tens—even hundreds—of millions of dollars. Was it possible that Earlham had so little faith in its alumni and traditional supporters that it did not believe it could raise $35 million for its endowment? Perhaps it was. On June 6, an Earlham alumnus wrote to the *Indianapolis Star*, "During the time I attended Earlham College, students were constantly told about the principles of equality, honesty and openness. Earlham's antics with Conner Prairie show that these principles are nothing but empty propaganda as far as the college administrators are concerned."[8]

There were obvious difficulties in making a case for a campaign that was based upon the need to replace endowment funds that the college had been using, but to which it had no right. As it turned out, the terms of the ultimate resolution of the dispute relieved Earlham of the need to look to new fund-raising to replace a substantial part of the endowment assets transferred to Conner Prairie.

In a letter to the *Indianapolis Business Journal* published in its June 7–13, 2004, edition, Save the Prairie's Douglas Church cataloged the results of Earlham's now year-old decision. Lilly Endowment had omitted Earlham from two rounds of grants that had benefited every other Indiana college and university. The college had embarrassed the museum by failing to carry on the Spirit of the Prairie program, had cost the museum over $100,000 in support from the Conner Prairie Alliance, and had devastated the museum's fund-raising efforts. Church concluded, "As members of the Earlham board of trustees gather this coming week for important meetings, one can only hope that they will reverse the direction of their president, establish independence for Conner Prairie and, in the process, restore some confidence in Earlham."

Church's hope was in vain. On June 7, Mark Myers wrote to the attorney general to report that the Earlham trustees, at their meeting, had adopted a minute that included the following: "Fully mindful of its fiduciary obligations, the Board believes that separating Conner Prairie from its governance would *not* satisfy [Lilly's intentions] *unless* the financial structures and division of assets, among other effects, resulting from such a separation were fully understood."[9]

How an understanding by Earlham of the "financial structures" of a settle-ment would change its views of Lilly's intentions was unclear, but at least it was now apparent that Earlham's problems with a separation of the museum from the college were financial in nature. Carter's tactics had not produced agreement on a new governance structure as the first step in a settlement, but they had succeeded in exposing Earlham's strategy of holding the museum hostage to an outcome in which the economic interests of the college would come first.

〜

It had now been one year since Earlham had dismissed the Conner Prairie board and almost six months since the attorney general announced that he would seek independence for Conner Prairie and filed his court petition seeking an accounting by Earlham of its trusteeship. He and Earlham had been in discussions for almost that entire time. But an outside observer would have concluded that the dialogue had thus far not produced much movement toward a resolution of the dispute. Earlham was resisting an accounting for its trust and had stepped up its public relations campaign in support of its continued control over the museum. The morale of the Conner Prairie staff remained at a low ebb. Earlham had rejected the attorney general's initiative designed to move the discussions along by first isolating and dealing with the future governance structure for the museum. The Earlham trustees were refusing to endorse that proposal without a settlement of the endowment issues. Earlham seemed to be unconcerned with the public relations damage that it was incurring. And, as long as this state of affairs continued, Earlham continued to draw over $10,000 per day from the Eli Lilly Endowment Fund for the support of the college's operations, including the cost of its lawyers and public relations advisors. It could afford to go on doing nothing for a very long time.

On the other hand, it seemed to us at Save the Prairie that the attorney general's legal case in support of Earlham's removal as trustee was stronger than we had first thought. Carter's accounting petition had laid bare the prospect that, if Earlham could not justify its management of the Lilly gifts, it would be exposed to claims for restitution of the monies withdrawn from the Eli Lilly Endowment Fund for use at the college. Earlham had refused to provide the accounting that would support—or refute—its claims. Earlham had not raised any credible argument that the college was not to hold the Lilly stock gifts as a part of the public charitable trust, which made the split of the endowment into two "shares" and the adoption of the spending rule indefensible. Earlham was in clear violation of several provisions of the

Indiana Trust Code. Why shouldn't Carter file his amended complaint, charge Earlham with breach of trust, and seek the college's removal?

Several countervailing considerations, the significance of each of which is difficult to assess, collectively argued in favor of continued negotiations. Earlham's public statements about its role in the development and operation of Conner Prairie demonstrated great pride not only in what it had done at the museum but in the college as an institution. It saw its motives as pure and unalloyed by any hint of self-interest. A lawsuit charging the college with breach of the fiduciary duties that it owed to Conner Prairie in its capacity as trustee of the public charitable trust would generate a furious response from Richmond. The college's public statements had evidenced little critical thought about the actual terms of Lilly's gifts or its management of them. If there were any moderates on the Earlham board, a charge of breach of trust made against Earlham by the state's principal legal officer could have driven them into the camp of the hardliners and assured the emergence of a bunker mentality.

Litigation is expensive. The attorney general's office did not have the staff to devote to a protracted lawsuit against Earlham. Carter had engaged outside counsel to represent the state in the accounting action, and would incur substantial additional costs if that litigation was expanded. Earlham, on the other hand, was represented by a law firm that specialized in business litigation, and in the form of the Eli Lilly Endowment Fund and its general endowment resources the college had virtually unlimited resources to devote to its defense, albeit at the expense of its other operational needs. But if that defense had proved unsuccessful, the result of a full-scale attack by the attorney general could have been devastating to the college, and Earlham had every incentive to fight to the last. For his part, Carter hardly would have viewed the demise of an Indiana college as an outcome that served the broader public interest.

Litigation also is time-consuming. With Earlham using every possible delaying tactic—including multiple appeals, which it later proved willing to pursue—it could have been several years before the matter found its way through the courts. In the meantime, Earlham's already fragile relationship with the museum's staff easily could break down, with the probable result that Conner Prairie could not continue to operate. Even if that did not happen, Earlham could disregard public opinion and close down major portions of the museum. While winning the battles, the attorney general could lose the war.

In urging a more aggressive approach by Carter, Save the Prairie was cognizant of all these arguments, and we viewed full-scale litigation as a last resort. But we also saw the threat of such an action as a powerful motivator and believed that Carter would not get the attention of the Earlham trustees until they understood that they faced the prospect of that lawsuit. Most litigation is eventually settled, and if Carter filed an amended complaint, there was at least the chance that Earlham would lose its appetite for the dispute and come to the table ready to talk.

We, however, had not been present in the face-to-face meetings with Earlham. We were prepared to yield to Carter's assessment of the prospects for an agreement based on his personal involvements with the college. In any event, all we could do was try to persuade and advise. The decision belonged to the attorney general.

～

On June 10, 2004, the attorney general held the first of the two public meetings in Fishers, with more than 200 people present. Carter outlined his governance proposals and distributed materials explaining them. Most of the speakers, several of whom represented local governmental entities and civic organizations, supported independence for the museum, some eloquently. The Conner Prairie staff appeared in force and a representative spoke on the museum's behalf, saying that Earlham's management threatened to cripple the museum and failed to respond to its needs. The staff was struggling to maintain the quality of the visitor experience, he said, and the future of the museum was at stake. Speaking for Save the Prairie, I argued that Earlham's future role in the museum's governance should be dependent on its level of cooperation with the attorney general's proposals for independence. Other speakers talked about the need for a timely resolution of the dispute in order to protect the museum and the community interest.

Some Earlham supporters attacked Save the Prairie and adopted the Earlham line that both issues—governance and money—should be resolved at the same time. Others wanted the attorney general to just go away. Some expressed concern that the plan for appointing new directors of the museum foundation and operating company was too political. Ann Kendall, the Earlham trustee who had resigned from the Conner Prairie board after Bennett's veto of the museum's 2002 budget, said that the discharged Conner Prairie board was the "most dedicated, passionate, caring, and thoughtful" board imaginable, and she did not see how a similar group could evolve from the attorney general's structure. Earlham officials were there, but none of them spoke. In his final comments, Carter pointed out that the constitution of the operating company board would be largely up to it, and that he thought that a "political" element was appropriate for the museum's governance, as it was a community asset.

The next day, June 11, was the anniversary of the dismissal of the Conner Prairie board of directors. About a dozen of the former directors and Herbst attended a "Dutch treat" luncheon at Persimmons, the museum's restaurant. The staff was delighted to see us, but the reaction of the finance committee of the Earlham board, eating at the other end of the restaurant, was more difficult to measure.

Perhaps anticipating which way the wind was blowing within its market, the Richmond *Palladium-Item* reacted to the Fishers public meeting with an editorial on June 11 chastising the attorney general for publishing his plan for the separation of the entities before responding to the governance proposal that Earlham had made back in March. The editorial writer accused Carter of playing politics with the situation and urged him to "replace his public posturing by serious negotiations with the college." In a second editorial the next day, the paper took offense at what it perceived to be the perception in Hamilton County "that a bunch of small-town rubes couldn't possibly run the museum and run it well." Earlham, it said, had run the museum well. All it needed to do was deal with the low morale at Conner Prairie. The next day the paper editorialized again, accusing Carter of "dishonesty" for not disclosing the full terms of Earlham's March proposal. This attack ignored the facts that it was Earlham, and not the attorney general, that had wanted those terms kept confidential, and that, if Earlham had believed that the release of the proposal's full text would have benefited the college, it could have done so. In none of these editorials did the newspaper explain why it had abandoned its earlier support for Conner Prairie's independence or its view that Earlham should provide some leadership, file its accounting, and resolve the dispute.

On June 16, two opinion pieces appeared in the *Indianapolis Star*, one by Bennett and the other by Save the Prairie. Bennett asserted that "we have been open to the possibility that there could be new arrangements, consistent with the terms of Lilly's gifts, in which Earlham would partner with others to allow the museum to do even better." He referred to Earlham's "comprehensive" March proposal and called for even more face-to-face discussions "as frequently and as long as needed." Any resolution, he said, "must also position the museum, the college and the school of religion each to continue to be successful."

In its piece, Save the Prairie noted that under the terms of Earlham's March proposal, the college would have appointed a majority of the new Conner Prairie directors, retained control of the William Conner House and retained for itself a substantial part of the museum's real estate and a majority of the endowment assets, and asked, "What is going on here? No wonder . . .

Carter cannot make any progress with Earlham. . . . Earlham is so blinded by its conflicts of interest that it cannot seem to understand that its role as a fiduciary with respect to the museum is to act in the best interests of the beneficiaries of its trust, the people of the State of Indiana." If Earlham wanted to "do the right thing," we said, it should immediately resign as trustee and then negotiate a "fair and equitable division of the endowment funds, a division that reflects Lilly's priorities and the needs and opportunities of the museum. It is unseemly for Earlham to be holding Conner Prairie hostage while insisting on a financial settlement on terms acceptable to it."

The attorney general held a second public meeting in Richmond on June 21. Save the Prairie was represented by Church, Hurt, and others, but at this meeting the audience was hostile to the museum and supportive of Earlham. There was almost no discussion of Carter's governance proposal, which was supposed to be the subject of the meeting. The spokesman for the Conner Prairie staff was booed when he finished his statement supporting independence. Church characterized the audience as angry, bitter, and mean.

Despite the controversy that had engulfed his college, Bennett left on his six-month sabbatical on July 1. The *Indianapolis Business Journal* reported in its June 21–27 edition that "he and others bristled at the notion that Bennett's sabbatical is a way for him to step aside so the talks can progress." Earlham trustee Morris Mills was quoted as saying, "I would hope that this thing gets settled before he gets back. They [the museum] need some permanent leadership."[10] As it turned out, Bennett never reappeared at Conner Prairie or as an Earlham spokesman except for one last letter to the editor of the *Indianapolis Star* in September. In the continuing discussions with the attorney general, Earlham chairman Mark Myers assumed the role of lead negotiator, with trustee emeritus Tom Gottschalk providing support.

The media coverage did not let up. In its July 26–August 1 edition, the *Indianapolis Business Journal* reported that "the Conner Prairie battle was still boiling," and quoted Carter as saying that, if Earlham was unable to provide an accounting for the operations of the 58-acre tract, "then its suitability to serve as trustee must be called into serious question. There is no reason why there should be further delay in finding this out."[11]

The attorney general's efforts attained a major milestone on September 20, when the Hamilton County Superior Court ordered that Earlham comply with Carter's demand for an accounting of its operations of the 58-acre tract and ruled against a motion by Earlham that would have excluded the Eli Lilly Endowment Fund from the ambit of the public charitable trust.[12] Save the Prairie hoped that these rulings would move Earlham toward a more cooperative attitude in its discussions with the attorney general, but this was not the result. On September 21, Earlham issued a press release bemoaning the work involved in complying with the judge's accounting order and claiming that the audited financial statements and "thousands of pages" of financial records that it had given to the attorney general should have been sufficient. It again raised the specter that the judge's order would have the effect of turning all college endowments into public charitable trusts. Earlham would continue to pursue its legal remedies, it said.

⌒

Attorney General Carter, whose four-year term of office was to expire at the end of 2004, was running for reelection. He was a very popular public official, having been the enforcer of a "no-call" rule that strictly prohibited solicitors from placing telephone calls to private residences if the homeowner put his or her name on a central registry. And he seemed to have benefited from the actions he had taken thus far in connection with the Conner Prairie matter. Nonetheless, no politician is comfortable with his or her prospects until the results are in, and Carter was waging an active reelection campaign. His opponent, Joe Hogsett, was a credible candidate, having been once elected as Indiana secretary of state and having served as chairman of the Indiana Democratic Party. He had also run for both the U.S. Senate and House of Representatives and lost. Save the Prairie did not know what views Hogsett might have with respect to Conner Prairie, but understood that Carter was committed to independence for the museum and had done a careful job managing the problem thus far. For his part, Carter did not seem anxious to make any dramatic moves and, as Election Day approached, campaign matters understandably diverted his attention. Earlham also had no incentive to take any action in advance of the election, as there always was the chance that Carter would lose. As a result, the Conner Prairie matter slid off to the side for a period of several weeks.

On September 29, Save the Prairie wrote to Mutz to say that if the election went "the wrong way," Carter owed it to the public and to the Conner Prairie staff to see the matter through to the filing of an amended complaint in his pending Hamilton County lawsuit seeking Earlham's removal as trustee. Doing so should be viewed as the completion of a commitment that he made when he decided to intervene, we argued. If this didn't happen, the alternative could only destabilize the already fragile situation at the museum and reward Earlham's intransigence. The staff needed to be able to see the light at the end of the tunnel, and this would be especially true in the context of the inauguration of a new attorney general. On October 20, the *Star* endorsed Carter for reelection, saying that he "doesn't flinch from tough cases" and citing Conner Prairie as one example.

Notes

1. Pam Klein, e-mail to the author, January 18, 2004.
2. William J. Booher, *Indianapolis Star*, "Earlham Agrees to Meeting," sJanuary 24, 2004, p. B3.
3. Earlham College board of trustees, meeting minutes, meeting held February 6–7, 2004.
4. Andrea Muirragui Davis, "Little Progress on the Prairie," *Indianapolis Business Journal*, March 15–21, 2004.
5. Editorial, *Palladium-Item*, April 30, 2004.
6. Save the Prairie, letter to the editor, *Indianapolis Business Journal*, May 10–16, 2004.
7. William J. Booher, "Conner Prairie Could Be on Its Own," *Indianapolis Star*, May 20, 2004.
8. Brian Maloney, letter to the editor, *Indianapolis Star*, June 6, 2004.
9. Emphasis in the original.
10. Andrea Muirragui Davis, "Museum Talks to Continue sans Bennett," *Indianapolis Business Journal*, June 21–27, 2004.
11. Andrea Muirragui Davis, "Conner Prairie Battle Still Boiling," *Indianapolis Business Journal*, July 26–August 1, 2004.
12. The court proceedings are more fully described in the next chapter.

CHAPTER THIRTEEN

~

The Hamilton County Lawsuit

In large measure, the foregoing narrative has followed the chronological sequence of events at Conner Prairie. At this point, we are going to step back in time to explore in more detail the events surrounding the attorney general's lawsuit against Earlham in Hamilton County Superior Court. We will pick up the chronological story in the next chapter.

The lawsuit commenced with the filing of a complaint on January 17, 2004, six months after the dismissal of the Conner Prairie board. As reported in the previous chapter, the attorney general's announcement that he had filed suit against Earlham was framed within the context of his dissatisfaction with the quality and timeliness of Earlham's response to his previous requests for the facts regarding its management of the Lilly gifts. In his complaint, the attorney general recited the relevant terms of the Lilly gift instruments and alleged that all of those gifts, including both the 58-acre tract and the Lilly stock, were part of the public charitable trust. He alleged that the assets of the Eli Lilly Endowment Fund were "clearly entrusted to Earlham for the benefit of the Museum" and that the terms of the gift instruments "subject Earlham to specific terms which give operation and maintenance of the Museum priority over the income and limit invasion of principal to only capital improvements for the Museum." Citing provisions of the Indiana Trust Code that required an accounting by trustees of charitable trusts with assets greater than $500,000 as well as other provisions of the code and his common law authority, the attorney general sought an order requiring that Earlham file a verified written statement of accounts with respect to the Lilly gifts, covering the entire period of its trusteeship from 1964 to the present.

The attorney general did not charge Earlham with breach of trust or seek any remedies other than the provision of the trust accounting. Nonetheless, this was an important step in laying the groundwork on which a settlement might be reached, or for further litigation, and it escalated the pressure on Earlham to resolve the matter. It seemed probable, given Earlham's submission to the attorney general of "thousands of pages" of contradictory and inconclusive data, that Steve Carter understood that Earlham either could not, or would not, provide a true trust accounting and that its failure to do so would badly damage its ability to defend its conduct.

In its answer to the attorney general's petition, filed March 10, Earlham admitted that the 58-acre tract was transferred to it in trust but denied that it held Lilly's other gifts as a part of that trust, asserting that they "were either outright gifts to Earlham or restricted endowment gifts for the benefit of both Earlham and Conner Prairie." It asked the court to dismiss the petition and to order the State to pay Earlham's attorney's fees.

On April 28, 2004, the attorney general responded to Earlham's answer by filing a motion seeking a partial summary judgment. As Earlham had agreed that it held the 58-acre tract in trust, the attorney general asked that the court compel the college to provide an accounting as to that property. In so doing, the attorney general expressly reserved the right to follow up on his demand for an accounting of the entirety of the Lilly gifts.

Now boxed into a corner, Earlham responded with its own motion asking the court for an order finding that the Lilly stock gifts were not part of the public charitable trust. In support of its motion, Earlham repeated its earlier arguments that the gift instruments did not use the word "trust," that Lilly did not expressly reserve the right to amend his original trust deed, that the college's consent was required for any such amendment, and that gifts to charitable institutions generally were not construed to be gifts in trust.

In his reply brief, the attorney general pointed out that there was no Indiana precedent that supported Earlham's contentions regarding the addition of new funds to an existing trust. Quite the contrary, in fact: prior Indiana cases established that the circumstances of the Lilly gifts dictated that they became part of the public charitable trust. No formal, technical language is needed to create a trust. The question was one of the donor's intent, and the language of Lilly's gift instruments was clear as to his primary purpose of providing for the operation and development of Conner Prairie. Lilly had rejected language proposed by Bolling that would have directed his first gift of stock to the Earlham general endowment, and instead had created a separate fund to be held by Earlham for the benefit of Conner Prairie. His subsequent gifts fell into the same pattern. There was a prior Indiana Supreme Court decision squarely on point.[1] And, most significantly, there was a trust relationship in place between Lilly and Earlham College at the time of the gifts of stock. Those gifts were not for the general purposes of the college, but were dedicated to the purposes of the trust.

The question of whether the Eli Lilly Endowment Fund was, or was not, a part of the public charitable trust was a crucial issue. If the fund was a part of an express trust, then the attorney general had both the common law and the Indiana Trust Code at his disposal in defining Earlham's fiduciary duties as trustee in the administration of that trust; he was entitled to a statutorily defined accounting from Earlham; and he would have available a broad range of remedies, including restitution, in the event that he could prove a breach of trust. From Earlham's perspective, a favorable ruling on its motion would have eliminated the need to provide the statutory accounting for its management of the Eli Lilly Endowment Fund. Furthermore, the college might have been able to persuade the court that it had more leeway in how it interpreted the terms under which it was required to administer the Lilly gifts. A desire to have this issue adjudicated as an abstract question of law, before the court had heard any evidence regarding Earlham's management of Conner Prairie, may also have influenced Earlham's choice of this tactic at this time. Once that information was in the record, it could have colored the court's view of the nature of the relationship.

But if the Eli Lilly Endowment Fund was not part of the public charitable trust, what was it? In its trial court pleadings, and later on appeal, Earlham argued that the Lilly gifts were "only restricted gifts." Nonprofit institutions frequently use the concept of a "restricted gift" as an accounting and fund management tool that sets the parameters for the gift's use. In that sense, the Lilly gifts to Earlham were restricted; but a computerized search conducted by Save the Prairie revealed that there was no law of restricted gifts in Indiana or elsewhere. Earlham's position raised this question: if the gifts were restricted, and their use was subject to some limitations, what was the nature of the obligation created? Legal obligations are accompanied by legal standards of conduct that define the rights and duties of the person having the obligation, including the obligations of a recipient of a restricted gift. Those standards would be applied to measure whether or not the recipient had complied with the terms of the gift. Earlham could not admit that the obligations created by a restricted gift were those of a fiduciary, or it again would have found itself governed by trust law. The college evaded that trap by remaining silent, never explaining under its view of the law what legal standard should be applied to measure its obligations in the administration of the Lilly gifts.

Both motions were scheduled to be heard by the court on August 23. But four days earlier, in an apparent attempt to establish compliance with the attorney general's original petition seeking an accounting for the entirety of the Lilly gifts over the full term of its trusteeship, Earlham filed an accounting with the court. However, the accounting was limited to what Earlham called the Conner House Trust, and it covered only the one-year period from January 1 to December 31, 2003. It showed receipts of $829,602 and disbursements of $918,296 and failed to explain how the deficit was made up. The report claimed that the trust had only income and expense and no principal either in the form of land and buildings or endowment.

The basis for this accounting and the data it contained were complete mysteries to Save the Prairie, for the accounting bore no relationship to the operations of the museum as we understood them. It was public knowledge that the total museum budget for 2003 was in excess of $8 million. In the budgeting and financial reporting of the operations of Conner Prairie, Earlham had never distinguished between the Conner House Trust and the rest of the museum. It appeared that in preparing this "accounting," Earlham had arbitrarily allocated a percentage of the museum's revenues and expenses to some part of Conner Prairie—presumably the 58-acre tract—and designated those operations as the Conner House Trust. If this was the case, and if the trust had no assets, then who owned the land, the William Conner House, and the other facilities located on that property? How could the Conner House Trust generate hundreds of thousands of dollars of income and expense without owning any assets?

At the hearing, the attorney general, acting on the court's suggestion, moved to strike Earlham's accounting from the record on the grounds that it had not been filed within the time allotted by the court. That motion was granted, thereby rendering moot the other questions raised by this document. After the hearing, Earlham's public relations spokesman stood outside the courtroom handing out a press release that said that Earlham had demonstrated that it had "handled its responsibilities for the Conner Prairie museum in a legal and highly ethical manner."

After listening to the arguments at the August 23 hearing, Save the Prairie decided that it should seek permission to file an amicus curiae, or friend of the court, brief supporting the attorney general's position. We filed the petition, but the court determined that our brief would not be timely as oral argument on the issues already had been held. Our brief would have cited additional cases to the court and would have directly responded to Earlham's contention that the Lilly gifts were "restricted" endowment gifts, but not held in trust. As it turned out, our contribution was not needed.

The judge, William J. Hughes, said that he would rule on the motions within 30 days and, on September 20, he granted the attorney general's motion and ordered that Earlham provide the statutory accounting with respect to the 58-acre tract. He denied Earlham's motion on the trust question, refusing to rule that the Lilly gifts were not part of the trust. The court also denied a motion by Earlham seeking permission to appeal the decision on the trust question. Earlham promptly appealed the order requiring the accounting, although that order did not seem to be subject to appeal at this point in the process. It also petitioned, for a second time, for permission to appeal the adverse order on the trust question. A hearing on this petition was set for November 16, 2004.

∼

The developments in the lawsuit did not escape media attention. Earlham's defense included the claim that the law did not require the filing of a charitable trust accounting unless the trust assets had a value in excess of $500,000. The college asserted that there was no evidence in the court record showing that the value of the assets on the 58-acre tract met that threshold. In a letter to the editor of the *Indianapolis Business Journal*, published in its September 13–19 edition, Save the Prairie attacked this defense as "the worst sort of hair-splitting," as Earlham's own records showed that millions of dollars had been spent on the development of that property.

In an editorial responding to the court's orders, published in its September 22 edition, the *Palladium-Item* again attacked Carter's management of the dispute and said,

> Had not Carter intervened, the dispute probably would have been resolved months ago by the college with little or no damage to the museum or the college. Now, though, Earlham and Conner Prairie have been damaged by uncertainty and public questioning of the college's motives and actions. Having thrust himself into the fray, it is imperative that Carter move it towards a productive solution that will allow the college and the museum to move forward.

It was clear, however, that it was Earlham and not Carter who was pursuing dilatory tactics and resisting any settlement of the matter. On the following day, an *Indianapolis Star* editorial pointed out,

> With controversy still stirring in January from its firing of Conner Prairie's board, Earlham College could have beat back accusations of unworthy stewardship of the museum by complying with Indiana attorney general Steve

Carter's petition for a full accounting. Instead, it spent eight months demanding that the case be dismissed.

Now Earlham says it will appeal [the court order] for Earlham to turn over
financial records related to Conner Prairie and its estimated $150 million in
assets. Stop it already.

Bennett weighed in with a letter to the editor of the *Star*, published
on September 27, in which he attacked the paper's editorial position and
claimed, again, that Earlham had "already complied" with the attorney
general's financial information request. It only disagreed as to "the form and
scope of the accountings," he said.

That same day, an *Indianapolis Business Journal* editorial said that the
court's order was a "welcome development" and that compliance by Earlham
would allow a resolution of "this increasingly ugly episode." Earlham's threat
of an appeal "only stokes the suspicions of those who wonder whether Earlham's been using more than its share of the generous trust at the expense of
Conner Prairie."

Resisting compliance with the accounting order may have been a necessary legal tactic for Earlham but it was a public relations nightmare. It put
the college in the position of attempting to convince the public of its sound,
fiscally responsible, and disinterested management of the museum while at
the same time refusing to comply with a court-ordered disclosure of its management decisions to which any trustee should have been willing and able to
respond immediately.

On October 1, the *Indianapolis Star* published side-by-side letters from
Save the Prairie and Frank Mazzi, the president of the Richmond-Wayne
County Chamber of Commerce; the *Palladium-Item* published those same
letters on October 5. Mazzi asserted that Earlham "operates with the utmost
integrity." The attorney general, he said, had injected the state of Indiana
"in a matter in which there is no legal wrong . . . without regard for the original intent of the donor," thereby endangering "the foundation upon which
philanthropy rests." The state was "infringing upon the rights and freedoms
of Earlham to govern the affairs of Conner Prairie." The attorney general's
office should "remove itself from this matter and trust Earlham to make the
decisions that are in the best interest of Earlham College, Conner Prairie and
the School of Religion."

In its October 1 letter, Save the Prairie pointed out that, contrary to
Bennett's assertion that Earlham had "already complied" with the court's accounting order, there never had been an accounting by Earlham with respect
to Conner Prairie. We noted that, if we had a true accounting, the public

would have the answers to some important questions: Had Earlham used for itself only the income from the Lilly gifts that was not needed at Conner Prairie, as directed by Lilly? Or had it used principal of the fund, contrary to the terms of his gifts? Why did Conner Prairie have operating deficits when Lilly's gifts provided for a first charge in its favor? Which institution was receiving more money—the college or Conner Prairie, the primary beneficiary of the gifts? How much, exactly, had each received? We noted that the mission statement of Earlham College said, in part, "Earlham emphasizes: pursuit of truth, wherever that pursuit leads; lack of coercion, letting the evidence lead that search; respect for the consciences of others; openness to new truth, and therefore the willingness to search; veracity, rigorous integrity in dealing with the facts. . . . The College strives to educate morally sensitive leaders for future generations. Therefore, Earlham stresses . . . peaceful resolution of conflict."

Save the Prairie observed that, in managing its relations with Conner Prairie, the Indiana attorney general, and the Hamilton County Superior Court, Earlham had closed its mind to any truth other than the mythology that it had created concerning the terms of the Lilly gifts. Its conflicts of interest blinded the college. But the most stunning failure to follow its own precepts lay in Earlham's threats of endless litigation over the production of a routine accounting, thereby holding Conner Prairie hostage to an outcome of the negotiations with the attorney general that benefited Earlham financially. Was this how a trustee was supposed to act? Wasn't this "coercion"? Was Earlham's strategy one that "stresses peaceful resolution of conflict"? Were its tactics productive in the education of "morally sensitive leaders for future generations"?[2]

The October 5 *Palladium-Item* also included a letter from Victor Jose, a Richmond journalist. He doubted that people in Richmond realized how "the reputation of Earlham College is being trashed through the Indianapolis news media." It was "time to stand up for Earlham," he said. The "so-called Save the Prairie group" had accused Earlham of "lying." Save the Prairie was writing "mealy-mouthed innuendo that Earlham is waiting for Conner Prairie to fail so that the college can have all the endowment." "Who are we to trust?" he asked. "Landrum Bolling or an Indianapolis society lawyer?" In an accompanying editorial, the *Palladium-Item* concluded that Carter was the "only impediment" to a resolution of the issues, and that he "should back out of the process and let Earlham resolve this situation."

Responding to this exchange, in a letter published in the *Indianapolis Star* on October 12, Myron Vourax, the former director of Conner Prairie who had presided over the construction of Prairietown, wrote,

In reading the public comments from Earlham College and Conner Prairie, there is a major point that has not been given serious attention. For the past 32 years, the quality, growth and creativity that are now characteristic of one of this country's premier outdoor settlements should be attributed to the existing and past management, staff and untold volunteer support of Conner Prairie.

Earlham College did not build Conner Prairie; it only held the financial strings. . . . Conner Prairie has built a life of its own and has left Earlham College behind.

Save the Prairie had one additional point to make regarding Earlham's litigation tactics. In support of its request for permission to appeal the order entered by the Hamilton County Superior Court on September 20, the college had cited the "substantial expense, damage, and injury" that it would suffer as a result of any further delay in resolving the issues. The damage in question, Earlham averred, was to Conner Prairie's fund-raising efforts. In a letter to the *Indianapolis Business Journal* published in its October 25–31 edition, Save the Prairie noted that these were the very efforts that Earlham shut down on June 11, 2003, when it fired Conner Prairie's board of directors and alienated the Conner Prairie Alliance, the museum's principal advocates and fund-raisers. "Having shot Conner Prairie in the foot," we wrote, "Earlham is now complaining about the bleeding!" If Earlham were truly concerned about restoring public support to Conner Prairie, we argued, it should resign as trustee of the public charitable trust and turn the museum, its properties, and its endowment over to an independent trustee that had no conflicts of interest—as proposed by the attorney general—and end this dispute.

⌣

Following the hearing on November 16, the Hamilton County Superior Court reversed its prior order and allowed Earlham to file an interim appeal of the court's denial of its claim that the Lilly gifts were not part of the public charitable trust. The court also stayed its order for the provision of the accounting, pending the outcome of that appeal. This decision surprised Save the Prairie, since the order in question did not dispose of any issues in the case and did not deprive Earlham of its right to raise this issue as a part of any appeal of a judgment on the merits. The court of appeals agreed to hear argument on this appeal, but matters went no further and the settlement agreement between Earlham and the attorney general ultimately rendered the appeal moot. Had the appeal reached the point of briefing the issues, Save the Prairie was prepared to seek permission to intervene as amicus curiae before the court of appeals, and we drafted a brief for that purpose.

Once the case reached the court of appeals, and even before the court had decided whether to hear it, Earlham solicited the intervention of its own amici curiae. In short order, Independent Colleges of Indiana, the Indiana Catholic Conference, the Association of Governing Boards of Universities and Colleges, and the National Association of Independent Colleges and Universities (of which Bennett was the chair-elect) each filed motions seeking to intervene in support of Earlham's legal position that the Lilly gifts were not held by it in trust. Their arguments adopted the position that Earlham had used in its previous attempt to drum up support from Indiana colleges: that a court decision in favor of the attorney general would turn all "restricted" endowment gifts into public charitable trusts.

This was the time for Save the Prairie to deploy the arguments that we had developed, but not used, in response to Bennett's May 27, 2004, letter to Indiana college presidents. We wrote to each of the prospective amici pointing out why the attorney general was seeking to isolate Conner Prairie from Earlham's conflicts of interest and that Lilly's gifts were not merely "restricted gifts" but were held as a part of an express trust. We went on to point out that, in making restricted gifts, donors assumed that the terms of those gifts would be honored. If those terms were dishonored, restricted giving would dwindle and charitable organizations would become increasingly dependent on unrestricted giving in raising contributed revenues. We further noted that although restricted gifts were held in a fiduciary capacity, they were not subject to the accounting requirements of the Indiana Trust Code on which the attorney general had relied in his case against Earlham; in fact, the statute expressly provided that it did not apply to such gifts. The outcome of the attorney general's claims against Earlham could have no bearing on the administration of restricted gifts. Earlham was using scare tactics to try to drum up support for its own purposes.

Save the Prairie believed that this response was very persuasive, but we later realized that we had misjudged the perspective of at least one of the recipients of the letter. In a story in the *Indianapolis Star* on December 23, Jon Fuller, a senior fellow with the National Association of Independent Colleges and Universities, one of the amicus petitioners, explained his organization's view that while schools that benefit from a restricted endowment gift typically follow the donor's intent, changing needs may require changes in the way college administrators use such gifts. If a school had to publicly disclose what it had actually done with restricted funds, he said, its actions might be "misconstrued" by other potential donors who might then decide not to give. It appeared that self-interest and lack of respect for donor intent were not limited to Earlham College.

On March 3, 2005, Earlham and the attorney general entered into the first of a series of stipulations that stayed any further developments in Earlham's appeals pending the outcome of the negotiations between the parties. As it turned out, the issues that generated the attorney general's lawsuit would not be resolved in the courts, and the litigation eventually was dismissed as part of a settlement agreement.

Notes

1. See *Sendak v. Trustees of Indiana University*, 254 Ind. 390, 260 N.E.2d 601 (1970), holding that a gift to a university for limited purposes specified by the donor was held by the recipient in trust and that the recipient was subject to the common law duties and privileges of a private trustee.

2. Berkley W. Duck, "Still No Accounting of Museum Records" (editorial), *Indianapolis Star*, October 1, 2004.

CHAPTER FOURTEEN

~

Positioning the
Dispute for Resolution

Our narrative left off at the point of the November 2004 election. The attorney general had assured Save the Prairie that Conner Prairie would be a top priority following that election, whether he won or lost. Steve Carter won, leading the state-wide Republican ticket by large margins even in Wayne County, the home of Earlham College and the Richmond *Palladium-Item*. With this mandate in hand, and while pursuing his litigation strategy, the attorney general continued with his efforts to resolve the dispute through an agreement with Earlham. But it was slow going despite his added leverage.

Earlham kept up the pressure by making more budget cuts at Conner Prairie and talking about closure of some of the museum's major attractions. The 2005 budget reflected a $350,000 reduction in expenditures, with programs and advertising taking the brunt of the cutbacks. Earlham planned to shut down museum operations for an additional six weeks beginning in mid-November and terminated cleaning services and routine maintenance contracts. Even with these measures in place, the museum's budget projected a $500,000 deficit for the year. Save the Prairie suspected that part of Earlham's negotiating strategy with the attorney general was to demonstrate that Conner Prairie could function on a greatly reduced scale, and thereby justify shifting a larger portion of the endowment resources from the museum to the college in any settlement.

Other management decisions seemed to reflect some confusion in the college's strategy at Conner Prairie. Earlham directed the Conner Prairie staff to begin work on a new five-year plan that would, over the long term, scale back the operations of the museum to a level with which the college was comfortable. Promulgation of a new strategic plan would reinforce Earlham's public position that it would remain in control of the museum. On the other hand, the college had to be able to convince the attorney general that it was acting in good faith in their negotiations if it was to forestall more aggressive litigation tactics on his part. It would be difficult to explain why the college was expending the museum's scarce resources on the development of a long-range plan that would be obsolete in the event of a settlement. Caught in this dilemma, Earlham terminated work on the plan shortly after it was to have begun.

Although the museum was able to preserve its staffing levels in the 2005 budget, the attorney general was concerned about morale at Conner Prairie, and he set up another meeting with the senior staff to encourage them to stay on. Save the Prairie also feared that Earlham's announcement of budget cuts at the museum would further destabilize the staff unless the attorney general took more aggressive action. We asked for another meeting with Carter to discuss our views. On December 14, 2004, Carter reported that although his recent discussions with Earlham had been "intense," he was optimistic. We discussed our analysis of the issues presented by Earlham's appeals of the Hamilton County court rulings and the role that Save the Prairie might play as amicus curiae. Regardless of developments in the court of appeals, we argued that the attorney general should immediately amend his complaint in the Hamilton County Superior Court and seek Earlham's removal based on breach of trust. Based on our understanding of the situation, a trial on the merits of a breach of trust action appeared inevitable, and at the November 16 hearing, Judge William Hughes had indicated that he would find an early trial date if either party wanted one. Further delays in arriving at a trial on the merits of the case only served Earlham's purposes. The college was benefiting from each delay in a final resolution of the issues and had no incentive to reach an agreement.

To address some of the adverse consequences of an escalation in the litigation, Save the Prairie suggested to the attorney general that in filing an amended complaint, he seek an interim court order that maintained Conner Prairie's support from the Eli Lilly Endowment Fund but cut off the distributions going to Earlham, pending a final outcome of the case. Such an order would provide for the continued operation of the museum and would remove Earlham's existing incentive to delay the outcome. We argued that the attorney general should also seek restitution to the Eli Lilly Endowment Fund of any distributions from that fund to which Earlham could not establish its entitlement, and we noted that the Indiana Trust Code also allowed the court to award to the attorney general his attorneys' fees. Pursuit of this strategy would put all of the issues where they belonged—in the trial court—and effectively moot the pending appeals. Earlham should not be allowed to obtain an appellate review of the gift-trust issue, we argued, without evidence in the record before the court as to its management of the trust. We recognized that these tactics were unlikely to be wholly successful, but we wanted the attorney general's team to aggressively consider its options.

We also suggested that the upcoming budget cuts at Conner Prairie, if not accompanied by decisive and aggressive action to end the stalemate, would further dishearten the staff, but that an aggressive challenge to Earlham's continued control over Conner Prairie would have a stabilizing effect. Carter was at risk that the staff and the public would conclude that his tactics thus far had failed to resolve the dispute. The filing of an amended complaint at this time would also position the matter for possible settlement in time for the Earlham trustees' meeting in early February 2005.

Carter responded by saying that his litigation strategy was fully developed and ready to be deployed. As to his timetable or the conditions under which he might make the decision to file an amended complaint, he indicated only that he expected some resolution of the issues within the next 60 days. That would mean some definitive action prior to the February trustees' meeting. It continued to be a concern among Carter's advisers that Conner Prairie could not survive extended litigation during which Earlham would follow, or accelerate, its strategy of steady retrenchment in the museum's operations. Save the Prairie urged that, at a minimum, the attorney general had to make it abundantly clear to Earlham that he was prepared to take it to court on the breach of trust issues and bring the full weight of public opinion—including national publicity—to bear.

At our meeting, Carter also explored Save the Prairie's views on the use of some of the Conner Prairie land as a bargaining chip in the negotiations with Earlham. We had suggested this possibility some months earlier. All of the museum's operations were east of White River. Between the river and River Road, to the west, there was a tract of about 170 acres of woods and fields, most of which was in the floodway. This tract would remain with the museum. An approximately 400-acre tract on higher ground, west of River Road, represented one of the largest pieces of undeveloped real estate in the township and would have substantial value to Earlham if sold. Conner Prairie had considered the possibility of using a portion of this tract for museum purposes, as a part of the development of a 1940s-era community, but it was remote from the museum's other attractions, presented some access issues, and in any event would have represented a significant investment of time, talent, and money to develop. The land between White River and River Road, to be retained by the museum, would provide an adequate buffer between the museum's major attractions and any housing or commercial development to the west. We also recognized that, notwithstanding what we believed to be compelling legal arguments in support of Conner Prairie's claims to this land, those claims would be the most difficult to enforce in any lawsuit. We encouraged the attorney general to develop this idea.

⌒

At the end of 2004 it had been a year and a half since the discharge of the Conner Prairie board of directors. Carter had another four-year term, and with the election out of the way, we hoped that 2005 would bring an end to the dispute. Even the attorney general's vast patience with Earlham seemed to be reaching its limits. The Earlham trustees would meet in February. We had no expectation that the trustees would suddenly realize how wrong they were on the facts and the law or how badly they had treated the board of directors, president, and staff of Conner Prairie as well as the beneficiaries of their trust, the people of the state of Indiana. But if Carter could frame the issues in such a way that the trustees could understand the benefits to Earlham of a settlement, the peril in which they had placed their college and the worst-case outcome if the attorney general filed his amended complaint, we might hope for closure.

⌒

On January 6, 2005, Carter invited Douglas Church, Stan Hurt, and me to meet with him and his staff five days later. At that meeting, Carter described his plan as it then stood: (1) the new two-tier governance structure for the museum, independent from any Earlham control, was unchanged; (2) Earlham would get the 400 acres of land west of River Road, and Conner Prairie would retain about 1,100 acres, including the Prairie View property, east of the road; (3) Earlham would transfer its interest in the Prairie View golf course project, estimated to have a value of $2.5 million, to Conner Prairie; (4) Conner Prairie would get approximately $91.5 million of the endowment, which had been valued as of December 31, 2003, at about $174 million; and (5) Earlham would receive the other $82.5 million. The fund had appreciated in value during 2004, and the appreciation would be split on the same basis as the rest of the endowment. Carter would present this proposal to Earlham prior to the February 4 trustees' meeting and would make a public announcement of its terms. If the college trustees did not accept this proposal, Carter was prepared to move "in a different way." To make his intentions clear to Earlham, Carter reported that, in their recent meetings, he had outlined his thinking about his litigation alternatives.

Carter had engaged the services of FTI Consulting, an international consulting firm, and he was relying on FTI's report in developing the economic terms of his proposal. FTI's assignment was to analyze the operations of Conner Prairie, determine the level of endowment distributions needed by the museum to support its present and future operations based on various assumptions, and then determine the size of the endowment fund needed to produce those distributions based again on certain assumptions as to how the endowment's assets would be managed. In a letter to Carter dated January 21, 2005, FTI confirmed that the criteria it had been given included the requirements that the allocation of the Lilly gifts should be faithful to the terms of those gifts, fair and reasonable, grounded in Conner Prairie's "financial realities," defensible and justifiable to the public as the beneficiary of the gifts, and focused on the future, rather than on what Earlham had done in the past. Faithfulness to the terms of the Lilly gifts included recognition of Conner Prairie's "priority right" to the income from the endowment funds, Earlham's interest in the residual income, Earlham's fiduciary obligation to operate the museum in the best interests of the public, and the interpretation of Lilly's use of the term "income" to mean interest, dividends, and rents. Under the consultant's methodology, once the determination had been made of the size of the endowment needed for Conner Prairie, the remainder of the Eli Lilly Endowment Fund was, by definition, equal to the value of Earlham's contingent interest in the fund.

As discussed in chapter 2, following Lilly's death Earlham adopted management policies for the Eli Lilly Endowment Fund under which distributions from the fund to Conner Prairie and to Earlham College were not based on the income earned by the fund but instead were determined by a "spending rule" under which Earlham calculated the amount of the distributions by multiplying the market value of the fund by an arbitrary percentage. The application of these policies had the effect of superseding Lilly's directions regarding the respective uses of "income" and "principal" of the fund. For over 25 years, Earlham had consistently described its policies in these terms, and it included this approach to fund management in its March 31, 2003, ultimatum to the Conner Prairie board. In its submissions to the attorney general during his investigation of the issues, Earlham claimed that its practices were sanctioned by an Indiana statute that was modeled on the Uniform Management of Institutional Funds Act (UMIFA); Save the Prairie had asserted that the statute could not be applied to the Eli Lilly Endowment Fund.

In his instructions to FTI, Carter had been careful to require the use of a model that was faithful to the terms of Lilly's gift instruments—a "natural income" model. But since UMIFA principles could be applied to an endowment that was held solely for the benefit of Conner Prairie, Carter also asked that FTI prepare a second analysis that applied those principles to determine the amount of future distributions.

Carter invited Save the Prairie to meet with FTI to discuss its analysis. During that meeting and subsequently, we put forth several objections to the use of the UMIFA model. That model would result in an endowment for Conner Prairie that was approximately $20 million less than that required under the natural income model. UMIFA contemplated the application to an endowment fund of modern portfolio management principles, under which investment decisions are focused on the "total return" of the portfolio. UMIFA enabled this approach by providing that, regardless of the terms of the gifts establishing a fund to which it applied, current distributions from the portfolio could include both natural income—interest and dividends— and realized and unrealized capital gains. This approach reduced the institution's dependence on natural income as an element of current distributions but increased its dependence on capital gains and, therefore, the portfolio's risk profile.

We argued to FTI that the natural income model was consistent with the terms of Lilly's gifts, which spoke of "income" and "principal," and the UMIFA model was not. The natural income model also was the more conservative approach and would produce an outcome that better served the public interest because an endowment division postulated on the use of the UMIFA model would force the board of directors of the restructured Conner Prairie into the use of the more aggressive UMIFA principles in order to make ends meet at the museum. We also argued strongly that the baseline museum operations relied upon by FTI in arriving at its conclusions reflected Earlham's historic practice of underfunding items such as staff salaries, maintenance, marketing, and facilities development, and therefore were destined to produce an unrealistically low assessment of the museum's future needs.

FTI's letter of January 21 suggested that Carter had adopted the natural income model in presenting FTI's conclusions to Earlham in a meeting between the parties held July 2, 2004, but also disclosed that the results of the UMIFA analysis had been reported at that same meeting. It was the UMIFA model that provided the basis for the settlement proposal described to Save the Prairie in our meeting with Carter on January 11.

In that meeting, we argued to the attorney general that he would get a better economic result if he litigated the issues. The methodology reflected in the proposed settlement structure did not strictly comply with the terms of the Lilly gifts, and a court would not split the baby. An outcome of a trial on the merits would have to reflect Earlham's historic practices in managing the endowment. There was no provision in the proposed settlement terms for restitution to the museum of any unauthorized withdrawals from the endowment by Earlham or compensation for the damage that Earlham had done to Conner Prairie's operations since June 11, 2003, both of which could have been elements of a court's judgment. We had seen nothing in the proceedings before the Hamilton County Superior Court or in the Indiana Court of Appeals that caused us to question our understanding of the law.

On the other hand, we recognized that a prompt conclusion of the dispute on the terms of Carter's proposal would preserve the museum's relationships with the staff and possibly the museum itself, both of which remained at risk as long as Earlham held control. Both the governance structure and the economic terms were significantly more beneficial to Conner Prairie than were the terms that Earlham had proposed and that the Conner Prairie governance committee had rejected in June 2003. Assuming the restoration of the public's financial support of the museum, these terms appeared to provide sufficient funds to resume operations at Conner Prairie at their former level, but they left no room for expansion of programs or facilities and made no provision for the substantial unfunded depreciation that Earlham had allowed to accumulate at the museum. The museum would have to meet these costs through other revenue sources. If Earlham did not accept all of these terms, we urged the attorney general to litigate, and he assured us that he was through negotiating.

When the attorney general's proposal was presented to the Earlham negotiators, they wanted further assurances regarding the value of the land west of River Road that would be allocated to the college. Earlham intended to immediately sell the land and convert its value into dollars that could be added back to the college's general endowment to partially replace the value being transferred from the Eli Lilly Endowment Fund to Conner Prairie. These inquiries would take some time but were expected to be completed prior to the February 4 meeting of the Earlham trustees. The attorney general assured us that Earlham clearly understood the consequences of a failure to endorse his proposal.

~

CHAPTER FIFTEEN

Sunrise

On Saturday, January 22, 2005, the attorney general held a press conference in which he laid out the economic terms of his settlement proposal and urged that the Earlham trustees approve it at their upcoming meeting. "We are not going to let this go, as it has, for another year," he warned, adding that it would not be in Earlham's interest if he had to take it to court. Steve Carter released to the press the January 21, 2005, letter from FTI reporting on the results of its analysis of Conner Prairie's needs and described the role that report had played in the development of his proposal, and he disclosed that the consulting fees he had paid thus far amounted to approximately $200,000.

Earlham reacted vigorously. Contrary to Save the Prairie's understanding that Earlham's representatives were pursuing outstanding questions that could leave it comfortable with the attorney general's proposal, Mark Myers issued a press release in which he claimed that the FTI report was based on "flawed accounting assumptions and projections that substantially inflate their estimates" of the museum's needs. Myers wanted to keep on talking. He fumed about Carter's public disclosure of his proposal. For its part, the *Palladium-Item* accused Carter of bad faith and urged Earlham to terminate negotiations and run the museum itself. If Carter files suit, it said, Earlham should just "pay whatever fine the judge deems and maintain its focus."[1]

It was at this point that the Indiana Court of Appeals announced that it had accepted Earlham's appeal of the Hamilton County Superior Court's refusal to rule that the Lilly gifts were not part of the public charitable trust.[2]

This news came as an unwelcome surprise, and it was certain to fuel the arguments of the Earlham hardliners.

Save the Prairie sent another letter to the editors of the *Indianapolis Star* and the *Palladium-Item* applauding the attorney general's efforts to resolve the dispute with the least amount of damage to both parties, but also noting that no one is happy with a compromise. Of course Earlham wanted to keep on talking, we observed, as it continued to draw from the Eli Lilly Endowment Fund while refusing to account for its management of the trust. Despite the heroic efforts of the Conner Prairie staff, it was clear that Earlham's operations of the museum over the past 18 months had been a failure. Earlham was in breach of its trust and should be removed as trustee. The time for negotiation was past, we asserted, for the attorney general would get a better economic result if he filed suit. We urged Carter to pursue his legal remedies if Earlham did not accept his proposal. As the February 4 Earlham trustees' meeting date approached, the attorney general's team was fine-tuning its litigation documents.

On February 5, Earlham issued a press release saying that the attorney general's proposal was "an acceptable framework in principle" for resolving the Conner Prairie dispute, subject to the contingency that Earlham could sell the land west of River Road. This condition was necessary, the release added, to ensure that the settlement would not compromise either Earlham College or its School of Religion.

At Carter's invitation, Douglas Church, Stan Hurt, and I met with him on February 8. The attorney general said that he hoped to have a definitive agreement signed by March 31, and we discussed some of the complexities that would have to be dealt with in the terms of that agreement. We had noted that the attorney general's press release and Earlham's response described the endowment split using dollar amounts based on the December 31, 2003, data and said nothing about the division of the appreciation of the fund during 2004 that Carter had outlined to us in our previous meeting. He assured us that he would protect the museum's interest—valued at several million dollars—in the endowment's 2004 appreciation. Carter also made reference to an Earlham request for some concessions regarding the use of the land that Conner Prairie was to receive in the settlement, but the nature of those concessions remained unclear until later.

Myers was quoted at some length in a story that appeared in the February 14–20 edition of the *Indianapolis Business Journal*. He said,

> We're just trying to put this behind us. We're satisfied. We were always concerned that . . . Conner Prairie be put in a good position with respect to its

future. But we had to get a settlement that would be fair to the college, the students and the faculty, since they are also beneficiaries. . . . We have been looking at it in terms of how can we fund [Conner Prairie] without causing harm to the College and the Earlham School of Religion.[3]

In Save the Prairie's view, Myers's statement amounted to an admission of breach of trust. As the museum's trustee, Earlham's primary obligation was to act in the best interests of the public as the beneficiary of the trust. The college's interest in the trust was remote and contingent and should not have been a factor in making decisions as to the future of Conner Prairie. But the standard applied in Earlham's consideration of the settlement proposal was the absence of "harm" to the college.

The Indianapolis Business Journal's account also suggested that Earlham had broader areas of disagreement with the terms of the attorney general's proposal. It appeared as though Carter was slipping back into negotiations, and we again urged that he set a firm, public deadline for reaching a signed agreement and make it clear what would happen if that deadline was not met. The Conner Prairie staff was skeptical, based on what it was hearing from Earlham. It turned out that Earlham's issues had to do with devices for maximizing the value to Earlham of the land that it was to receive in the settlement. The college wanted some of the land east of River Road that was to go to Conner Prairie under the terms of Carter's proposal or, alternatively, Carter's agreement to impose development restrictions on that land that would allow, in turn, a greater population density on the Earlham land west of the road and therefore increase its value.

After about three weeks of creative work on the part of Mark Mutz and the attorney general's team, they were able to craft a resolution of the real estate issues that did no harm to Conner Prairie's interests and met Earlham's objectives. But when the discussions turned to the split of the endowment appreciation, Earlham balked again. It would give up some of that appreciation to Conner Prairie, but not its full share. Earlham had no objective criteria supporting this demand; it just wanted another million dollars of the endowment. We again argued to Mutz that Earlham was not dealing in good faith and urged that Carter set a firm deadline and stick with it. When the attorney general refused to agree to another extension of the stay of the appellate proceedings, Earlham filed a unilateral request with the court of appeals. The Conner Prairie staff was steeling itself for what seemed to be an inevitable lawsuit to resolve the issues.

As March 31 came and went with no agreement, we renewed our suggestion that Carter should file his lawsuit. Doing so would at least get the parties back to talking about donor intent, conflict of interest, and breach of trust, rather than who got the last million dollars. But Earlham ultimately caved in and agreed to the attorney general's terms. Another 30 days were spent haggling over the process by which the parties would arrive at a definitive agreement. The parties agreed to file a joint stipulation with the court of appeals seeking a further stay of the proceedings to June 15.

On May 4, 2005, the attorney general released to the press a letter he sent to Myers two days earlier. In that letter, Carter pointed out that, without a signed, enforceable contract, there was in fact no agreement and no procedure in place to get to a closing. He recited all of the steps that had to be completed prior to closing and noted the need for "a high degree of cooperation" in order to have a signed agreement by the June 15 deadline. Meeting this timetable was, in Carter's view, crucial for the future of Conner Prairie. If Earlham was not able to sign an agreement by that date, then "we need to face up to the reality that we may be unable to resolve the matter without further court involvement."

Carter's threat had the desired effect and, although the June 15 date came and went, a definitive agreement was signed at Conner Prairie on July 5, to the cheers of the staff and museum supporters. Earlham was represented by Myers; Douglas Bennett was not in attendance. This was an emotional moment for the leadership of Save the Prairie who, in that capacity and as board members and supporters of Conner Prairie, had invested so much of their time, energy, and financial resources in the future of the museum. Since June 11, 2003, we had dreamed about walking back into the Museum Center under circumstances in which the future of the museum as an independent entity was assured. And here we were.

∼

The terms of the agreement created two new entities: Conner Prairie Foundation, Inc., and Conner Prairie Museum, Inc. Earlham's existing subsidiary, Conner Prairie, Inc., would be dissolved and all of its assets—principally artifacts and equipment—would be transferred to Conner Prairie Museum, Inc. The members of the boards of directors of the new entities would be selected according to the process that the attorney general had proposed earlier. The Conner Prairie Foundation would own the museum's land and buildings and manage its endowment, and Conner Prairie Museum, Inc., would operate the museum. The foundation also would serve as the trustee of the public charitable trust, but the trust would be reformed to include only the William Conner House and approximately five acres of surrounding land. None of the endowment would be included as part of the trust, and both the museum's share of the Eli Lilly Endowment Fund and the balance of the 58-acre tract would be conveyed to the foundation free and clear of the trust Lilly had created. Although the settlement agreement did not set forth any reason for the reduction in the scope of the trust estate, the rationale for this change may have arisen from a provision of the agreement under which Earlham was to act as the successor trustee in the event of the resignation, disqualification, or removal of the foundation from that position. Minimizing the assets held in trust meant that Earlham's obligations to maintain the trust, in the extremely unlikely event that it should have to assume the duties of the trustee, would be negligible.

Conner Prairie was to receive 48.25 percent of the value of the Eli Lilly Endowment Fund at the closing of the agreement, but not less than $85 million, and a promissory note from Earlham for an additional $6.5 million payable within five years.[4] The note would be secured by a mortgage on some of the land retained by Earlham. Conner Prairie would get all of the land east of River Road, and Earlham would retain the land west of the road. Conner Prairie would receive all of the interests in the limited liability company that owned the property leased to the Prairie View golf course, valued at $2.5 million. Earlham would forgive all of the debt of approximately $5.8 million owed by Conner Prairie. The agreement was subject to approval by the Hamilton Superior Court and neither party could appeal the court's order, which had to be "reasonably satisfactory" to both parties.

The settlement agreement provided that Earlham would file with the court a "summary" of an "accounting" that it was to prepare in order to comply with the outstanding court order regarding its management of the 58-acre tract. The accounting itself would not be made public. The agreement recited that the attorney general had reviewed the "documents that are the sources of the information that will be used in the Accounting" and that the attorney general would not object to the summary as compliance with the court's order if the summary was based on and "accurately summarizes" those documents.

The summary revealed little about Earlham's administration of the trust. The report covered the entire history of the museum on a year-to-year basis in three separate categories: (1) a statement of the current balance in the Eli Lilly Endowment Fund and of the income on the fund for the year, (2) a "trust property inventory" that reported only on the value of the real estate and improvements within the 58-acre tract, and (3) an operating statement. The statement of balances in the Eli Lilly Endowment Fund did not contain a reconciliation to the operating statement, making it impossible to ascertain how the income on the fund had been applied to museum operations. The summary also said nothing about the amounts distributed from the endow-ment for the operation of the college. Beginning in 1993, the report also in-cluded balance sheets of the trust's assets and liabilities. The data contained in these statements bore little relationship to the historic operating state-ments for Conner Prairie, and the amounts involved reflected only a small percentage of the museum's total operating budget.

The settlement agreement was filed with the Hamilton County Superior Court, and the judge set the matter for hearing on August 31, 2005. The judge invited public comment on Earlham's accounting summary, but not on the other terms of the agreement.

The board of directors of Save the Prairie met on August 19 to consider its position on the terms of the agreement. After the meeting, we reported to the attorney general that we had concluded that the settlement deserved our support, although we noted that there were various elements of the settle-ment with which we were not in full agreement. Our objections arose out of our reading of the terms of the Lilly gifts, the assumptions used in arriving at the economic terms of the settlement, Earlham's previous actions regarding the allocation of the land between itself and Conner Prairie, and our views as to the appropriate governance arrangements for the new Conner Prairie. We also reported that we were not satisfied with the accounting summary. As we read the document filed with the court, the reports of operations bore no relationship to any previously produced budgets or financial reports of the museum. It was impossible to ascertain from the filing whether, to what extent, or on what basis Earlham had distributed assets of the Eli Lilly En-dowment Fund to itself. With only this summary in the record, Earlham had successfully avoided any meaningful accounting for its administration of the Lilly gifts, or for the remainder of the public charitable trust, over the past 25 years.

Our disagreements notwithstanding, we recognized that the terms of the settlement would achieve our paramount goals—the removal of Earlham College as trustee of the public charitable trust and transfer of the Conner Prairie endowment, land, and operations to independent ownership and operation. We noted that we continued to have serious concerns for the survival of the museum under its current ownership structure and Earlham's management policies, and said that we believed Earlham would not flinch from dismantling Conner Prairie if it were to conclude that the museum had lost its value as leverage in extracting a division of the Eli Lilly Endowment Fund that the college found acceptable. We also expected that Earlham would aggressively defend any additional litigation initiated for the purpose of determining whether it had breached its duties as trustee and that further litigation would push a final resolution of the matter into the distant future. Finally, we noted that the attorney general's role as the public's lawyer in the pending proceedings, with the weight of his office behind the presentation of the settlement for approval by the court, meant Save the Prairie had little to gain from any protest of its terms.

At the hearing, the lawyers for Earlham and the attorney general described the settlement to the court in general terms and outlined the procedures to be followed to arrive at a final closing. The court asked the members of the public present in the courtroom—mostly Conner Prairie staff and supporters—if there were any questions; there were none. After discussing a procedural question with counsel for both sides, the court approved the agreement. The judge then asked if there were any objections to the accounting summary. There were none, so the court also approved it. Pending a final report to be filed by the parties when the transaction had been closed, the Conner Prairie litigation was over.

Notes

1. *Paladium-Item*, "Steve Carter Shameless in Dealings on Endowment," January 30, 2005.

2. See chapter 13.

3. Andrea Muirragui Davis, "Sides Nearing Peace on the Prairie," *Indianapolis Business Journal*, February 14–20, 2005.

4. At the closing of the settlement agreement on December 30, 2005, Conner Prairie received investment assets valued at $106 million, including the Earlham note.

CHAPTER SIXTEEN

~

The Organization of
New Conner Prairie

Under the new governance structure for Conner Prairie that became part of the final settlement, the makeup of the board of directors of Conner Prairie Foundation, Inc., would determine the values and policies of the new Conner Prairie for the indefinite future. Although the foundation was to have no active role in the management of the museum, it would set the investment policies and spending formula for the museum's endowment. Of equal immediate significance, the foundation's board of directors was to control the selection of 10 of the 11 members of the initial board of directors of Conner Prairie Museum, Inc. Once seated, those 11 directors could then reorganize the museum board as they saw fit, determine its size, and elect their own successors. That board would have the responsibility for meeting Conner Prairie's needs for operating and capital funds, including the generation of the significant contributed revenues needed to balance the budget; for the development of a new strategic plan for the museum; and for all of the other structural and operational needs of the museum.

The initial board of directors of the foundation was comprised of seven persons. The governor of Indiana, the chief justice of the Indiana Supreme Court, and the judge of the Hamilton County Circuit Court (rather than the entire Hamilton County judiciary) each were to appoint one director, and Earlham and the attorney general each would appoint two directors. The terms of office of the attorney general's appointees would expire in December 2006, at which time the board of directors of the museum corporation would select their successors.

174

Earlham College would name one of the eleven directors of the museum board. The foundation board would supply two directors to the museum's board, one of whom would be one of the two Earlham appointees to that board. The remaining eight directors would be persons nominated by the governor, the mayors of Indianapolis and Carmel, the Hamilton County Board of Commissioners, the Fishers Town Council, the convention and visitors bureaus of Indianapolis and of Hamilton County, and the Conner Prairie Alliance, and then elected by action of the foundation board.

Deep suspicion remained within Save the Prairie regarding Earlham's ultimate designs on Conner Prairie. Although we were confident that the attorney general would use his influence and his two appointments to the foundation board to assure that control of the museum would not fall back into Earlham's hands, the fact remained that if two of the other five foundation appointees turned out to be persons sympathetic to Earlham, those persons acting in concert with the Earlham appointees would control the foundation and, therefore, the museum.

When it became apparent, following the meeting of the Earlham trustees in February 2005, that the attorney general's negotiations with Earlham were on course to produce a settlement, Save the Prairie turned its attention to the selection processes for the boards of directors of the new governance entities. In our view, it was important that the foundation board consist of persons who knew and understood Conner Prairie's history and mission and who would exercise their powers as foundation directors to address the museum's immediate needs. We intended to use whatever influence we had to assure that control of the foundation board of directors wound up in the hands of persons sympathetic to Conner Prairie.

We visited the individuals who would appoint the three independent members of the foundation board—the judge of the Hamilton County Circuit Court, the chief justice of the Indiana Supreme Court, and a senior member of the governor's staff—to explain their roles in the process, detail our views as to the needs of the new Conner Prairie, and outline the desirable qualifications for foundation directors. We received a warm and attentive reception from each of them and did not shy away from suggesting that the principals of Save the Prairie would be well qualified to play important roles at Conner Prairie. We also contacted the officials—the governor, the mayors of Indianapolis and Carmel, the Hamilton County Board of Commissioners, the town council of Fishers, the convention and visitors bureaus of Indianapolis and of Hamilton County, and the Conner Prairie Alliance—who were to nominate the directors of the museum for appointment by the foundation board to inform them of the issues surrounding their decisions.

Upon the approval of the settlement agreement by the Hamilton County Superior Court, the attorney general immediately filed articles of incorporation for the new entities and applied to the Internal Revenue Service for determinations that the entities qualified for tax-exempt status under section 501(c)(3) of the Internal Revenue Code. The receipt of these rulings was the major condition precedent to the closing of the settlement, the transfer of the assets to the foundation, and the delivery of control of the museum to the new boards of directors. As this process could take several months under normal conditions, the attorney general also sought expedited review of the applications.

In the meantime, the staff at Conner Prairie convened task groups consisting of former members of the board of directors of Conner Prairie, Inc., and others to guide it in the development of plans for independence, preparation of the 2006 budget, and fund-raising. By mid-November there was increasing pressure to designate the persons who would serve on the new boards of directors so that they could begin the work of organizing those boards, selecting management for Conner Prairie, and planning the future of the museum. On November 18, 2005, the attorney general held a press conference at which he announced the new members of the foundation board. Coincidentally, that morning his office received official confirmation from the Internal Revenue Service that the tax rulings had been issued, so he was able also to announce that fact.

The persons named to the board of directors of the foundation were: Stan C. Hurt, appointed by Governor Mitch Daniels; Douglas D. Church, appointed by Chief Justice Randall Shepard of the Indiana Supreme Court; Sarah Evans Barker, judge of the U.S. District Court—Southern District of Indiana (and a former member of the board of Conner Prairie, Inc.), and Bobby Fong, president of Butler University, both appointed by the attorney general; and Morris Mills and Thomas Fisher, both appointed by Earlham. Judge Judith Proffitt of the Hamilton County Circuit Court appointed me as the seventh director. Dr. Fong was the only person having no prior relationship with the museum.

The foundation directors met for the first time on December 8, 2005, in the midst of a snowstorm. Fisher nominated Judge Barker for election as chairperson of the board, in what seemed to be one last attempt by Earlham to avoid further evidence that control of Conner Prairie had returned to the hands of the people that Earlham had cast aside. Hurt nominated me. Barker announced that she was not willing to serve in that capacity and that she favored my election as chairman, which is what happened. Mills was elected as vice chairman, Hurt was elected as treasurer, and Church as secretary.

The meeting moved on to the appointment of the initial members of the board of directors of Conner Prairie Museum, Inc. The 11 nominees designated in the manner described in the settlement agreement were as follows:

Douglas D. Church	Appointed by the board of directors of the foundation
Berkley W. Duck	Nominated by Carmel mayor Jim Brainard
Thomas G. Fisher	Designated by Earlham as its foundation board appointee also to be appointed to the board of the museum
Steven A. Holt	Nominated by the Hamilton County Board of Commissioners (Holt, an attorney in Noblesville, was one of the directors removed by Earlham in 2003.)
Stan C. Hurt	Nominated by Governor Mitch Daniels
Walter Kelly	Nominated by the Fishers Town Council (Kelly, a managing partner of an accounting firm and a long-term member of the town council, also was a director removed by Earlham in 2003.)
Brenda Myers	Nominated by the Hamilton County Convention and Visitors Bureau, of which she was the executive director (Myers was a former member of the staff at Conner Prairie.)
Peggy Neal	Nominated by the Conner Prairie Alliance, of which she was the president
Jerry D. Semler	Nominated by the Indianapolis Convention and Visitors Bureau (Semler, a former board member of Conner Prairie, Inc., was the chairman of American United Mutual Insurance Holding Company.)
Dr. Eugene R. Tempel	Nominated by Indianapolis mayor Bart Peterson (Dr. Tempel was executive director of the Center on Philanthropy at Indiana University.)
John G. Young	Appointed by Earlham College (Young, an Earlham appointee to the board of Conner Prairie, Inc., was a businessman in Portland, Indiana.)

With the approval of the foundation board, these persons became the initial board of directors of Conner Prairie Museum, Inc., which convened for the first time on December 19. I was elected as chairman and Ellen

Rosenthal as president and chief executive officer. Church would serve as secretary. As the final stroke in the reorganization of the museum, the board then passed a resolution inviting back as directors of Conner Prairie Museum, Inc., all of the persons that Earlham had fired on June 11, 2003; with only one exception, all accepted.

CHAPTER SEVENTEEN

~

Assessments

The ultimate outcome of the Conner Prairie dispute grew out of many decisions made and positions taken over a long period of time by the administration and trustees of Earlham College, by the advisory council, by the board of directors and managers of Conner Prairie, by Save the Prairie, and, finally, by the Indiana attorney general. This chapter explores and assesses some of those decisions and positions as well as the views and objectives that could have influenced the parties to act as they did.

~

Eli Lilly's initial decisions regarding the terms of the transfer of the Conner Prairie property to Earlham is the logical starting point. Hindsight and a modern-day perspective on the organization and governance of major arts organizations make it tempting to criticize Lilly for not being more careful and thorough in setting the terms upon which he transferred the Conner Prairie property to Earlham. If he was prepared to invest over $30 million (in 1970s dollars) into the development and operation of Conner Prairie, why didn't he create an independent, stand-alone entity for that purpose, with its own board of trustees, staff, mission statement, endowment, investment managers, and all of the other accoutrements of a present-day museum? Why did he transfer the property to a small liberal arts college, 70 miles away?

The likely answer is that he did not and could not realize where his initial decisions would lead. At the time of the initial transfer to Earlham, Lilly's objectives were limited and no money was involved. He sought only to preserve the William Conner House and the other historic structures and artifacts that he had acquired for the property and to assure continued public access to the facility. But Lilly did feel strongly enough about his objectives that he created an express public charitable trust as the vehicle for the transfer of the 58-acre tract that contained the important historic elements of the museum. In choosing to use a public charitable trust for this purpose, Lilly consciously or unconsciously selected a form of ownership for the museum that imposed upon its custodian, Earlham College, more stringent fiduciary duties than would have been the case had Lilly transferred the property to a separate nonprofit corporation.

Instead of providing an endowment for Conner Prairie, Lilly transferred the remainder of his Hamilton County land to Earlham without deed restrictions and later wrote that he expected—consistent with Landrum Bolling's proposal in his initial memorandum to Bubenzer in October of 1963[1]—that Earlham would sell the land and use the proceeds to fund an endowment for the museum operation. Had Earlham been content with these terms, sold the 1,371-acre tract, and transferred the proceeds to its own endowment fund, it could have drawn on those funds for the modest needs of the version of Conner Prairie that it had accepted in trust, and neither Lilly nor anyone else would have had any basis for questioning its decisions. The structure Lilly had put in place would have been adequate for his original purposes.

But that was not the way Earlham elected to view the relationship. At this distance from the events and the participants, it is difficult to speak with any certainty as to why Earlham did what it did, but several factors may have come into play. With the mid-1960s move to suburbia in full flower, it would not have been surprising for Earlham to have been reluctant to sell the 1,371-acre tract immediately. Property values for a parcel of that size, strategically located on one of the main arteries between Indianapolis and Noblesville, the next county seat to the north, might have seemed low to someone with a long view and no immediate need to sell. Earlham reported to Lilly that buyers were interested in the property. It was not going to become any less valuable.

More importantly, perhaps, Earlham had just been handed the opportunity to become a partner with one of Indiana's most wealthy and generous citizens in a project that was dear to his heart. There is no element of surprise in Earlham's decision to test the extent of Lilly's interest in future gifts to the college by using Conner Prairie as a vehicle to explore ways of enhancing its relationship with him. Keeping Conner Prairie as it had received it and selling off the land would have been counterproductive to this strategy, for it would have closed the book on Lilly's original plan and signaled an end to any future relationship based on the development of the museum.

After one false start in which Bolling approached Lilly for a gift to the college's general endowment fund and was turned down, Earlham found an approach that worked—tying requests for Lilly contributions to the operation and later the expansion of the museum. The first significant Lilly gift—$3 million in 1969—was intended both to subsidize the operations of the museum in substantially the form in which Earlham received it in 1964 and to seed its expansion.

It is understandable that the circumstances of this gift would not have caused Lilly to reexamine the structure of the relationship between Earlham and the museum, or between himself and Earlham. As a result of Lilly's original gift, Earlham held title to the original Conner Prairie property as its trustee and it owned outright the land that was to be used for the museum's expansion. It would have been awkward, at best, for Lilly to have suggested at this point that Earlham should transfer the property to a new, independent trustee that would take over the ownership of the William Conner House and the development and operation of the Prairietown project, and thereby become the primary recipient of Lilly's future gifts. It also would have been cumbersome for Lilly to have established an endowment fund independent of the college and given the managers of that fund the ultimate authority over spending decisions at a museum of which Earlham was the trustee.

However, Lilly rejected Bolling's proposal for a gift in the form of an outright transfer to Earlham's general endowment and created, instead, a special fund to be held by Earlham separate from that endowment and under terms that specifically provided that the income and principal of that fund were to be expended for the operation and development of Conner Prairie. We will never know if Lilly held the contemporaneous view that this gift became part of the public charitable trust or if he expected that Earlham's duties in the administration of this separate endowment would be governed by trust law. In its dispute with the attorney general, Earlham argued that Lilly's failure to use the term "trust" in the gift instrument required the conclusion that this was not the case. But the gift created a trust relationship as a matter of law and, if Lilly intended otherwise, the only way of assuring that it did not become part of the trust would have been for him to have included a specific disclaimer to that effect.

Thinking about the financial and operational consequences of a proposed major expansion of the museum's operations, in 1970 the Conner Prairie advisory council urged that Earlham support the creation of a separate organization and discrete funding for the museum in the form of a $2 million endowment, conceding that the new organization could be controlled by Earlham appointees. Wilson, the chairman of the Earlham trustees, recognized the "desirability and perhaps necessity" of doing so, but nonetheless attempted to close the door on any approach to Lilly along these lines. When pressed to do so by the advisory council, the Earlham trustees appear to have reluctantly broached the subject with Lilly. From its own perspective Earlham had no incentive to advocate a reorganization of the museum even if it received the remote, contingent interest in the project funding that eventually became a part of the relationship. Had Earlham transferred Conner Prairie to a separate foundation, future funding for the museum's development would have been directed to the new entity. Earlham could have anticipated few if any benefits from that funding, even if it controlled the foundation's management. Earlham can be excused if it gave little weight to advisory council chairman Johnson's argument that the restructuring could cause Lilly also to "consider more funds for Earlham." It seems likely that Earlham saw it had nothing to gain from any restructured relationship, and chose instead to put its energies into the pursuit of Lilly funding within the existing framework.

As a result, Lilly's 1973 gift instrument reiterated the substantive terms of his 1969 gift, as did the gift under his will. Lilly admired and trusted Bolling, and he respected what Earlham stood for. Even though Lilly rejected Earlham's initial proposal for a gift to its general endowment, and later refused to accept its proposal for a fifty-fifty division of the 1973 gift, it seems probable that Lilly anticipated that the size and terms of his gifts would result in some economic benefit to Earlham after provision for the needs of Conner Prairie. Lilly strongly approved of Earlham's decisions not to sell off the 1,371-acre tract, to keep the property intact, and to use the surrounding land to expand the museum operations. It is not surprising that Lilly left Conner Prairie in Earlham's hands.

There is, however, a final irony in Earlham's management of its relationship with Lilly. In order to continue in Lilly's favor, the college had to invest the proceeds of his lifetime gifts in the growth and development of the museum. Given the jump start provided by Lilly's agreement to fund the creation of Prairietown, Conner Prairie's operations continued to expand over the years following Lilly's death. The growing scope of operations at Conner Prairie, both before and after Lilly's death, represented, in turn, an escalating threat to the college arising out of its view of the terms of the Lilly gifts, the museum's potential demands on the Eli Lilly Endowment Fund, and Conner

Prairie's growing sense of its own identity and confidence in its management capabilities. These forces ultimately collided on June 11, 2003.

～

In its coverage of the Conner Prairie dispute, the press frequently suggested that the issues surrounding the respective interests of Earlham and Conner Prairie in the Eli Lilly Endowment Fund were the result of a failure on Lilly's part to be sufficiently precise as to how the fund was to be allocated between the institutions. The benefit of hindsight lends an element of truth to this assertion, but the terms of the gifts were clear enough on this point, had they been administered by a disinterested trustee. The principal difficulty with the Earlham–Conner Prairie relationship was that Lilly had created a conflict of interest by naming Earlham as a contingent income beneficiary of the gifts, while giving it the power to determine the size and scope of the museum's operations. The temptation to manage the Lilly gifts in its own favor might have proven irresistible to the most dedicated and least needy of trustees, but Lilly's fundamental mistake seems to have been his reliance on the ability of Earlham College to manage this task.

～

Lilly's refusal to dictate specific plans for the development of Prairietown and the language of his gift instruments that left those decisions up to the Earlham trustees provided the college with one of its principal arguments in its dispute with the attorney general: that Lilly had given Earlham the "discretion" to manage both Conner Prairie and the endowment gifts as it saw fit and that, because of this discretion, Earlham was free to deal with the museum and the endowment without regard to any interest other than its own. This was, however, an erroneous view of the college's legal obligations under the terms of the gifts.

Earlham was a trustee of Conner Prairie and obligated to manage the resources given to it by Lilly for the benefit of the public. Most trustees have some discretion in the management of their trusts. The use of the trust mechanism and the selection of a trustee usually reflect the donor's understanding that the exercise of some discretion will be required to accomplish his objectives and the donor's confidence that the trustee possesses the judgment and experience that will enable the trustee to effectively carry out the purposes of the trust. The means chosen by Lilly to accomplish his objectives at Conner Prairie fell within this model. His gift instruments contained language that vested broad discretion in the Earlham trustees, but the gifts also were clear in setting forth his objectives: the maintenance and operation of the museum (1969 and 1973 gifts and gift under the will); educational programs at the museum (all gifts); capital improvements at the museum (all gifts); and the construction, reconstruction, and restoration of the museum (1972 gift and gift under the will). The discretion given to the college trustees related to *how* the trustees were to accomplish those objectives.[2] The means of pre-serving, protecting, expanding, and operating Conner Prairie, and even the decisions as to the size and scope of the operation, were left up to Earlham. But this grant of discretion did not extinguish Earlham's fiduciary obligations to manage the resources of the trust for the benefit of the public and for the purposes enumerated by Lilly.

Earlham might have done less than it did in developing Conner Prairie, as long as it fulfilled its mandate of applying to Conner Prairie the resources that were appropriate and necessary in light of Earlham's commitments and representations to Lilly, the museum experience for its visitors, and the public response to its operations. Had Prairietown been a failure, attract-ing no public interest and no critical acclaim, no one would have suggested that Earlham should continue to pour the trust's resources into the pursuit of the Prairietown strategy. But its success obligated Earlham as trustee of the museum to preserve and protect that investment and to look for new, thematically consistent opportunities to meet Lilly's objectives of promoting public education and authentic early Midwest history. Certainly the size of the subsequent Lilly gifts suggests that, as a result of his interactions with Earlham and his personal observations of what had been done at Prairietown, Lilly had a very expansive vision of what Conner Prairie could become.

Unfortunately the college trustees exercised no strategic judgment or discretion over the 25 years following Lilly's death. Instead, they adopted a mechanistic approach to the administration of their trust, dividing the endowment into "shares" and determining distributions from those shares by the automatic application of a spending rule that suited the purposes of the college but ignored the needs of the museum. Earlham itself characterized the division of the Eli Lilly Endowment Fund as having been made pursuant to a "rule of thumb." In its submissions to the attorney general, the college asserted that it could change the allocation as the museum's needs changed. But once they established the allocation shortly after Lilly's death, there is no evidence that the Earlham trustees ever considered making a change. This was not the result of inattention. Instead, the college had become dependent upon the distributions it was receiving under its initial allocation, and any consideration of a change would have attracted increased attention to its conflict of interest. A shift in the ratio in favor of Conner Prairie would have exacerbated the "chronic budget troubles" at Earlham College,[3] and a shift in favor of the college would have met stiff resistance from the museum's advocates and raised new questions regarding the college's trust management policies.

What happened at Conner Prairie over the 25 years following Lilly's death was not the result of the conscientious oversight of the museum's operations by the college or the thoughtful application to the museum of the resources available for its development and operation. The Earlham trustees never questioned whether the division of the Eli Lilly Endowment Fund into the Earlham share and the Conner Prairie share, or the adoption of the spending rule, was an appropriate discharge of their fiduciary duty. They never considered any other resource allocation techniques. With only a few exceptions, the contribution of the college trustees to the museum's fiscal management during this quarter century was limited to the one-time allocation of the Eli Lilly Endowment Fund into two shares and the adoption of the spending rule. This blunt instrument represented the trustees' only exercise of the discretion that Lilly vested in them and expected them to use, in good faith, in perpetuity.

The outcome of the 1974 negotiations between Lilly and the college also called into question Earlham's reliance on its discretion to justify the division of the Lilly gifts between the museum and the college. At the end of those negotiations, Lilly had rejected a mechanistic solution to the question of the extent of Earlham's participation in his largess and reconfirmed his intent that the college trustees were to develop Conner Prairie on a basis consistent with its needs and opportunities, committing to the museum from his very generous 1973 gift whatever level of funding was appropriate to realizing its potential. Lilly obviously did not regard a fifty-fifty split of the endowment funds between the college and Conner Prairie as a proper exercise of the discretion that he had given to Earlham. Lilly did not endorse that proposal when it was made to him by Earlham in its June 12, 1974, letter, and Earlham abandoned that approach in its September 1974 letter reporting its agreement to manage Lilly's 1973 gift on a basis consistent with its original terms. Even if a fifty-fifty split of the endowment had been a viable exercise of Earlham's discretion prior to 1974, it was not thereafter.

Under these circumstances, what their fiduciary duty demanded of the Earlham trustees was the diligent review and assessment of the effectiveness of their policies and procedures in carrying out Lilly's objectives. This would have been a fact-based inquiry requiring the continuous collection and assessment of a wide variety of data bearing upon the operations of the museum—attendance trends, peer evaluations, market conditions, competition, pricing, costs, the effectiveness of museum programs and policies, condition of facilities, and other relevant factors. Once developed, these standards should have been updated and revised by Earlham as the operations of the museum expanded and its circumstances changed. This seems to be exactly the approach that Lilly was pressing for in his May 6, 1974, letter to Bolling relating to Earlham College's management of his earlier gifts, in which he said that "relations between the two institutions are decidedly nebulous" and suggested a review of investment income, operating income, and budgets as a part of "planning what the Village is to get" so that it will not be "absolutely at the mercy of the Trustees of the College." It is reasonable to assume that this is what Lilly thought he had received from Earlham as a result of the negotiations that followed Earlham's receipt of this letter.

The Earlham College trustees did create the Conner Prairie advisory council, hired staff at the museum, and later created Conner Prairie, Inc., and established a community-based board of directors. However, the trustees largely ignored the expertise and advice of these constituents. The trustees warned each other to be on guard against the enthusiasm of the advisory council. An Earlham board committee listened to reports from the museum staff and the full board held one meeting each year at the museum, but it did little else. The college trustees did not make regular, systematic assessments of the needs and opportunities presented by the museum's operations, nor did they inquire as to whether their policies had or had not been effective in achieving Lilly's objectives. Instead, they limited the museum's operational budget to the distributions available to it under Earlham's spending rule and reacted to the museum's pleas for capital resources only when they could no longer be ignored. Adherence to the spending rule ultimately resulted in Earlham's refusal to use any part of the Eli Lilly Endowment Fund for capital improvements at the museum, despite Lilly's directions regarding the use of endowment principal to support Conner Prairie, as the college's dependence on the distributions it received under that rule left no room for any other use of the endowment resource.

Nothing in Lilly's gift instruments authorized the use of the spending rule device. The plain language of the Lilly gift instruments and contemporaneous documents, including the 1974 letter written by Edward Wilson and Franklin Wallin, speak of fund distributions in the traditional terms of "principal" and "income." Under the express terms of its 1974 agreement with Lilly and the terms of his will, Earlham College had three fundamental obligations: (1) maintain the Eli Lilly Endowment Fund as a single account; (2) direct income and principal to Conner Prairie as needed for its development and operation, as determined by the Earlham board of trustees; and (3) distribute any leftover income but no principal to the college. This would have been a simple and logical implementation of the gift instruments, and the outcome most consistent with Lilly's instructions.

～

By investing in the museum during Lilly's lifetime, Earlham was nurturing its relationship with Lilly and sustaining his financial support. By expanding the museum Earlham also was balancing potential returns on investment in programs and facilities, in the form of admissions and other earned income, against potential returns on endowment investments in the financial markets. Successful development of new programs and facilities could offset the museum's demands on future endowment income, but the failure of this strategy would increase the museum's endowment demands.

The risk that Earlham was running by investing in the museum became quantifiable at the time of Lilly's death in 1977. By that time, it was apparent that Conner Prairie was not going to pay for itself and that, if there was any endowment income left over for the college after providing for Conner Prairie's operations, it might not meet Earlham's needs. Having received the gift under Lilly's will, there would be no additional resources forthcoming for development or operations at Conner Prairie. Investment in the museum, while effective in inducing the gift under the will, could not continue without jeopardizing Earlham's access to future endowment distributions.

So Earlham College abandoned the use of the discretion that Lilly had given to it, gave up on any further effort to determine the size and scope of the museum by the application of subjective judgments regarding its operations, terminated any further investment in Conner Prairie, split the 1973 gift—and all of Lilly's other gifts, including the gift under the will—into shares, and adopted the spending rule. Doing so guaranteed that Earlham would receive a steady stream of distributions from the Eli Lilly Endowment Fund—just as it did with its own endowment. This was not consistent with Earlham's representations to Lilly; it was not what Lilly provided for either in the original terms of the gift instruments or in the 1974 correspondence; and it was not what Lilly intended.

Lilly's gifts did not give the Earlham College trustees discretion as to how much to *spend* at the museum; their good faith determinations as to the *needs* of the museum's programs and facilities were to drive that decision. Earlham's view of its discretion necessarily leads to the conclusion that it was not *required* to expend *any* of the Lilly gifts on the development or operation of the museum. But if this was Lilly's intent, why did the terms of his gifts speak as they did?

～

In its submissions to the attorney general following June 11, 2003, Earlham defended its administration of the Eli Lilly Endowment Fund on the grounds that it had acted in accordance with the principles of the Indiana version of the Uniform Management of Institutional Funds Act (UMIFA). If applicable to the Eli Lilly Endowment Fund, UMIFA would have allowed Earlham to ignore Lilly's careful delineation between the uses of the principal and the income of the fund and sanctioned Earlham's policy of making distributions from the fund of a specified percentage of its market value.

However, there were several barriers to the application of UMIFA to Earlham's administration of the Eli Lilly Endowment Fund. Earlham began to operate under its principles in 1978, more than a decade before the Indiana legislature adopted the statute. More importantly, UMIFA applied only to an endowment or institutional fund held for the "exclusive use, benefit, or purposes" of a single institution. Earlham's reliance on UMIFA was premised on its view that Conner Prairie and the college were "one and the same," and Earlham argued to the attorney general that the museum had no separate existence from the college. This argument was tenuous on both legal and factual grounds, as it ignored the terms of Lilly's original gift under which Earlham acquired the 58-acre parcel, not in its corporate capacity, but as the trustee of a public charitable trust; the terms of Lilly's subsequent gifts under which the college and the museum held separate and distinct interests in the fund; and Earlham's practice of utilizing different management structures for the college and the museum. Further, UMIFA specifically provided that it did not apply to a fund in which a noninstitutional beneficiary had an interest. The public, as the beneficiary of the Conner Prairie public charitable trust, had an interest in the Eli Lilly Endowment Fund, and the public is not an "institution" as defined in the act.

⌢

Earlham's failure to view the Eli Lilly Endowment Fund as a trust led it into another error that seems to have had a profound effect on the college's thinking about its relationship to Conner Prairie and its decision in 2003 to seize direct control of the museum's operations. Although the concept that the Eli Lilly Endowment Fund could be divided into a Conner Prairie share and an Earlham share was flawed, Earlham correctly understood that exhausting the Conner Prairie share of the endowment would expose the Earlham share to the needs of the museum under the first charge language of the gift instruments. It became apparent in its negotiations with the Conner Prairie governance committee and in what Earlham later said in defense of its action in terminating the museum's board of directors, that Earlham believed that Conner Prairie was on a course that would use up not only its share of the endowment but also the Earlham share, and that the college then would have to dip into its tuition revenues or other resources in order to honor its commitments to Lilly. From this perspective, firing the Conner Prairie board, taking direct control of the museum, and then scaling down the museum's operations were necessary steps in order to protect the college's other revenues.

Lilly's gifts were explicit on this point, had Earlham read them correctly. Pursuant to the gifts' terms, Earlham was to establish the Eli Lilly Endowment Fund as an "entity separate from [Earlham's] other general and special endowment resources." It seems likely that Lilly imposed this requirement in order to insulate the museum's resources from the demands on Earlham's general endowment made by the college and the Earlham School of Religion. But these terms also had the effect of insulating Earlham College and its other resources from the demands of the museum, if the gift was one held in trust.

Had Earlham viewed the museum and the Eli Lilly Endowment Fund as assets held in trust, its concerns would have evaporated. A trustee has no legal obligation to expend its own, separate resources in the discharge of its duties as trustee. If the principal and income from the Eli Lilly Endowment Fund had been expended to fund the operation and development of Conner Prairie, the museum would have had no claim on the separate endowment or earned revenues of the college. In this sense, Earlham's view that Lilly did not want Conner Prairie to become a financial drain on the college was consistent with what Lilly did.

Under this view of the relationship, at some point the college would have been put in a difficult situation as the size of the trust fund and the distributions in support of Conner Prairie diminished and, ultimately, disappeared. As that date approached, Earlham, in its capacity as the museum's trustee, would have been called upon to develop alternative funding and operational plans for the museum. Assuming that the college had strictly adhered to the terms of the Lilly gifts and otherwise used its best efforts to deal with the circumstances, in making these decisions it would have been insulated from any legal claims made on behalf of the museum. Earlham's options could have included a reduction of museum operations to a level that could be supported solely by Conner Prairie's earned and contributed revenues, or even its closure. As unpleasant and unpopular as these actions would have been, any outcome arrived at within this framework would have been understandable and morally and legally defensible. It seems that this is where Earlham thought matters stood in June 2003, but its actions at that time were dictated not by the exhaustion of the Eli Lilly Endowment Fund for the purposes of Conner Prairie but by Earlham's interest in preserving the Earlham share of the fund, at its then-current value, for its own use and in putting almost all of the Conner Prairie share behind a "firewall."

This view of the relationship leaves open the question whether Earlham would have had any continuing obligation, independent of the Eli Lilly Endowment Fund, to fund the maintenance and operation of the William Conner House under the terms of Lilly's original deed of trust. It seems likely that a court, presented with this question, would have viewed that commitment as subsumed by the subsequent events and Lilly's later establishment of the Eli Lilly Endowment Fund for the purpose of maintaining and operating Conner Prairie as a whole. In any event, the maintenance of the William Conner House did not entail a significant financial commitment, and this obligation would have posed no threat to Earlham's other operations.

Was the Eli Lilly Endowment Fund held as a part of the public charitable trust, or wasn't it? If it was, then in its capacity as trustee, Earlham had a fiduciary duty to manage the fund in the best interests of the beneficiary of the trust—the public—and to subordinate its personal financial interests to the interests of that beneficiary. As Earlham could not defend its fund management policies under these standards, the college hotly disputed the attorney general's assertion that the gifts were held in trust and appealed the adverse decision on this issue by the Hamilton County Superior Court. Because the dispute was settled and the appeal dismissed, the Indiana Court of Appeals did not have the opportunity to rule on the question. So we are left with the trial court's ruling in favor of the attorney general's position and the arguments advanced by the parties as described in chapter 13.

Save the Prairie strongly supported the attorney general's view of the matter. So that the reader may assess the legal arguments and authorities supporting its position, appendix B contains a draft of an amicus curiae brief that Save the Prairie prepared and intended to seek leave to file in the Indiana Court of Appeals, had the legal proceedings gone forward.

⌒

Earlham's arguments to the attorney general raised an additional question: did it make any difference whether or not Earlham followed the terms of the Lilly gifts? Earlham's defense of its administration of Conner Prairie and the Eli Lilly Endowment Fund included the argument that, under its stewardship, Conner Prairie had become one of the nation's leading outdoor history museums and one of its best endowed on a per-visitor basis (using for this purpose the Conner Prairie "share" of the Eli Lilly Endowment Fund). In making this argument, Earlham was attempting to convince the attorney general and the public that, even if Earlham had complied with the terms of the Lilly gifts, Conner Prairie could not have been a better place and that the damages flowing from any proven breach of trust would have been minimal.

But a trustee cannot defend a claim of breach of trust by attempting to show that nothing would have been different had it complied with its fiduciary duties. Such a defense, if accepted, would gut the legal principles that underlie the law of fiduciary duty. In considering whether or not to expend the time and effort needed to discharge its trust and the confidence placed in it by the creator of the trust, a trustee could elect to do nothing and hope that subsequent events would cure its defaults. This argument ignores the premise upon which trust relationships, including the Lilly–Earlham relationship, are based: that a trustee will follow the terms of its trust and will devote the highest levels of loyalty and care to its administration. A trustee does not have the luxury of ignoring its duties and looking to subsequent, unrelated events to bail it out. Earlham's assertion that it did no harm because its decisions produced an acceptable result at Conner Prairie was disingenuous at best.

Since Earlham did not administer the Lilly gifts in accordance with their terms, we will never know what might have resulted had the college done so. It is certainly possible that Conner Prairie received more resources than it would have under a strict interpretation by Earlham of its mandate from Lilly. But it also is possible that careful attention to the museum's programmatic and capital development needs and opportunities, and the liberal application to the museum of the income and principal available under the terms of the Lilly gifts, would have produced an even more talented staff, a wider range of programs, additional and better-maintained facilities, more extensive advertising, broader audience exposure, more visitor amenities, increased revenues, and a greater share of all of the other elements that make for a successful museum operation.

⌢

In his management of the Conner Prairie dispute, the attorney general chose to frame his positions as ones grounded in public policy and to avoid a legalistic approach. By employing a delicate balance between persuasion and coercion, Steve Carter preserved his options and created a climate that allowed settlement by agreement. In this way, the ultimate resolution could be nuanced, the competing issues balanced, and the damage controlled in a manner that might have been impossible had a judge been required to apply the law to the facts.

As with all compromises, the terms of the settlement agreement between the attorney general and Earlham were less favorable both to the college and to Conner Prairie than those sought by the advocates for either institution. Although the museum's supporters generally agreed with the attorney general's methodology of determining the present value of Earlham's share of the Eli Lilly Endowment Fund and the allocation of that value to the college as part of an agreement for the museum's independence, they challenged the assumptions used by the attorney general's consultants to determine Conner Prairie's needs and the application of UMIFA in the calculation of the distributions available to the museum. Those assumptions failed to reflect the years of deferred maintenance, suppressed staff salaries, and other decisions forced upon the museum by Earlham's endowment management policies. For its part, Earlham thought that the museum could get by on far fewer resources than it had been receiving under the spending rule. These were, however, points on which reasonable persons could differ, and the attorney general chose to rely on the opinions of his experts.

The museum's supporters also believed that all of the Hamilton County land given by Lilly to Earlham had been dedicated by Earlham for the use of the museum, except for the 80-acre tract in the northwest corner of the property that Earlham had reserved for its own use. Accordingly, they believed that the settlement could have resulted in the outright transfer of all of the dedicated land to the museum. This would have been the weakest link in the attorney general's case, however, had he gone to court to reform the trust. Earlham had never divested itself of the legal title to the land, and the museum's claims rested on general equitable principles. Conner Prairie's ability to effectively use the land west of River Road as a part of its operations was problematic. It is doubtful that the museum would have disposed of that land, however, as there was a possibility that it might be needed at some future date and the museum might have faced a serious public relations problem had it sold the property for development purposes. Earlham, on the other hand, felt no such constraints. The parcel had only an intangible value to the museum but represented great monetary value to Earlham.

In this context, Carter's decision to leave this parcel in Earlham's hands and position it for sale by the college did no material damage to the museum and allowed the shift to Earlham of the additional resources that it wanted as part of a settlement. Earlham immediately sold the parcel, generating $24 million to replace part of the endowment value transferred to Conner Prairie in the settlement.

∽

The museum's supporters believed that the Lilly gifts were held as a part of the public charitable trust and that Earlham could not have proven that it had administered those gifts in accordance with their terms and its duties as their trustee. Had Earlham failed to do so, the court could have ordered restitution to the museum of any amounts wrongfully distributed to the college. This possible outcome provided the background for the battle over the initial rulings by the Hamilton County Superior Court. The point of departure for any resolution of these questions was the accounting that the attorney general sought from Earlham, which was ordered by the court and which Earlham refused to provide. The settlement, reached during a stay of Earlham's appeals of the court's orders, did not resolve these questions. The "summary" accounting that Earlham filed with the Hamilton County Superior Court in accordance with the settlement agreement provided only a fragmentary explanation of how the principal and income of the Eli Lilly Endowment Fund had been distributed, and it disclosed nothing regarding Earlham's use of the fund for its own purposes.

This was, however, the final resolution of the issue. The agreement provided that the attorney general would not object to the summary as representing Earlham's compliance with the court's order as long as it was "consistent with" the thousands of pages of accounting records that Earlham had dumped on the attorney general. The court invited public comment on the summary, but there was no basis on which to challenge the Earlham filing without the benefit of the original documents and records on which the summary was based and the application to their analysis of substantial time and expertise. None of this was available to Save the Prairie or any other public representatives. Furthermore, had the court found the summary to be incomplete or inadequate, that finding would have allowed Earlham to walk away from the settlement agreement, leaving the attorney general back where he started.

The settlement was, therefore, a forward-looking agreement that dealt only with the structure, properties, and funding of New Conner Prairie. The agreement did not provide a basis for a critical examination of Earlham's administration of the Eli Lilly Endowment Fund over the past 40 years, and therefore no determination could be made whether Earlham had received distributions from that fund to which it was not entitled. No claim for restitution could be made. Earlham was not required to defend its fund management practices, and it certainly did not volunteer to do so. This element of the Lilly–Earlham–Conner Prairie relationship will likely remain unexamined forever.

But if the settlement did not fully satisfy Conner Prairie's advocates, neither did it reflect Earlham's views. It was obvious from Earlham's conduct and public statements that losing control over Conner Prairie and its endowment was not what the college had in mind when its trustees fired the board of directors and president of the museum on June 11, 2003. College spokesmen said on many occasions before and after that event that, in their view, the terms of the Lilly gifts did not permit the replacement of the college as trustee of the public charitable trust and that any transfer of endowment assets to the sole ownership of the museum was not only contrary to the terms of the Lilly gifts but unacceptable to the college. According to their view, Earlham was entitled to act as trustee of the museum in perpetuity and to continue to manage the Eli Lilly Endowment Fund as it saw fit. Earlham wanted to be left alone with the power to do with Conner Prairie whatever it wished and to continue to administer the Eli Lilly Endowment Fund for the benefit of the college. Earlham and its supporters relentlessly attacked the attorney general for having intervened in the matter, and the college spent over one and one-half million dollars on lawyers and public relations advice related to the governance dispute.[4] Nonetheless, following the signing of the settlement agreement, Earlham asserted that it was "proudly bequeath[ing]" Conner Prairie to the community.[5]

∽

Ironically, Earlham probably would have remained in control of Conner Prairie and continued to administer the museum and its endowment indefinitely, but for its actions in firing the museum board. Over the course of 25 years, Earlham had successfully resisted efforts by the museum's staff, by the Indianapolis volunteers who served on the museum's advisory council, and by the board of directors of Conner Prairie, Inc., to change the college's policies toward the museum. Earlham had ignored their attempts to persuade the college to more closely adhere to the terms of Lilly's gifts and their pleas that Earlham honor his intentions with respect to Conner Prairie. At least one director of the museum quit in frustration over his inability to secure for Conner Prairie the support that it needed and deserved from Earlham, and more than one person who supported the museum with volunteer time and money ultimately withdrew that support as a result of Earlham's policies. Earlham had successfully met these challenges by simply doing nothing or by hiring replacements as managers quit and making incremental concessions to self-governance that were sufficient to suppress any community unrest while retaining full control over Conner Prairie and its endowment. For their part, the museum's supporters had no standing to effect any change in Earlham's policies. Absent some catalyst that would bring the full power of public understanding and opinion to bear, this state of affairs might have continued indefinitely.

Earlham itself provided that catalyst. Encouraged perhaps by its past successes in quelling dissent at Conner Prairie, misled by its unwillingness to objectively examine the terms of the Lilly gifts, frustrated by its inability to bring the museum's board of directors into line with its objectives, and underestimating the consequences of its actions, Earlham did the unthinkable. The college engaged in a power play for complete control of an institution that was loved and respected by the community and thought of as a community asset. As a means of advancing its own interests, Earlham unceremoniously fired the popular and effective president of the museum and publicly humiliated the volunteer board of directors who had devoted their time and financial support to the institution. Such an event could not, and did not, escape public notice. Earlham's actions thrust the problem into the public arena in a very visible, and perhaps decisive, manner. But for Earlham's tactics, it is doubtful that matters ever would have reached the desk of the only person with the power to effect fundamental change at the museum—the Indiana attorney general.

Earlham's tactics also had the effect of galvanizing the former Conner Prairie directors into a cohesive and dedicated advocacy group. As volunteers, and with many other worthwhile activities to which they could devote their time, it would not have been surprising if the directors had accepted Earlham's actions at face value and drifted away from their roles at Conner Prairie after June 11, 2003. But, to a person, they immediately transformed themselves into the board of directors of Save the Prairie, Inc., and in that format continued their campaign for Conner Prairie's independence. Their motives for doing so may have varied from person to person, but collectively they understood that, given the terms of the Lilly gift instruments, the college's ultimate objective could have been the dismantling of the museum. Then, with no first charge obligation to worry about, Earlham could have devoted all of the resources of the Eli Lilly Endowment Fund to the operations of the college. To their credit, the directors refused to allow this to happen.

The college denied that it had designs on Conner Prairie or on the Eli Lilly Endowment Fund. But Earlham knew that Conner Prairie could not continue to operate on a basis that remotely resembled its pre–June 11, 2003, activities unless its philanthropic and corporate support continued at their preexisting levels. It also had to know that, by firing the board and president of the museum, it was putting those revenues at risk. Earlham's plan for "fiscal integrity" at Conner Prairie necessarily encompassed a substantial contraction of the museum's operations. It immediately brought in a consultant to assist in the development of a new business plan for the museum. Earlham persistently maintained that the size and scope of Conner Prairie were matters within Earlham's sole discretion, and the unspoken implication of this view was that its discretion included the right to tear down what it had built with Lilly's funds. Only the public outrage triggered by Earlham's tactics deterred the college from executing on this plan.

The Conner Prairie dispute was, therefore, a life-and-death struggle. And Conner Prairie lived. It emerged from the settlement with its own, separate endowment that was expected to be sufficient for the museum's immediate needs so long as public support of its operations resumed. It was given the land that historically had been considered as the core museum real estate, that encompassed all of its current operations, and that provided an adequate buffer from the development surrounding the museum.

Most importantly, Conner Prairie emerged from the dispute with its independence from Earlham College. Freed from the college's management policies and the taint of its conflicts of interest, Conner Prairie could now approach the community for talent, for leadership, and for financial support on its own merits and manage the museum with only the public interest in view.

Notes

1. See p. 7 infra.
2. The terms of Lilly's will did not explicitly grant "discretion" to the college board with respect to the objectives of that gift.
3. See "Report of the Strategic Planning Committee, Earlham Campus Draft 1," August 30, 2002.
4. Internal Revenue Service Form 990 reports of Earlham College for the years 2001 through 2005
5. Mark Myers, "Earlham Offers the Past as a Present" (editorial), *Indianapolis Star*, July 10, 2005.

~

Epilogue

Following the completion of the attorney general's agreement with Earlham College on December 30, 2005, Conner Prairie's most immediate need was to develop a comprehensive plan to guide the board of directors and staff in the future growth of the museum's facilities and programs. To that end, the museum engaged a team of site planning experts and simultaneously began to seek public input on the shape and content of programming. These efforts, which began in late 2006, merged into the preparation of a new strategic plan that the board of directors approved on September 19, 2007.

The completion of the strategic plan enabled Conner Prairie, in turn, to submit its application, which had languished since the Earlham takeover, for reaccreditation by the American Association of Museums. The reaccreditation was granted in April 2008, and the association's report on the museum's operations included glowing comments regarding its management, fiscal practices, governance, and programs.

The museum's development efforts had been decimated by the Earlham dispute. Annual giving dropped almost 85 percent following June 11, 2003, and Conner Prairie had not mounted a capital campaign since the construction of the Museum Center in 1987. Reconnecting with supporters was critically important to the museum, both for annual operating support and for the groundwork necessary to raise funds to pay for the construction and maintenance of the new facilities and programs contemplated by the strategic plan. As the museum's endowment was committed to operating support, the strategic plan objectives must be met by tapping new resources. In 2006, the museum's first year of independence, donations to Conner Prairie were 490 percent higher than in 2005, and that trend continued throughout the next three years with increases of 10 percent, 5.8 percent, and 13.8 percent in 2007, 2008, and 2009, respectively.

Conner Prairie Foundation, Inc., the new entity created to hold and manage the museum's endowment and its real estate, inherited from Earlham a pro rata share of each of the investments held as of the closing date in the Eli Lilly Endowment Fund. The foundation engaged in a national search for an investment management consultant, ultimately hiring Cambridge Associates, Boston. Acting on the recommendations of Cambridge, the foundation began a gradual process of realigning the portfolio investments to better match the museum's needs. The value of the investment assets increased from $99.5 million as of December 31, 2005, to $106.5 million as of December 31, 2007. That value declined to $77.7 million as of December 31, 2008, as a part of the general economic contraction, but rebounded during 2009 to $85 million. Following recommendations from the board of directors of the museum, the foundation provided $4.8 million, $5.3 million, $5.6 million, and $5.5 million to support the museum's operations in 2006, 2007, 2008, and 2009, respectively, reflecting an average spending rate of approximately 5 percent of the value of the foundation's investment assets over the trailing 12 quarters. The financial terms of the settlement have given the museum access to resources that otherwise would have been denied to it.

At the time of the museum's acquisition by the foundation, its physical plant was suffering from approximately $1.2 million in deferred maintenance expense. During 2006 and 2007, almost all of that deficiency was cured, and Conner Prairie's properties were in their best condition in many years.

Turning its attention to the elements of the new strategic plan, in 2009 the museum constructed a major new exhibit, the 1859 Balloon Voyage. The exhibit, which draws upon an historic balloon ascension in Lafayette, Indiana, that carried the first successful delivery of air mail, and on the science of balloon flight, culminates in a 350-foot-high ride in a tethered, helium-filled balloon. The balloon exhibit opened in June 2009 and greatly exceeded expectations in its first part-year of operations. During 2008, a rebranding initiative resulted in the adoption of the descriptor line "Interactive History Park" as a means of better describing Conner Prairie's diverse activities and programming.

The most impressive measure of Conner Prairie's progress since independence has been its operating results. Overall attendance, admissions, special events, memberships, and contributions each showed double-digit gains in both 2006 and 2007, and continued trending upward in 2008 and 2009.

These results flowed from many sources including innovative thinking on the part of the staff in creating new guest experiences and the implementation of the museum's Opening Doors initiative. This initiative, which began during John Herbst's administration, generated a guest interaction training program now used by over 1,000 museums around the world. Operations have produced surpluses in each of the years following independence. Conner Prairie's recent successes have earned it national and local recognition for sustainability, innovation, and business excellence.

Ellen Rosenthal has proven to be an effective and popular leader. Her energy, intelligence, and enthusiasm have served Conner Prairie well. She stepped into a challenging task in accepting the chief executive officer position in a new entity organized for the purpose of rebuilding an institution with long and confusing history and in the glare of a great deal of public attention. There were many, including some with close ties to Conner Prairie, who doubted the museum could survive the trauma of its reorganization. But Ellen grabbed the reins and effectively led Conner Prairie through the strategic planning process and the development, adoption, and implementation of countless other plans and policies. Conner Prairie's current successes are a testament to her abilities.

After two years leading the Indiana State Museum, in 2006 John Herbst became the chief executive officer of the Indiana Historical Society, another institution of which Eli Lilly was a major benefactor. The society, headquartered in an expansive building in downtown Indianapolis, is a private, nonprofit membership organization that houses the nation's premier research library and archives on the history of Indiana and the old northwest. Under Herbst's leadership, the society has implemented a variety of new visitor experiences that supplement its function as a research facility.

Douglas Church, Stan Hurt, and I continue to serve on the board of directors of Conner Prairie Museum, Inc., and Conner Prairie Foundation, Inc. I served as chairman of the museum board for the first two years of its independence and continue to act as chairman of the foundation board. Church continues to practice law as the senior partner of his firm. He served as the president of the Indiana State Bar Association in 2007. Hurt is now retired. We each continue to serve in volunteer capacities in other nonprofit organizations.

It will be years before any definitive judgments can be passed on the outcome of the struggle for control of Conner Prairie. At present, Conner Prairie's experience stands in stark contrast to that of other major outdoor history museums, which are seeing declines in attendance and membership in an industry confronted with multiple challenges. Conner Prairie is certainly not immune to broader economic and societal changes, but events since the 2005 settlement have made it clear that independence has allowed the directors and staff of Conner Prairie to engage in thinking, planning, and actions that would have been impossible under Earlham College.

⌒

The Conner Prairie dispute was not an isolated event. Unfortunately, instances of abuse of donor intent and mismanagement of nonprofit organizations come to light with distressing frequency. The experiences of the Barnes Museum in Pennsylvania and the Bishop Trust in Hawaii provide two recent examples, each of which shares some elements in common with Conner Prairie. But there are reasons to hope that these situations were products of their time.

Following the disclosure of mismanagement and accounting scandals in the for-profit sector, the governance practices of business corporations have come under increased scrutiny and new legislation addresses the perceived deficiencies. The federal Sarbanes-Oxley Act of 2002, in particular, established many new requirements that affect how boards of directors of publicly owned corporations conduct their businesses, and those principles have begun to spill over into the development of best practices for nonprofit corporations. As a result of the efforts of the National Conference of Commissioners on Uniform State Laws, the provisions of the 1972 version of the Uniform Management of Institutional Funds Act was updated and expanded in a revised version adopted in 2007, subsequently enacted in several states including Indiana, and the several inconsistencies between the law of trusts, the laws dealing with prudent investment of trust funds, and the laws related to the management of trust principal and income have been reconciled. Accounting and law firms have developed practice areas that focus specifically on service to the nonprofit sector. Auditing standards have been tightened. The Internal Revenue Service has become more aggressive in policing the activities of organizations operating under tax exemptions.

As a result, nonprofit corporations are becoming much more attentive to how they manage their affairs. They now conduct their operations in a more disciplined fashion, paying closer attention to the development and distribution of agendas for board meetings, requiring attendance at meetings, permitting delegations of authority only within prescribed limits, using committees more effectively, and constituting governing boards in a more thoughtful manner. Once fairly rare, most nonprofits now have formal policies that deal with conflicts of interest, the acceptance of gifts, and the protection of donor intent and whistleblowers. Many nonprofit organizations now employ development officers trained in the ethics and responsibilities of fund-raising and gift management. Institutions with endowment funds have become more disciplined in managing those funds and in deciding how to employ their endowment resources for use by the institution. Many now have special investment committees (or separate supporting organizations) for this purpose that are comprised of persons with experience in investment management and have some degree of separation from the day-to-day management of the institution benefited by the fund. The relationship between donors and the institutional objects of their charity has been the subject of a great deal of scholarly work and has become much better understood. And, finally, prospective donors should now understand the need for clarity and enforceability in creating the terms of a major gift.

The board of directors and management of a nonprofit corporation, if presented today with the opportunity to develop a relationship with a donor such as Eli Lilly, would have many more tools at their disposal than did Earlham College in the 1960s.

APPENDIX A

~

Operative Terms of the Lilly Gifts

Lilly Gift	Purpose	Provisions Benefiting Conner Prairie	Provisions Benefiting Earlham College
Deed of gift, January 24, 1969 (40,000 shares = $3 million)	To be "held in perpetuity . . . to maintain and operate" Conner Prairie, as a "special endowment fund"	Twenty percent of corpus for capital improvements; income on the balance "shall be used in the first instance" to support operating budget of Conner Prairie	"All remaining income . . . *may* be used" for educational purposes at the college
Receipt and agreement, July 20, 1972 (20,000 shares = $1.4 million)	To be "kept separate" from the general college endowment; income and principal for (1) capital improvements at Conner Prairie; (2) educational programs at Conner Prairie and (3) certain educational programs at the college	(1) and (2) under "Purpose"	(3) under "Purpose" *No* income or principal to be used for capital improvements at the college

Lilly Gift	Purpose	Provisions Benefiting Conner Prairie	Provisions Benefiting Earlham College
Agreement, June 4, 1973 (200,000 shares = $16.7 million)	To establish a "special Eli Lilly Endowment Fund . . . as an entity separate" from Earlham's other resources	"First charge upon the income" for support and maintenance of Conner Prairie	Remaining income allocated to educational purposes at the college
		Principal, if necessary, for capital improvements at Conner Prairie	No principal to be used for capital improvements at the college
Letter agreement regarding 1973 gift, September 9, 1974	No change	Principal and income on half of gift for capital and operating purposes at Conner Prairie	Income on half of gift for operation of the college, subject to first charge
		And first charge on income on *entire* gift for operation and development of Conner Prairie	*No* principal for support of the college
1973 gift (13,000 shares = $1 million)	Outright gift to Earlham College	None	One million dollars to construct a science building
Last will and testament (approximately $10 million)	Created a "fund" to support operations and capital improvements at Conner Prairie	First charge on principal and income as needed for Conner Prairie	Income not needed for purposes *may* be used for support of the college
			No principal for support of the college

APPENDIX B

~

Draft of *Amicus Curiae* Brief Prepared by Save the Prairie, Inc.

Note: This draft was prepared by Save the Prairie, Inc., for filing in the Indiana Court of Appeals in *Earlham College, as Trustee v. State of Indiana, ex rel. Steve Carter, Attorney General.* As no brief was filed by Earlham College in support of its appeal, this draft anticipated that the college would rely on the arguments made and authorities cited in its lower court filings.

I. THE TERMS OF THE GIFT INSTRUMENTS ESTABLISHING THE ELI LILLY ENDOWMENT FUND AND TRANSFERRING PROPERTY TO THAT FUND CREATED A TRUST RELATIONSHIP.

Mr. Lilly's initial gift to the College created a public charitable trust. In relevant part, the deed of gift states that the transfer is:

IN TRUST, IN PERPETUITY *for the Benefit of the public upon the trusts and uses* stated in the following covenant of the Grantee [the College], *as trustee,* to-wit:

The Grantee covenants that it will hold this parcel of land in perpetuity *as a public charitable trust;* that it will keep and maintain all improvements situated thereon and related to the Conner House and Monuments in a state of good repair in all respects; and that it will permit *all members of the public,* while in good behavior, to have access to said property and buildings at reasonable times and under such rules and regulations as it shall promulgate. (Emphasis added.) (Tr. p. ___)

The College formally accepted this gift and its appointment as trustee of the property on terms stated. (Tr. p. ___)

Subsequently, the College solicited additional gifts from Mr. Lilly, and he ultimately made three additional transfers that, taken together, now constitute the Eli Lilly Endowment Fund.

Mr. Lilly's first major gift to the Eli Lilly Endowment Fund (40,000 shares of Eli Lilly and Company, valued at about $3 million) was made in 1969. (Tr. p. ___). The relevant terms of that gift agreement provide that the shares "constitute the initial corpus of this gift" which "shall be held in perpetuity" by the College along with the proceeds of any reinvestment of the initial corpus. The purpose of the gift is—

> . . . to enable Earlham College to maintain and to operate the Conner Prairie Farm Museum complex in Hamilton County, Indiana, which I have heretofore given to the Donee,[1] on a basis which, in the judgment of the Board of Trustees of Earlham College, will effectively and appropriately communicate to young people and to the general public the record of Indiana's early history.

A percentage of the "initial corpus" of the gift could be "appropriated" for "capital improvements in the physical facilities of the Conner Prairie Farm Museum complex" that would be—

> . . . directed toward providing and preserving for posterity a comprehensive exhibit of the homes, outbuildings, artifacts and such other features as will faithfully reflect the life of a pioneer settlement in the early years of the State of Indiana.

> The remainder of the gift shall be assigned for the establishment of a special endowment fund to be managed by the Board of Trustees of Earlham College . . . the income from which shall be used in the first instance to support the annual operating budget of the Conner Prairie Farm Museum complex . . .

including staff salaries, repairs and maintenance, development work and publications. Only the "remaining income" from the endowment could be used by the College for its educational purposes.

An additional gift was made by Mr. Lilly in 1973 (200,000 Lilly shares, or approximately $16.7 million). (Tr. p. ___). The terms of that gift agreement provide for the establishment of "a special Eli Lilly Endowment Fund to be kept and managed as an entity separate from [the College's] other general and special endowment resources." The instrument provides for a "first charge" upon the income from the Fund for "the support and maintenance" of "the Conner Prairie Pioneer Settlement" and its operation "as a historical site for the education and enjoyment of the public. . ." Principal of the Fund may be used, if necessary, "for construction and reconstruction projects involved in the operation" of the Settlement, but "none of the principal of this gift shall be used for the construction of buildings on the Earlham College campus" and only "that portion of the income from the Fund not, in the judgment of the Earlham Board of Trustees, needed for the rightful and reasonable operation" of the Settlement shall be allocated to educational programs at the College.

Mr. Lilly died in 1977. The gift under his Last Will and Testament (approximately $10 million in Lilly shares) was made—

> . . . on the express condition that the income and principal, if necessary, of the fund hereby given shall be subject to a first charge in such amounts as may reasonably be required from year to year for the general maintenance, support, construction, reconstruction and restoration of the William Conner Residence and surrounding grounds and structures in Hamilton County, Indiana, for the construction, reconstruction, restoration, maintenance and support of any additional buildings which the College may wish to erect in the area, and for the exhibition thereof as an historic site for the education and enjoyment of the public. Any income from such fund (but no principal) remaining after performance of the foregoing provisions ... may be used for the general support of EARLHAM COLLEGE as its Trustees shall determine. (Tr. p. ___).

In none of these gift instruments (other than the original deed) did Mr. Lilly use the words "in trust." However, the language he did use, in light of the relationship of the parties and the facts and circumstances set forth in those instruments, requires the conclusion that the gifts were made in furtherance of the public charitable trust and, as a matter of Indiana law, became a part of that trust. As discussed below, these gifts should be viewed as additions to the public charitable trust; but even construed standing alone the gifts meet the conditions for the imposition of a separate trust or trusts on the fund created thereby.

Whether the stock gifts became part of the original public charitable trust, or constituted one or several new trusts, seems to be irrelevant. The law supports either conclusion.[2]

A. The stock gifts as additions to the original trust.

Under the Indiana Trust Code (Indiana Code §30-4) (the "Trust Code"), "trust property" means "property either placed in trust or purchased or otherwise acquired by the trustee for the trust *regardless of whether the trust property is titled in the name of the trustee or the trust.*" I.C. §30-4-1-2(16). (Emphasis added.) The Trust Code (which is to be "applied to the terms of the trust so as to implement the intent of the settlor and the purposes of the trust") also provides that the trustee has the power to "receive additions to the trust estate." I.C. §30-4-1-3 and I.C. §30-4-3(a)(2). Also, "the law is well settled that the provisions of instruments purporting to establish charitable trusts are to be given a liberal construction. . ." *State ex rel. Emmert v. Union Trust Co. of Indianapolis*, 74 N.E.2d 833, 836 (Ind. App. 1947).

Under the language of the Trust Code, the fact that the gift instruments did not title the property in the name of the public charitable trust, or in the name of the College "as trustee," is irrelevant. The gifts became part of the trust by operation of law, as they were acquired by the trustee for the purposes of the trust.[3]

B. The stock gifts as a new trust or trusts.

Under I.C. §30-4-2-1(b), "no formal language is required to create a trust, but its terms must be sufficiently definite so that the trust property, the identity of the trustee, the nature of the trustee's interest and the purpose of the trust may be ascertained with reasonable certainty." This language reflects long-standing common law principles.

In *Holsapple v. Shrontz*, 65 Ind. App. 390, 117 N.E. 547 (Ind. Ct. App. 1917), real estate was transferred by a mother to a son under a deed that included the following language:

> Said party of the second part [the son] agreeing to use the rentals of said property to support the family and to educate the girls and if finally sold, to divide the price received therefor equally among the then living heirs or members of the family if of age, otherwise hold said shares till minors become of age.

The other children of the grantor claimed that the property was held by the grantee in trust, and the court had no difficulty concluding that this language created an express trust.

> The term "express trust" signifies a trust created by the direct and positive acts of the parties as evidenced by some deed, will, or other instrument, wherein the language employed either expressly or by plain implication evinces an intention to create a trust.

Implied trusts are those which, without being expressed, are deducible from the relation of the parties and the nature of the transaction as matters of intent, or which by operation of law are deduced from the transactions of the parties as a matter of equity independent of the particular intention of the parties. 1 Perry, Trusts (6th ed.) §§73-82; 39 Cyc 17, 24, and cases cited; 28 Am. and Eng. Ency. Law 848 *et seq.*

The creation of a trust does not depend upon the use of any particular language or form of expression, but upon the meaning of the language employed when fairly construed in the light of the circumstances, relation, and situation of the parties. If the intent to create a trust is clear and the essential elements may be fairly deduced from the language employed, the trust will not fail for the lack of more adequate expression. *Grant Trust, etc., Co.* v. *Tucker* (1911), 49 Ind. App. 345, 352, 354, 96 N.E. 487; *Gaylord* v. *City, etc.* (1888), 115 Ind. 423, 428, 430, 17 N.E. 899; *Anderson* v. *Crist* (1888), 113 Ind. 65, 67, 15 N.E. 9; 1 Perry, Trusts (6th ed.) §§82, 83.

When the settlor, or person creating the trust, the trustee, or person who takes and holds the legal title to the property for the benefit of others, the *cestui que trust,* or person for whose benefit the trust is created, the property transferred to the trustee, and the object to be attained, all appear with reasonable certainty from the writing, the requirements of the law are satisfied and an express trust is thereby established, which the courts will recognize and enforce. *Gaylord* v. *City, etc., supra;* §4012 Burns 1914, §2969 R. S. 1881; 1 Perry, Trusts (6th ed.) §§82, 83. . .

The language of the deed when fairly construed is not open to any other inference or reasonable conclusion than that above announced. When viewed in the light of the circumstances, relations and situation of the parties, as we have the right, and are in duty bound, to do, the conclusion is inevitable that a valid express trust was created in the land conveyed, for the purposes designated in the deed in favor of the children and grandchildren of the grantor. . .

Id., at p. 549.

The court also noted that the fact that the son was given a personal interest in the property conveyed did not defeat the trust, and found that the language of the deed was sufficient to put a third party purchaser of the real estate on notice of the existence of the trust.

All of the elements essential to the creation of a trust, as enumerated in the Trust Code and in the *Holsapple* decision, are present in the circumstances and terms of Mr. Lilly's gifts of stock to Earlham College and, in addition, *there was a trust relationship in place* between the donor and donee at the time of the gifts. The College's position—that a gift made by the settlor of a trust, to the trustee, and for the purposes of developing and operating the trust assets, is not a gift held in trust—defies both the law and common sense. As noted in *Holsapple*, Earlham's remote, contingent interest in the "left over" income from the trust assets does not change the legal character of the gifts.

The principles of the *Holsapple* decision were affirmed in a subsequent decision by the United States Court of Appeals for the Seventh Circuit. Applying Indiana law, that Court said:

> The omission of the word trust is not material . . . It is not essential that the purpose should be described in legal phraseology. Any agreement or contract in writing made by a person having the power of disposal over property, whereby such person agrees or directs that a certain fund or particular parcel of property shall be held or dealt with for the benefit of others, in a court of equity raises a trust in favor of such other against the person making such agreement.

Todd v. Citizens' Gas Co. of Indianapolis, 46 F.2d 855, 864 (7th Cir. 1931) (citations omitted).

The terms of Mr. Lilly's gifts are replete with trust concepts. The 1969 gift instrument (Tr. p. ___) speaks in terms of a "corpus" of the gift that is to be held "in perpetuity;" that the purpose of the gift is to "maintain and operate the Conner Prairie Farm Museum complex . . . which I have heretofore given to the donee" (in trust), and in such a manner as to promote the public educational purposes of the initial trust; that the portion of the "initial corpus" not "appropriated" for capital improvements at Conner Prairie (for the purpose of furthering its educational mission) is to be held in "a special endowment fund to be *managed* (emphasis added) by the Board of Trustees of Earlham College" for the benefit of the Museum. Note particularly that the College's power with respect to the gift is limited to its *management*. This language is not consistent with an outright gift, even if viewed as a "restricted gift."

Under the terms of the 1973 gift (Tr. p. ___), it is to be placed by the College in "a special Eli Lilly Endowment Fund to be *kept* and *managed* as *an entity* separate from its other general and special endowment resources." (Emphasis added.) Again, the College's power with respect to the Fund is limited to its *management*. The gift terms speak of the use of income and principal "of the . . . Fund." Note that the Fund is a separate *entity* from the general Earlham College endowment. The terms create a "first charge" upon the income of that Fund "for the support and maintenance of the William Conner residence and surrounding buildings that form the Conner Prairie Pioneer Settlement . . ." with the principal of the Fund, "if necessary," for the construction and reconstruction of projects at the Settlement. The College is barred from using the principal of the Fund, and its interests are limited to any income remaining after the "first charge" commitment has been honored.

The gift under Mr. Lilly's will is characterized as a "fund." (Tr. p. ___). Under the terms of the will, "income" and "principal" of that fund are subject to a "first charge" to be used as required for the operation and development of the Museum "as an historic site for the education and enjoyment of the public," thereby linking that gift to the objectives of the public charitable trust created by Mr. Lilly's original deed.

The terms of these gifts clearly meet the conditions for the imposition of a trust.

The decision in *Stockton v. Northwestern Branch of Women's Missionary Society*, 127 Ind. App. 193, 133 N.E.2d 875 (Ind. Ct. App. 1956) also is instructive, as it delineates the conditions under which a gift will *not* be found to create a charitable trust. In that decision, the court said:

> There is a difference between an absolute devise and one in trust to a charitable institution. In the former, the property becomes an asset of the corporation to be used in such manner as the corporation deemed best, while in the latter, the property is held by the corporation, not as its own, but in the capacity as a trustee, or as an instrumentality of the settlor in carrying out the directions. . . .

> We view the devise to the appellees, being charitable, non-profit corporations which have for their purposes missionary work in foreign fields and for the United States and territories, as being a gift absolute without restrictions as to use. The testatrix *did not designate a particular use or condition to which the devises were to be applied within the corporate purposes of appellees*, such as education, either for boys or girls, construction purposes, hospitals, health or sanitation, or the many other purposes which this court can take judicial knowledge of what such societies as appellees are concerned with in carrying out the purposes of their respective corporations, *but, to the contrary, left the devises to be used for the general purposes, that of missionary work.* (Emphasis added.)

Id. at 133 N.E.2d 875, 879.

In his gift instruments, Mr. Lilly specifically provided that the income and principal of his gifts was to be used by the College to develop and operate the Museum,[4] and he carefully distinguished between those uses and the use of the "left over" income of the gifts (but no principal) for the general purposes of the College as an educational institution. The gifts were not made for the "general purposes" of the College.

The Restatement (Second) of Trusts, §351, notes that "no particular form of words or conduct is necessary for the manifestation of intention to create a charitable trust. . . . A charitable trust may be created although the settlor does not use the word 'trust' or 'trustee.'" (Comment b.)[5] The Restatement, §25, includes this comment in discussing the question of the settlor's intention:

> On the one hand, the settlor may manifest an intention to create a trust; on the other hand, his manifestation of intention may amount merely to a suggestion or wish that the transferee should use or dispose of the property in a certain manner, leaving it to the transferee to follow the suggestion or comply with the wish only if the transferee desires to do so. No trust is created if the settlor manifests an intention to impose merely a moral obligation. In determining the intention of the settlor the following circumstances among others are considered: (1) the imperative or precatory character of the words used; (2) the definiteness or indefiniteness of the property; (3) the definiteness or indefiniteness of the beneficiaries or of the extent of their interests; (4) the relations between the parties; (5) the financial situation of the parties; (6) the motives which may reasonably be supposed to have influenced the settlor in making the disposition; (7) whether the result reached by construing the transaction as a trust or not a trust would be such as a person in the situation of the settlor would naturally desire to produce.

Measured against the standards described in the Restatement, it is clear that Mr. Lilly's words were sufficient to bring his gifts of Lilly stock within the ambit of the public charitable trust. The words used are imperative; the property is definite; the beneficiary and the extent of its interest are definite; the relation of the parties is that of grantor and trustee under an earlier deed of trust; the settlor's motives are clear; and the relationship of trust is that which the settlor would naturally desire to produce.

C. The stock gifts as "restricted gifts."

In the College's view, the stock gifts are not held in trust but are, instead, "restricted gifts." We have found no Indiana decision in which the term "restricted gift" (or "restricted endowment") is used to describe a legal relationship between a donor and a gift recipient, and the College offers no alternative legal theory to characterize the relationship.

The only case cited by the College in support of its view is *Ebenezer's Old People's Home v. South Bend Old People's Home, Inc.*, 113 Ind.App. 382, 48

N.E.2d 851 (1943). But the Court found in that case that the gift had been made for the general purposes of the donee "*without* restriction or limitation." (Emphasis added.) *Id.* at 855. Therefore, the gift was not a "restricted gift" and this decision does not stand for the proposition that "restricted gifts" are not gifts held in trust. See also, *Bible Institute Colportage Ass'n of Chicago v. St. Joseph Bank & Trust Co.*, 118 Ind.App. 592, 75 N.E.2d 666 (1947), discussing and distinguishing the *Ebenezer's* decision and finding that a gift to a charitable organization "to be used in the publication and dissemination of evangelical Christian literature" created an express trust and not an outright gift.

There is no "restricted gift" concept in Indiana law because, in this State, the type of gift described by the College as a "restricted gift" is a gift held in trust and trust law defines the duties of the recipient of the gift. In *Sendak v. Trustees of Indiana University*, 254 Ind. 390, 260 N.E.2d 601 (1970), the Indiana Supreme Court was presented with the question whether the acceptance of gifts of stock by Indiana University conflicted with the Indiana constitutional prohibition against the State becoming a stockholder in any private corporation. Earlham College is not a state institution, and there is no constitutional issue presented by its management of the Fund. However, there is language in the *Sendak* decision that is relevant in determining the character that such gifts have in the hands of an educational institution. In relevant part, the *Sendak* decision says:

> The facts are undisputed. From time to time, during the University's more than one hundred years of existence, the appellee has received and accepted and now holds and administers property transferred to it in trust by private gifts, bequests and devises. Such privately donated property is held by the appellee for educational and charitable purposes, such as for the benefit and the use of the students, faculty and various activities of Indiana University, as specified in the terms and conditions under which the gifts are made. The property is in many cases given for specified purposes, the corpus to be preserved, and in other cases the corpus to be expended for specified purposes in the educational field, such as endowing academic chairs, promoting research and offering educational help and opportunities to students and the faculty at Indiana University. In some cases this property so received includes common and preferred stock of commercial and industrial corporations.

After discussing relevant constitutional and statutory provisions, the court goes on to say:

> Under this legislation and related legislation it appears clear to us that the Board of Trustees of Indiana University acts in a dual capacity, first as direc-

tors and managers of the University operation; second, as trustees of *private trusts created by private donors*. In the first capacity it is a corporate body politic governing Indiana University, as fixed by the statute. In the second capacity *it has the common law duties and privileges of a private trustee* to administer funds which the statute authorizes it to accept on terms and conditions fixed by private donors. (Emphasis added.)

Id., at p. 602.

The terms of the Lilly gifts are exactly as described by the *Sendak* court: they consisted of securities of a public corporation, and were given to an educational institution to use for specific charitable purposes (in fact, purposes that are within the scope of the College's duties as the trustee of a public charitable trust) that were spelled out in the terms of the gift instruments, with different rules governing the use of corpus and income. The circumstances of the Lilly gifts require the conclusion that those gifts are held by the College "in trust."

However, the conclusion reached by the College that the legal relationship of trust that flows from a "restricted gift" to charity, as described in the *Sendak* decision, results in all "restricted" charitable gifts becoming public charitable trusts (and therefore subject to the accounting and other provisions of the Trust Code) is erroneous. The rules of law contained in the Trust Code do not apply to trusts created by operation of law, which is the trust relationship described in *Sendak*. I.C. §30-4-1-1(b)(1). The "duties and privileges" of the trustees of such trusts are, as noted in *Sendak*, governed by common law principles, and the Trust Code expressly preserves the general equity powers of the courts over the administration of trusts. I.C. §30-4-3-30. By contrast, the Lilly stock gifts are held as part of an *express* trust, as described under subparagraphs (a) and (b) above, to which the Trust Code *does* apply.

The College's argument that restricted gifts are not held in trust also must fail for public policy reasons. Donors of charitable gifts do not have individual standing to enforce the terms of their gifts. The law has long recognized that the power to enforce a public charity resides in the office of the Attorney General, and that an individual member of the public has no right to maintain a suit of that character. *Boyce v. Mallers*, 121 Ind. App. 210, 96 N.E.2d 343, 345 (1950). Charitable institutions in the State of Indiana receive millions of dollars annually in the form of restricted gifts. If the donors of those gifts cannot themselves seek to enforce the terms they imposed, and if the recipients of such gifts do not hold them under a fiduciary obligation to apply those gifts in the manner specified by the donor (i.e., in trust), then the law provides no assurance that donor intent will be honored and there would be no restricted giving to eleemosynary institutions. The result sought by the College would severely undermine the foundations of charitable giving.

Notes

1. This was a transfer in trust, as described above.

2. For reasons of economy and simplicity in the administration of the public charitable trust, the stock gifts should be viewed as part of that trust and held by the trustee of that trust for the use and benefit of the public in accordance with their terms.

3. The fact that the college has a contingent interest in the fund does not affect its character as a trust.

4. The fact that the size and scope of museum operations was left to future determination by the Earlham College board of trustees is not relevant to the question of whether the gifts are held in trust.

5. The "Illustrations" to this section include the following: "A bequeaths $10,000 to B and also bequeaths the residue of his property to B 'desiring him' to apply the property to a charitable purpose. In the absence of evidence showing a different intention of A, B holds the residue upon a charitable trust."

Index